As If

As If

The importance of
make-believe for children
(and other human beings)

David Kuschner

Also by
David Kuschner

The Child's Construction of Knowledge: Piaget for Teaching Children
(with George Forman)
THE NATIONAL ASSOCIATION FOR THE EDUCATION OF YOUNG CHILDREN, 1983

From Children to Red Hatters®: Diverse Images and Issues of Play
(editor)
UNIVERSITY PRESS OF AMERICA, 2009

International Perspectives on Children's Play
(co-editor with Jaipaul Roopnarine, James Johnson, & Michael Patte)
OPEN UNIVERSITY PRESS, 2015

Handbook of the Study of Play (Volumes 1 and 2)
(co-editor with James Johnson, Scott Eberle, & Thomas Henricks)
ROWAN & LITTLEFIELD, 2015

Being In Time With Children: Reflections on the Moments Between Us
STICKY EARTH BOOKS, 2019

COVER PHOTOS:
FRONT Emily Kuschner
BACK   David Kuschner (color)
       Lauren Harel (black and white)

Published by
STICKY EARTH BOOKS
Exton, Pennsylvania
StickyEarth.com

Paperback ISBN 978-0-9986449-5-0
Library of Congress Control Number: 2019950391

to Lily and Jake

for being beyond my wildest dreams

Acknowledgments

I HAD THREE professional "homes," if you will, during my academic career. The time spent at those stops provided the foundation for the ideas you will encounter in this book. There were many people at each of those stops who provided mentorship, collegial support, and friendship. I would like to take this opportunity to thank a few of those people.

At the University of Massachusetts - David Day, Peter Wagschal, and especially George Forman for his guidance, inspiration and friendship.

At the University of North Dakota - Maurice Lucas, Walt Prentice, Sara Hanhan, Steve Harlow, Vito Perrone, Cecelia Traugh, Amy Dell, and the late Steve Goldberg, who I miss more and more as time goes by.

At the University of Cincinnati - Anne Dorsey, Vicki Carr, Darwin Henderson, and Peg Elgas.

I had another professional home during my career and that was *The Association for the Study of Play*. I cannot overstate how important the conferences and conversations at those conferences were to my thinking and professional development. I would particularly like to thank Michael Patte, Jim Johnson, Dorothy Sluss, Marcia Nell, Walter Drew, Olga Jarrett, John Sutterby, Rick Worch, Fraser Brown, and Alice Meckley for their friendship all these years; I have learned more from all of you than you probably realize. I owe a special thanks to Fraser Brown for reading a pre-publication version of this book and for the kind words he allowed me to use on the back cover. I would also like to thank Tom Henricks for a great friendship that developed over our once-a-year walks around whatever city in which we found ourselves. Perhaps we should write a book someday about what happens when an early childhood educator and a sociologist go for a walk together.

There are also a number of people with whom I had the good fortune to cross paths along the way, however brief those meetings might have been, and whose words in print and in person provided inspiration and the proverbial food for thought. My thanks go to David Elkind, Eleanor Duckworth, Ben Mardell, Richard Rodriguez, Valerie Polakow Suransky, Patricia Carini, Brian Sutton-Smith, and Jaipaul Roopnarine.

I need to thank Annette Murray of Sticky Earth Books, once again, for taking my words on a computer screen and masterfully formatting them to look good between book covers. She also gets all the credit for designing the book covers themselves.

Finally, I thank my wife Leslie. When she signed on to this life almost fifty years ago the vows didn't include living with someone who would try to write a book. But here is the book and here she is.

Table of Contents

Introduction

Human beings are good at making stuff up. If we are Charles Dickens we make up a story about a man named Scrooge and if we are Mark Twain, about a boy named Huck. If your name is Alice Walker, you make up a story about a girl named Celie and the color purple. The Steven Speilbergs among us will create an *E.T.*, and an amusement park full of dinosaurs while the Rod Serlings among us will tell stories from the *Twilight Zone*. If we are lucky enough to be a Robert Frost we will describe a road not taken on a snowy day and if we have the talent of an Arthur Miller we will relate the sad tale of a salesman named Willy Loman.

But making stuff up doesn't have to be confined to what we can do with words. George Balanchine took the movement possibilities of the human body and created dances about Apollos and nutcrackers. The master mime, Marcel Marceau, used movement and gesture to tell entire stories in complete silence. George Gershwin could combine musical notes and rhythm to conjure up a rhapsody in blue and an American in Paris. Colors and space were used by Vincent Van Gogh to portray a vision of the stars in the night sky while Pablo Picasso used his colors and space to tell the horrors of war in his masterpiece, *Guernica*.

Of course the human ability - and urge - to make stuff up also means that we tell tall tales, little white lies, and sometimes perjure ourselves in courts of law. You might be a president who denies having had a relationship with THAT woman or a president who insists there are weapons of mass destruction someplace in THAT country. If your name is Bernie Madoff, you take people's money and promise to make them rich; if your title is snake-oil salesman, you take people's money in exchange for pills and potions that promise to cure all their ills. The ability to make stuff up means you can be Benedict Arnold who says, "I work for you," while all the while working for them, and you can be Clifford Irving who found it more interesting to write Howard Hughes' autobiography than his own, and spent more than two years in prison for doing so.

We human beings are good at making stuff up but the truth is we don't have to wait until we are grown, mature adults to do so. Dickens, Twain, and Spielberg, might be acclaimed geniuses at making stuff up but many young children could give them a run for their money. Spielberg may have had his *E.T.*, but many a young child has his or her imaginary friend. The novels of Dickens and Twain may be populated by a cast of interesting characters but the same is true for the miniature dramas created by children in their make-believe play. The Van Goghs of the world may be revered for their artistic creativity but as the refrigerator doors in many homes can attest, children are quite capable of using color and space to create representations of worlds of their own making. And just like Balanchine and Marceau, children can use movement to represent ideas.

I saw her that Saturday morning, walking with her mother around the store's rug and carpet displays. She looked to be about 4-years-old and I watched as she moved away from her mother's side and approached a pile of round rugs stacked about three feet off of the ground. Without any hesitation, this little girl climbed up onto the top of the pile, lay down on her stomach and proceeded to move her arms and legs in a circular motion, in and out from her body. As her arms and legs were moving along the braided surface of the rugs, she proclaimed, "Butter melting on pancakes!"

There have been many words used to describe the activity of that young girl in the home improvement store. You could call it make-believe play, imaginative play, pretense, fantasy play, or dramatic play and most people would understand what you were describing. There might be subtle differences between and among those descriptors but for the most part they are used interchangeably when we talk about how children take on roles and use objects in unique and creative ways. This book is about that kind of play, about the play of make-believe and pretense, about children making stuff up. This is a book about those pancakes and about the child who is able to conjure them up with her mind, body, and words. This is a book about the make-believe play of children. But this is also a book about human beings.

The play of children has long been a topic of interest to people studying children's development. Browse through such research oriented journals as *Child Development* and *Developmental Psychology* and you will find article titles like, "Fathers and mothers at play with their 2- and 3-year-old children: Contributions to language and cognitive development," and "'This is a bad dog, you know...': Constructing shared meanings during sibling pretend play." Browse the shelves of the local bookstore for books written for mainstream audiences and you might find such titles as, *Play: How It Shapes the Brain, Opens the Imagination, and Invigorates the Soul*, and *A Child's Work: The Importance of Fantasy Play*. Educators have also been interested in the play of children. Consult the policy and position statements of the National Association for the Education of Young Children (NAEYC), the foremost professional organization in the field of early childhood education, and you will read the following about best practices for programs serving young children: "Play needs to be a significant part of the young child's day - and part of a developmentally appropriate classroom." Peruse the alphabet soup of professional organizations and you will find the following acronyms: TASP (The Association for the Study of Play), IPA (International Play Association), and ICCP (International Council for Children's Play). The fact is that play has long been a topic of interest to professionals who work with children in a variety of settings.

Parents, of course, are also intimately familiar with the fact that play is a major part of childhood. They often spend not insignificant amounts of time watching their children play, buying the toys that support the play, furnishing playrooms, playing with their children, serving as the audiences for their children's play, cleaning up after their children's play, taking their children to playgrounds, arranging play dates, and uttering such statements as, "It's time to finish up your playing and get ready for bed," and "Stop playing with your food!" Most parents don't need to be told that children play; they are well aware of that fact and are not always happy about it.

There is somewhat of a paradox about play, however; even though it is a major part of almost all children's childhoods, it is very difficult to define. As the saying goes, "we know it when we see it," but coming up with an operational definition that distinguishes 'play' from 'not play' has been a challenge for those who study the phenomenon and for anyone who informally tries to pin down a definition. It's easy to say that play is when children are having fun, but children seem to be enjoying themselves when engaged in activities we wouldn't necessarily label as play. It's also easy to say that play is anything that's not work (which itself is not easy to define), but watch a child spending hours building a complex structure out of Lego bricks and you will see someone evidencing the seriousness and intensity of activity we usually associate with things we call work. The task of defining play can be so challenging that some researchers and theorists have even gone as far as to say that arriving at a precise definition is an impossible undertaking. As Brian Sutton-Smith, one of the founding fathers of the field of play studies has written, "We all play occasionally, and we all know what playing feels like. But when it comes to making theoretical statements about what play is, we fall into silliness."

Looking at various attempts at definitions, however, there is one characteristic that is often included: play is frequently defined as the suspension of reality; play is said to have a non-literal orientation, and an *as if* quality. Returning to that scene in the home improvement store - the rugs weren't pancakes and there was no butter in sight, but this didn't stop the child. For a brief moment, that little girl suspended reality. She was no longer on an errand in a home improvement store with her mother. She could, for that moment, enter the world of *as if*; she could act *as if* the rugs were pancakes and *as if* her moving arms and legs were the melting butter. She could remove herself from that specific time and place and for a moment she could act *as if* she were sitting at the kitchen table in her own house eating breakfast. Or perhaps she was acting *as if* she were the pancakes and butter. This book, then, is about that particular characteristic of play; this book is about *as if*. Through *as if*, a child is able to transform an object into anything she wants it to be and transform herself into anyone she chooses to be. The rugs can become pancakes and her limbs can become melting butter. For another child the pencil can become an airplane or the towel around a neck can turn you into Wonder Woman. This book is about the moments in the play time of children when they can suspend the reality they are in and transform their world into a reality of their own making.

The power of *as if*, however, is more than pretending rugs are pancakes or pretending you are Wonder Woman. This book is about other ways in which the ability to engage in *as if* thinking is important to the development of children. It's about the child's use of all types of symbols to represent his or her ideas; to use a symbol *as if* it is the object or idea it represents. A child can draw you a picture of his dog and then proceed to tell you all about his pet *as if* the dog were right there. The drawing, a symbolic representation of the dog, stands in for the real thing; it can be related to *as if* it were the dog. That same child might even be able to write a story about his beloved pet just by printing the dog's name on a piece of paper; those marks serving as yet another symbolic representation of his dog. A drawing, a spoken name, a written word - all of these are symbols that represent, that *re-present* the idea of his dog - and all of these are symbols that the child can use to act *as if* his dog is right there by his side.

The power and importance of *as if* also extends into a child's social and emotional experiences. For example, *as if* is part of a child's ability to feel empathy, to be empathic. One dictionary defines the word empathy as "the ability to identify oneself mentally with a person or thing and so understand his feelings or its meaning." To feel empathy, therefore, you must be able to understand how another person is feeling, you must be able to understand the situation *as if* you are standing in the other person's shoes. Being able to understand perspectives other than your own requires that you consider things *as if* you are seeing the world through the other person's eyes. This book is about the connection between that young child picking up a pencil and using it *as if* it is an airplane and his ability to feel empathy and consider the perspectives of others, *as if* he is seeing the world from the other person's point of view.

But this book isn't just about the *as if* play of children. Children engage in make-believe play and *as if* thinking not because they are children but because they are human beings. As we leave childhood, it might no longer occur to us to climb on those rugs and play butter melting on pancakes (well, it might occur to us but we realize that doing so might not be a socially acceptable act for a grown-up), but *as if* is still very much a part of who we are and what we do; *as if* is there when we make plans for our vacation, have expectations for our new job, worry about our children, work with spreadsheets in our businesses, or even read this book. The focus of the chapters to follow will be on the make-believe and *as if* play of children but the "other human beings" of the book's title will also be part of the story. I believe that the act of *as if* is a fundamental characteristic of being human and such a ubiquitous aspect of our functioning as human beings that most of the time we aren't aware that we, too, are engaged in a bit of make-believe.

AFTER THE FIRST chapter, which covers the nature of make-believe *as if* play in general, I have chosen to explore the play and power of *as if* by focusing on eight particular manifestations of the phenomenon. Chapter Two, titled, *This Stands for That*, looks at how symbols and representation are very much a function of *as if* and pretend play, and how *as if* underlies such ideas as the object substitutions of make-believe play (using a cardboard box as a truck), transitional objects (the importance of blankies), and the understanding of metaphors (think, "Fog comes on little cat feet," by Carl Sandburg).

In Chapter Three, *Standing in the Other Person's Shoes*, I discuss how much of social interaction and the understanding of other people's perspectives is grounded in the ability to see the world *as if* you are standing in the spot, or shoes, of the other person. A decrease in self-centeredness and an increase in multicultural understanding both depend on considering the other person's experience *as if* you are in their shoes. Chapter Four, *The Truth Isn't the Only Option*, focuses on the telling of lies and how this ability emerges from the same foundation as make-believe play and the act of *as if*. It turns out that no matter how much we parents might want to emphasize the importance of honesty and truth-telling, children will become liars just like the rest of us (including their parents).

Chapter Five, *Real Friends Aren't the Only Option*, examines the phenomenon of the imaginary friend and how this creation by perfectly normal children builds on and further develops their ability to conjure up alternatives to reality as they know it, and to understand the minds of others. There is also a discussion in the chapter of how the childhood power to create imaginary companions can come in handy in the waging of war.

In Chapter Six, *Superheroes, Tales of Fairies and Monsters*, I discuss children's attraction to power and monsters of various sorts. The chapter explores these themes by looking at superhero play, children's love of fairy tales, and why young children want to go into the deep, dark woods every now and then for a good scare.

Chapter Seven, *The Simulation of Reality (and the Reality of Simulation)* looks at how the pretend play of young children, which is in effect a form of simulation, lays the foundation for the sophisticated simulation environments developed for such worlds as video gaming, medical education and training, and military preparedness.

Chapter Eight, *Making It Through the Dark and Stormy Night*, highlights how make-believe play and *as if* continues to exist for children (and adults) even under what one author called some very "startling circumstances." The purpose of this chapter is to show that the ability to imagine alternative realities and to transform one's reality through make-believe play proves to be a very powerful tool for coping with a variety of life's challenges and, at times, is even a tool for survival.

The final chapter, *Being a Head Taller*, brings the discussion to an end by illustrating how playing *as if* can be a force and process that promotes personal growth and development. For example, President Theodore Roosevelt suggested that the way to conquer a fear is to pretend that you are not afraid. There are research studies that suggest we can feel happier by smiling and acting *as if* we are happy even when we don't feel happy. The message is that we don't have to accept reality as it is but can, in effect, change that reality by making believe it is different, by acting *as if* it is different, and ultimately, causing it to be different.

IT IS IMPORTANT to note, and to give you, the reader, an advanced 'heads up,' that although the chapters that follow are organized by topic, there are number of themes that weave their way through these chapters. The first is the overarching theme that reality isn't the only option. As will be discussed in greater detail in the next chapter, in make-believe play children are really taking or announcing a 'stance towards reality.' Whether it is saying that the wooden block doesn't have to be just a wooden block or that words spoken don't have to represent the truth, make-believe play at its heart is the act of considering alternatives to reality.

Closely related to the idea that *reality isn't the only option*, is the concept of *distancing*. Through make-believe play and the act of *as if*, children are able to distance themselves from the realities of the here and now and by creating this distance, engage in the important processes of reflection and communication.

Finally, and perhaps most importantly, the ability to pretend and act *as if* - to distance oneself from the here and now and consider alternative realities - is not simply a function of being young and perhaps immature but is fundamentally a part of what it means to be human. We can pretend that a wooden block is a truck, make-believe that we are a superhero, tell lies and create imaginary beings because of our very human ability to suspend a present reality and create, even if for just a moment, a *possible* reality. This very same power was what led President John F. Kennedy to announce in 1962 that the United States would explore the surface of the moon by the end of that decade. Space exploration was at its nascent beginnings in 1962 but President Kennedy was asking the nation to imagine what might be possible and to begin acting *as if* landing on the moon was a reachable goal. Neil Armstrong's first footstep on the moon in 1969 began with a nation pretending, imagining, it was possible.

We humans, therefore, have the power to imagine a reality that may not currently exist but one that may in the future. As the psychologist Alison Gopnik has written, "The uniquely human evolutionary gift is to combine imagination and logic to articulate possible worlds and then make them real." This book is about that "uniquely human gift."

CHAPTER 1

As If, or, Reality
Isn't the Only Option

Sometime during the second year of life, a fascinating behavior emerges in the life of a child, a behavior that will characterize much of the child's activity during the early childhood years. This behavior is referred to by a variety of terms: pretend, fantasy, imaginary play, and dramatic play. It is the type of play that lets a child remove herself from the immediate here and now and enter the worlds of 'once upon a time' and 'lands far, far away'. It is the play of carpets becoming a stack of pancakes and a cardboard box becoming a car. It is the play of a red towel tied around your neck turning you into a superhero and the play of a crying baby doll needing the comfort of your parental arms. It is the play of two friends going off to fight dragons in the far regions of the backyard. It is the play of make-believe, the play of *as if*.

Living in two worlds

WE HUMAN BEINGS actually spend our lives moving back and forth between two worlds. One is the world of the here and now; the world of stimuli, sensations, and responses. Sensations of hunger lead to a fussy baby. Stubbing a toe on the corner of the coffee table may bring a less-than-polite string of words out of our mouths, no thought required. Hearing the dentist's drill may cause anxious feelings even if you aren't the one who will be sitting in his chair. These feelings of hunger, pain, and anxiety are sensations that are part of our right here and right now experience and are generally beyond our consciousness and oftentimes beyond our control.

But we human beings can also inhabit another world, a world that is removed from the here and now of stimuli and sensations, a world that is built on the power of *as if*. This is the world of pretend and make-believe, of fantasy and the imagination, as well as the worlds of prediction and planning, and worry and foreboding. This is not the world of what is actually happening but rather a world of what could happen, might happen, and a world of hoped-for-happenings, the "woulda-coulda-shouldas of life, all the things that might happen in the future, but haven't yet, or that could have happened in past but didn't quite." As the psychologist Alison Gopnik has written, "Human beings care deeply about these possible worlds - as deeply as they care about the real actual world." And as Jonathan Gottschall has written, we human beings will spend a good deal of time in this second world.

> You might not realize it, but you are a creature of an imaginative realm called Neverland. Neverland is your home, and before you die, you will spend decades there...While your body is always at a particular fixed point in space-time, your mind is always free to ramble in lands of make-believe. And it does.

Whenever we do one of the following we are entering that 'other' world: planning the clothes we pack for the upcoming vacation; depositing money in the retirement savings account; creating a 'to do' list for the next day; or losing ourselves in an author's imagined world of historical or science fiction. All of these actions in this second world of our existence as human beings involve the act of *as if*. I plan my vacation clothes by imagining what it will be like to be lounging on that beach of my dreams and I write down my tasks for tomorrow *as if* I am already working in that tomorrow, trying to get done what I want to accomplish. We also enter the *as if* world when we find ourselves worrying about something that hasn't happened yet. Any stress or anxiety that we experience results from thinking about the event *as if* it has already actually occurred; we feel the anxiety in the here and now only because we allowed our minds to enter that other world, the world of *as if*.

Children generally begin to enter and explore this other world, the world of make-believe, pretend, and *as if*, sometime during their second year of life. An early form of make-believe play may look something like this: in the middle of the afternoon, long before her regular bedtime and shortly after she has arisen from a nap, the young girl pretends that she is tired and going to sleep. She lies down on the sofa, places her hands under her cheek, and closes her eyes. How do we know that she is only pretending that she is sleeping? Because while her eyes are closed, she also has just the slightest smile on her face. We also know that she is pretending because she doesn't 'stay asleep' for very long and soon bounces up and giggles. We also know she is pretending because as her parent, we know that this is not the usual time of day (or place) for bedtime or her midday nap.

What exactly is happening in this commonly occurring scene? This little girl is using the abbreviation or imitation of an action *out of the normal context* for the behavior (more on that later in this chapter) to *represent* the action and context (more on representation in the next chapter). The actions of lying down and closing your eyes are both part of the real process of going to sleep and the hands under the cheeks represent the pillow that is part of the context of sleeping. This little girl may not yet be using words as part of her make-believe, but with actions and gestures she is able to act, or play, *as if* she is going to sleep.

From these beginnings, children's ability to pretend grows and expands. There will be more imitative actions; for example, raising two hands up to the mouth to pretend that you are drinking from a cup. Children will also develop the ability to employ what is called *object substitutions,* which is when they use one object to represent another object. For example, a wooden, rectangular block is pushed along the floor *as if* it is a car; the block, in other words, is used to represent a car. The play of *object substitutions* then becomes more complex with the combination of object substitutions: two smaller blocks (the driver and passenger) placed on top of the larger one (the car). Even more complexity can occur when the child uses a doll (representing a person) to push the car carrying two people across the floor. Before the incorporation of the doll into the play, the child was the *agent* of the action (car traveling on a road); now the doll is the agent of the action. The child is not only pretending that the block is a car but is also pretending that the doll is a person capable of making the car move; the child is capable of combining multiple instances of *as if* in her play.

Once the child becomes more fluent with language, she will begin to create pretend worlds around her object substitutions and make-believe actions. The child is no longer simply pushing a pretend car across the floor on pretend roads; now the child will tell a story about the car and its passengers. These passengers will have destinations and reasons for being in the car in the first place. Perhaps a mother and daughter are going to visit grandma and grandpa. Or maybe two friends are going to the zoo so they can visit their favorite animals. Language gives children the power to incorporate their pretend actions into the fictional stories of the imagination and at the same time the power to change the pretense of the actions themselves, as when the car with two passengers is transformed into a boat with two giraffes. All this is done simply by announcing with language that the change has taken place.

One of the more important developments in pretend play occurs when a child engages in make-believe play with another child (or perhaps adult). This is a type of *as if* activity frequently referred to as *sociodramatic play*. In sociodramatic play a child isn't just imagining her own alternative possibilities and realities but must coordinate her creations with those of the other player. If two children are playing store, for example, the type of store needs to be determined (does the store sell food or shoes?); the pretend roles need to be negotiated (who will be the store owner and who will be the customer?); and an ongoing 'script' for the story needs to be managed as the children play out their mini-drama together. Coordinating your own *as if* with the *as if* of another player exercises the ability to take and understand the perspective of the other person, a topic we return to in Chapter 3.

As children move back and forth between these two worlds - the world of the here and now and the world of *as if* - they step in and out of what has been called the *play frame*. The English anthropologist and linguist Gregory Bateson used the metaphor of a picture frame to describe how children move in and out of their pretend play. The *play frame* communicates the message that what is taking place, for example the fighting between superheroes or the interaction between a store owner and customer, is, in fact, play and not for real. Children often send this message through such metacommunicative devices as smiling and giggling, or by simply pronouncing, "Let's pretend..."

As the play episode unfolds, children can flow in and out of the play frame, what Peter Gray refers to as moving back and forth from "time in" to "time out". For example, they may step out of the play frame in order to resolve a disagreement about the actions of one of the characters in their mini-drama ("You own the store. You can't go out the door!") or about the evolving plot of the drama itself ("No, you haven't run out of all the ice cream, just chocolate ice cream.") Once the play is back on track, the players reenter the play frame and continue on with their pretend play.

The play frame is where the children act on their power of *as if*; the play frame establishes a place and time where possibilities can be explored and children can "draw on forms of thinking and logic not related to the real world." One of the most powerful aspects of the play frame for children is that they know that whatever transformations they employ within the play frame - e.g., turning the dining room table into Batman's cave and themselves into Batman and Robin - can be reversed once they step back out of the play frame. The dining room is once more just a table and they are once more just good friends in the real world. They also know that sometime in the future, when another play frame is established with the words, 'Let's pretend,' that very same table may no longer be a table or Batman's cave but is now transformed into a tent in the desert and they are no longer superheroes but are now treasure hunters following clues to the hidden chest of gold. As Stuart Brown wrote in his book, *Play: How it Shapes the Brain, Opens the Imagination, and Invigorates the Soul*, "Part of the freedom to alter the natural order of things...is the knowledge that order will be restored again afterward."

It is important to note, however, that when children enter the play frame, when they enter this second world, and use their power of *as if* to explore possibilities, they don't do so empty-handed (or empty-headed), so to speak. Children bring their experiences and knowledge of the 'real' world with them as they create their pretend worlds. To act *as if* you are a mother taking care of her child presupposes that you know something about the role of mothers and the relationship between mothers and their babies; in other words, "the child who pretends to bathe a doll needs to know something about water and baths." Generally speaking, children bring with them into their imaginary play their current knowledge of how the physical world of objects and how the social and emotional world of people work. Their knowledge may be the incomplete understanding of the 3-year-old but nevertheless it is what they know and what they know serves as the starting point for their exploration of possibilities. As Paul Harris writes in his book, *The Work of the Imagination*, "Children, like novelists, are inspired by actual events." And like novelists, children may take those actual events as the starting points for the creation of their own stories and dramas. In other words, "we use the predetermining elements of the life space in other than a predetermined way to create something other than what is predetermined."

Reality isn't the only option

WHEN CHILDREN CREATE their own pretend stories, when they enter the magical world of *as if*, they are making a statement about, and are taking a stance towards, reality. Children entering the play frame are, in effect, making the statement that reality as they know it isn't the only option. Their make-believe play can be one at the same time a *suspension* of reality, a *transformation* of reality, and a *distancing* from reality.

Suspending reality. As just discussed, human beings live in two worlds and a child at play is a child in that 'other' world. Whether by invoking the words, 'Let's pretend...', gathering the needed props together, or by donning just the right hat and shoes, the playing child steps out of world dictated and dominated by the demands of the here and now and crosses over into a world created through and ruled by the imagination. Her time in this other world may last a few minutes or go on for hours, and during this time in the 'other world,' imaginary characters come and go, fantastic lands are built and destroyed, and life battles are won and lost. Whether it is for minutes or for hours, the pretending child plays *as if* the real world doesn't exist and *as if* the make-believe world does. Whether it is just for a few moments or for a few hours, when children are pretending, reality is suspended.

Transforming reality. The pretending child may suspend reality as she steps into the play frame but the tools of make-believe play consist of the 'stuff' of reality: the objects of the physical environment, the child's knowledge of the people of her social environment, and the child's own life experiences. In pretend play, children transform the 'stuff' of this reality to fit the needs and goals of their play and these transformations can take one or more of the following forms.

The first type of transformation focuses on the physical environment. In this case, the child uses an object or some other aspect of the environment *as if* it is something else, something other than its real 'being.' For example, once co-opted for make-believe play, the cardboard box that functioned as a container for the new set of dishes her parents recently purchased is transformed into a truck moving furniture to a new house. The cardboard box is used *as if* it is a big truck. This transformation doesn't even require any physical change to the box itself; all it may take to transform or 'change' the box into a truck is the child sitting inside of the box, making truck noises and narrating the actions of her story. The transformation of objects is common feature of children's pretend play: wooden blocks become airplanes, Tupperware containers become corrals for farm animals, and bits of crumpled paper can stand in for food on the dinner plates (which may be represented by pieces of cardboard). And as mentioned earlier, dining room tables can become a superhero's cave or a tent for explorers. Each of these transformations is an act of *as if*; the child is acting *as if* the block is an airplane, the plastic container is a place for animals to sleep, and the wadded up paper is a serving of steak and mashed potatoes.

The second type of *as if* transformation involves the people of pretend play. Not only is the cardboard box transformed into a truck but the child sitting in the box has transformed herself into a truck driver. When that young girl establishes the play frame by sitting herself in the box and announcing that she has to drive the furniture to the new house, she is in essence making the statement that, "I am going to act *as if* I am a truck driver moving furniture." She may effect this transformation by using her voice to make engine noises and getting out of the 'truck' to load and unload the furniture. In a similar way, another young child ties a towel around his neck and begins to act *as if* he is a superhero while another child fills a box with wooden sticks and acts *as if* he is selling a box of nails in the hardware store. And in the latter case, the box of nails is being sold to another child who has transformed himself into a paying customer in the hardware store; this child is acting *as if* he needs the nails for the house he is building down the street. In effect, as Bateman writes, the child herself becomes a sort of prop for her pretend play: "Role-taking...is a kind of play predicated upon imagining oneself as a primary prop."

The final type of transformation is one which focuses on the child's experiences and life circumstances. In pretend play, children are often times imitating and reproducing what they have seen or heard in real life. The child playing moving van driver may have observed a real moving van in her neighborhood or experienced a recent move herself. The children playing Batman and Robin underneath the dining room table may have watched a Batman cartoon on television. Children very often transform an object and themselves in order to reenact a scene or experience from real life. The children playing hardware store may be imitating what they have observed on trips to a real hardware store with their parents, for example.

There are forms of make-believe play, however, where children aren't simply reenacting real life but are using their imaginations to alter their known experience in some way. In these cases, children may not be playing life *as it really is* but life *as they would like it to be*. An anecdote from one of my university classes powerfully illustrates this type of transformational pretend play.

One of the courses that I frequently taught during my years of university work focused on the role of play in early childhood education. I taught this course at both the undergraduate and graduate level. As a way of introducing the importance of play in the lives of children, I would have the students write a brief play autobiography. The assignment asked them to describe a type of play that was important to them between the ages of four and nine. They were required to identify the nature of the play, where it took place, whether or not any special materials were needed for the play, whether the play involved other children, and why this play might have a special place in their childhood memories. Students seemed to enjoy the assignment and one of the interesting results was that frequently students learned that they shared common play experiences with some of their classmates; for example, discovering that you weren't the only one who had a large collection of Barbie dolls growing up.

One year a graduate student used this assignment to describe how she would play with dolls and create fictitious families and then play out various life scenarios with these *as if* families. As she wrote her paper and reflected on these play memories, she remembered that very often she would take on the role of a married adult in her play drama. Here is what she had to say about this childhood play memory.

There were many factors that I believe urged me to pretend I was a married, or engaged adult...There was a fair amount of fighting between my parents...My father was present for my childhood but not necessarily there. In my pretend world, I wanted a friend in a husband. A husband who would be kind and funny...so, I made one... the way I wanted him to be...

"In my pretend world...so, I made one...the way I wanted him to be..." This is perhaps the most powerful type of transformation that is part of make-believe play, the most powerful kind of *as if*. This graduate student was remembering a time when she played *as if* her family was a happy one, *as if* her father was kind and funny and *as if* her parents had a relationship that didn't include frequent arguing. In her pretend play, within the play frame, she used the power of the imagination to take what was part of her life reality and transform it into something different, something that for her, was better. It is difficult to know how this play may have benefitted her at the time; perhaps it served as a respite from the real world or perhaps it was practice for a future life. It seems likely, however, that since she still remembered this play activity more than thirty years later it was indeed important to her.

It can be a mistake, therefore, to look at a young child playing a doctor examining a patient or playing a mother feeding her baby and simply chalk it up to imitation. There is certainly an element of imitation or mimicry in the play and "much of their play will involve mirroring events they have seen and experienced...or perhaps observed, for instance by watching television." Children, however, "also transform events and people through their enactments."

In thinking about what children do in their *as if* play it is helpful to consider the distinction between *re-enacting* (or *re-capitulating*) and *re-inventing* (or *re-imagining*). When children *re-enact*, in the narrowest sense of the word, they may be repeating an experience as close to the way the event occurred as possible. Lenore Terr, a psychiatrist who has worked with children of trauma, writes that these kinds of re-enactments often characterize the play of children who have experienced difficult life events. The children feel a need to re-live the experience precisely as they had experienced it the first time.

When children *re-invent* or *re-imagine* their life experiences through play they are exerting some control over what has happened to them and they explore the possibilities within the experiences. Terr suggests that it is this type of play that can help children cope with and move past the traumatizing events that they are represent-ing in their play. The real power of *as if* occurs when children trans-form the 'facts' of their experience and "reinvent [this] experience in order to learn where it might lead." The essayist Roger Rosenblatt captured this distinction when he wrote that, "The imagination has different levels. You can imagine something that has never been seen before. And you can imagine something that has always been seen, yet never in the way you see it."

Distancing from reality. When children enter the play frame, when they step into the world of make-believe, in addition to suspending and transforming, they are in effect distancing themselves from real-ity. The important point to this distancing is that children are lessen-ing the grip that the immediate here and now has on their thinking and actions. As the Russian psychologist Lev Vygotsky wrote, "In play, things lose their determining force. The child sees one thing but acts differently in relation to what he sees. Thus, a condition is reached in which the child begins to act independently of what he sees." There is enormous power in this liberation from the here and now for both the child and human beings in general because "the imagination liberates us from the tyranny of this place, these chores, these people." When children engage in pretend play, they are not bound by the conventional and socially acceptable uses of objects or conceptions of who people are and how they behave; a pencil can be an airplane and a shy four-year-old can be a star ballerina. Chil-dren even distance themselves from the words that serve as labels for things; the usual name for an object is set aside as the object is re-ferred to by its new label within the play scenario. The cardboard box is no longer referred to as a cardboard box, it is now a truck. When children enter the play frame and conjure up their imaginary worlds, therefore, children, "learn to act not just in response to external stimuli but also in accord to internal ideas."

Imagine what the world and life would be like if we did not have this ability to distance ourselves from the constraints and dictates of the immediate here and now. (Yes, I am asking you to engage in a bit of *as if* thinking.) We wouldn't be able to think about what we wanted to do for fun on the weekend let alone plan for retirement that might be years down the road. All of those students who found my university lectures to be boring wouldn't have been able to use their powers of daydreaming - another form of *as if* and make-believe - to lift themselves out of that boredom. If we happened to live where winter temperatures were low and winter snow plentiful, we wouldn't be able to look forward to our summer vacation on the beach. As bad as that would be for we adults, "things are even worse for a baby," writes Paul Bloom, "because even the most stressed-out adult can choose to think of something else; we can look forward to getting back to the hotel; imagine how we would describe our trip to friends; fantasize, daydream, or pray. The baby just is, trapped in the here and now. No wonder babies are often so fussy." And no wonder long car rides can be a form of torture for young children (and the adults in the front seat).

As we will see in later chapters, this ability to distance oneself from the pull of the immediate here and now is a theme that runs through many manifestations of the act of *as if*, and is characteristic not only of young children's play but of much of human activity. The human being's ability to "move in perception and thought away from the concrete given, or 'what is,' to 'what was, what could have been, what one can try from, what might happen' and ultimately to the purest realms of fantasy - is a touchstone of that miracle of human experience, the imagination." It is the "special mystery of how we develop our human capacity for mental travel through time and space."

The rules of pretend play

ALTHOUGH CHILDREN SUSPEND, transform, and step away from the 'givens' of reality while engaged in pretend play, that doesn't mean their make-believe is devoid of structure or is totally free from rules. One of the fascinating characteristics of *as if* play is its rule-bound nature. Just because children may be exploring imaginary possibilities, transforming their worlds, and considering alternative realities, that doesn't mean they do so in in a willy-nilly fashion. This is especially true when two or more children are involved in the activity of sociodramatic play. The rules that children follow in their make-believe role play aren't the codified rules found in the instruction pamphlets for board games like *Candyland*; they are the rules that the children assume and create for themselves as they negotiate their joint exploration of *as if*.

Consider the following scenario, for example. Three children are 'playing house.' The first negotiation that occurs addresses who will play what role; in other words, who will be the mother, who will take on the role of father, and who will be the baby of the family. Once these roles are assigned then the actors in this drama must follow the 'rules' of what these characters can and cannot do. If the family is going to get in the car and drive to the store (with three chairs standing in for or representing the seats in the car), then it can only be the 'mother' or the 'father' who can drive the car; as much as the child who is playing the baby wants to be the one who drives the car, he can't. If the play is to be maintained then all the children must play within the rules and "accept premises established...and respond in consequential fashion." As Vygotsky wrote, "The child [who] imagines himself to be the mother and the doll to be the child...must obey the rules of maternal behavior."

Even though we often attach words like 'free' and 'spontaneous' to this type of children's play we can see from this example how *as if* play actually exercises children's impulse control. The child assigned the role of the baby in the family may want the excitement and sense

23

of control that being the driver of the car brings but if the play is to continue, he will need to suppress the impulse to want the 'cool' job of driving. He will need to maintain his performance as the baby by following the rules of what it means to be a baby. This child must delay his need for gratification and wait his turn to play the parent who gets to drive the car. Even though this second world of a child's life can be thought of as the 'anything goes' world of the imagination, the world of *as if* serves as a fertile training ground for the development of such important abilities as impulse control and the delay of gratification. Vygotsky went as far as stating that, "A child's greatest self-control occurs in play. He achieves the maximum display of will-power when he renounces an immediate attraction in the game."

What makes us human

IT IS EASY to take the make-believe play of children for granted, easy to overlook all that is happening when children pretend. Sometimes it seems as if young children are playing at make-believe almost all their waking hours. They walk around with their dolls and action figures, sometimes talking to them and sometimes moving them about in some fabulous world of heroes and villains. Some children retreat to their bedrooms or playrooms and read stories to their invisible (at least to the parents) classroom of children. Other children take their make-believe play outdoors and create dramas with neighborhood friends that take place on the stage of backyard trees and fences. If truth be told, as parents, we may actually welcome the fact that our children get engrossed in their imaginary worlds for large chunks of time; while they are occupied with their fantasies, we are able to take care of the things we need to get done in the very *real* worlds of our lives.

But the fact that we might take the make-believe and *as if* activity of children for granted, shouldn't mean that we underestimate the important transformational activity that happens when a child picks up a shoebox and calls it a truck or puts on a pair of eyeglass frames and proclaims himself a teacher. By using words and props, the child is making the statement that the world, including herself, doesn't have to be taken as a given; by transforming the shoebox and her own identity she is exerting her will, expressing her ideas, and altering her reality. She is taking a step back from the *world as is* and thinking about a *world that could be*. She is saying, in effect: "I don't have to simply react to the world as the objects and people in that world want me to react. In my moment of pretense, in the play frame, I can choose how I want my world to be and I can choose how and who I want to be." The child at play, in other words, moves "from the 'just so' to the 'as if'."

Chapter 2

This Stands for That

George had come right up to me when he saw me enter the day care center classroom. He and I had a bit of a relationship from previous visits so he was not at all shy about approaching me and initiating a conversation. On that day he wanted to know if I had brought a particular toy with me, a toy that I had shared with the children the last time I had been at the center. When I told him that, no, I didn't have the toy with me, he asked if I would be returning to the center the next day. When I replied that I would be returning, he said that he wanted to find a piece of paper and a pencil. I asked him what he needed the paper and pencil for and he explained that he wanted to write a note for me to take so that I would remember to bring the toy back with me the next day.

George was a somewhat precocious four-year-old so I wasn't surprised by his verbal ability or his memory. I also wasn't surprised by his willingness to speak his mind and make his request. I was surprised, however, by his suggestion that he write a note to serve as a reminder for me. What I didn't realize about George at the time was that he apparently understood the power of the written symbol and how writing as representation can affect the world at a place and time removed from the here and now.

George understood that by making some marks on a piece of paper - marks that would stand in for and represent his wishes - he could potentially affect my behavior in a place he had never been (my office) and at an imagined time removed from the present (the future). In a fundamental way, George understood that when I would look at the note while sitting in my office, it would be *as if* he were there himself, expressing his desires directly to me. It likely was an unconscious understanding on his part, but his request to write a reminder note made it clear that on some level he did understand that representations on a piece of paper took a wish from the immediate here and now and transported it to some other place and some other time. It's *as if* George were saying, "Let's pretend that this note is me standing next to you when you are about to leave your office tomorrow. And let's pretend I'm telling you, 'Don't forget the toy.' "

The importance of representational competence

TO BE A functioning human being, let alone a successful one, children like George must develop the skills of what is known as *representational competence*. Narrowly defined, representational competence would include what we think of as the components of literacy: developing an oral language, and learning how to read and write. But representational competence is broader than just learning how to speak, read and write in your native language. Representational competence involves the understanding of symbolic activity in all of its forms. Representational competence involves understanding that you will need to be both a decoder of symbols presented to you by your environment (public symbols) and the creator and producer of your own symbols (personal symbols) that you will use to communicate your own ideas. Fundamentally, representational competence means that you understand, in all of its variations, that *this* can *stand* for that; that you can think about this, *as if*, it is that. The beginning of that understanding, of how *this can stand for that*, has its roots in action.

Sometime around the age of 12 months, give or take, children begin to produce an interesting type of gesture or action. These actions are imitations, often abbreviated imitations, of an action the child has emitted or observed at some time in the past; hence, the label, *deferred imitations*. A child, for example, might be sitting in her mother's lap in the living room and begin to act *as if* she were brushing her own hair. The child doesn't need the hairbrush to communicate what is happening; all she needs are the actions of folding her fingers together to represent holding the hair brush and then moving her arm up and down. Using the terminology introduced in the preceding chapter, the child's actions are *distanced* from the original circumstances and experience. The child pretending to brush her hair is doing so *distanced* from the typical **time** the action occurs (right before bedtime or in the morning) and **place** the action occurs (in her bedroom). What is significant about deferred imitation is that it "involves a familiar and well-practiced behavior detached from its customary context." In other words, I'll pretend, or act *as if*, I am brushing my hair even though it's not the right time or place and even though I'm not actually holding a hairbrush.

These deferred imitations are perhaps a child's first effort at *this stands for that*. In other words, these deferred imitations are *representations;* the child who is sitting in the living room pretending to brush her hair is representing an activity that usually happens in another time and place. The abbreviated action of moving a hand up and down her hair *stands in* for the real and actual act of hair brushing. Ultimately these actions are the foundations for all of the representational abilities to follow.

NOT LONG AFTER the emergence of deferred imitations, children begin to use another type of representation in their play, a form of *this stands for that* called *object substitutions*.

Object substitutions occur when a child uses one object to represent, or stand in for, another object. When a child pushes a block across the floor, for example, and says that he is driving his car to the store, this is an example of an object substitution. The child is using the block to represent the car.

For the most part, object substitutions don't occur randomly or willy-nilly. Children often prefer to use realistic props in their pretend play; if a toy car is available the child would most likely choose to use it for his pretend car driving instead of the block. As children develop their pretend play skills, however, they are increasingly able to use non-realistic props in support of their play; this is another example of how children are able to distance themselves from reality. The plain, rectangular piece of wood can stand in for a car even though it doesn't have wheels or doors or a steering wheel. The child can play with the piece of wood *as if* it is a car simply by imagining it, or mentally transforming it, to be a car.

The wooden block does, however, have some resemblance to what it is representing, the car. If given a choice between a rectangular block of wood and a soft, woolen ball, for example, a child would likely choose the block of wood to represent the car because its shape is closer to the shape of a car. In some sense the child can see more 'carness' in the wooden block than in the ball. That doesn't mean that a child couldn't use the ball to represent a car if he wanted to or if no other suitable object were available. The power of imagination is so strong and flexible that one day this very same child will be able to let the word 'car' stand in for and represent a car even though that word has even less resemblance and connection to the real object than the woolen ball does. (At least the woolen ball is a concrete object.)

As children become skillful players, their object substitutions become more complex and flexible. They begin to use double object substitutions, for example. Two pieces from a checker game are placed on top of the wooden block to represent the people riding in the car. Think about the complexity of what may seem to be a fairly simple form of play. There are at least three *as if* components to this play: the wooden block is being used *as if* it is a car; the checker pieces are being used *as if* they are the people/passengers riding in the car; and the block of wood (car) carrying the checker pieces (passengers) is pushed along the floor *as if* it is being driven down the highway. The wooden block and the checker pieces are the props and support for the play but the engine of the car play, if you will, is the child's imagination, the child's ability to let one object stand in for another.

Children also become very flexible with their ability to use object substitutions and it's easy to see how this flexibility is related to the development of creativity. The wooden block, for example, isn't relegated to a life as a pretend car; on another day, the child might use the very same block as a bed for one of his dolls or as a roof for a house he is building. The power of the imagination allows the child to use one object as a stand in, or a representer, for a variety of objects. At the same time, one object can be represented by a variety of other objects. One day the idea of a car is represented by a toy car and the next day by a wooden block. And as mentioned above, that same child will one day represent that same idea of car by the use of three letters, c_a_r.

The ability to use one object to stand in for many different things and to have one thing represented by a variety of objects is one of the great powers of the imagination. Consider an everyday object, the shoe, for example. For most of us, under most circumstances, the shoe is an object with a singular and obviously utilitarian function: it goes on our feet to help us walk and to protect us from uncomfortable and sometimes harmful surfaces. For some of us, there might be the ancillary function of making a fashion statement. But there are times when we can distance ourselves from the inherent function of a shoe and see that it can serve other purposes. If our fear and disgust overwhelms our reverence for all living things, we can wield a shoe like a weapon and deal with the spider crawling across our living room floor (the shoe is used *as if* it were a fly swatter). If we are Nikita Khrushchev, former head of the Soviet Union, and we don't like what someone is saying about our country at the United Nations in 1960, we can use our shoe to pound the table as an expression of our anger (the shoes is used *as if* it is a gavel). And when you come upon the pile of several thousand shoes in the United States Holocaust Museum, you instantly recognize that in this particular context, this pile of a common everyday object is so much more than a pile of utilitarian shoes. It is a symbolic representation of unfathomable horror and we stand there and look at those shoes *as if* we are looking at the victims.

It also turns out that the young child's ability to use one object to represent another can be good practice for later life. Think about the young child who can represent a gun with a pencil, a stick, or a pointed finger. That kind of pretend play may have been good training for some of the early inductees into the Army during World War II. They didn't have real weapons to use for their training exercises and had to make do with mop handles as make-believe anti-aircraft guns; they used these mop handles *as if* they were the real thing. Even though the purpose of their training was quite serious, it was a good thing that these recruits had practiced their object substitution skills when they were younger.

THE YOUNG CHILD who moves her hands up and down *as if* she is brushing her hair and pushes a wooden block across the floor *as if* it is a car will then become the young child who makes marks on a piece of paper *as if* those marks are the ideas she wants to express. Take, for example, the first word our daughter wrote down on a piece of paper.

FVBT. Those four letters were the first word, other than her name, that our daughter wrote (printed) on a piece of paper. I no longer remember the context in which this word appeared; I know the house in which it was written but not the reason it was written. It lives more than thirty-five years later because it was the first.

FVBT. To you, the reader, these four letters undoubtedly look to be just that, four random letters, not a recognizable word. But I was there. I knew what this young child was trying to write, what idea she was trying to represent with those four letters. And as an academic who studied and taught classes about children's development, I knew a little bit about how she was going about that process of representation.

As children enter the world of literacy and begin to read and write, they often create, or construct, some fascinating word spellings. When held up against the conventional spelling of words found in the dictionary, these word constructions are clearly errors or misspellings. It is often possible, however, to figure out the logic behind these misspellings, a logic which reveals how a child is actively trying to represent or symbolize the sounds she hears in the spoken language around her. These spelling mistakes, which are really the products of very active minds, have been referred to as children's *invented spellings*.

Invented spellings typically emerge between the ages of three and five, after children have been exposed to oral language, learned the names of the letters of the alphabet, and have had some experience with the processes of reading and writing. Our daughter had, at that point in her development, three things at her disposal when she was motivated to represent that word with written marks on a piece of paper: she knew the word she was trying to spell from hearing it spoken; she knew the letters of the alphabet; and she had had a good deal of practice in her play using one object to stand in for another. The challenge, then, was for our daughter to represent those spoken sounds with the letters of alphabet.

Which brings us back to FVBT. In the process of creating their invented spellings, children acoustically analyze the word they want to spell and then go 'look' for those sounds in the letters of the alphabet. One of the patterns of invented spellings found across children is that in searching for the letter needed to represent a particular sound, children often find what they need in the beginning or first half of the sound of the letter name. In my daughter's FVBT, she found the following sounds in the letter names.

/F/ = ev

/V/ = vee

/B/ = ba

/T/ = tee

It made perfect sense to my daughter to use FVBT (ev vee ba tee) to represent the word she was to trying spell - EVERYBODY. She used the same process to arrive at the first written representation of her own name, MLE. In this case, she found the sounds she needed in the full letter names and simply used the letter itself.

/M/ = m (name of the letter)

/L/ = l (name of the letter

/E/ = e (name of the letter)

MLE = Emily

It could be argued that MLE is more parsimonious and makes more sense than the actual spelling.

Here is another interesting example of how children find the sounds they need for their word spelling. One of my former college students collected this invented spelling from a young child: CY-MEN. No one in the college class could guess what the child was spelling until I suggested that they slow down their pronunciation of the letters and focus on the first halves of the sounds of the letter names. By doing so, the students could see how the child found the representation of the /s/ sound in the letter /C/ and the representation of the /w/ sound in the letter /Y/. From there, it was easier to see what the child was trying to spell: SWIMMING.

As children progress in their literacy development, particularly as a result of formal reading instruction in school, their invented spellings will fade away and be replaced by the conventional and socially acceptable word spellings that are found in dictionaries. The spelling of a word - the way in which you represent sounds with letters - will no longer be a personal creation but rather be a word that resides in the public pool of words. The transition from the personal to a public spelling of words is ultimately necessary for communication among people to occur. But the invented spellings of childhood are an important example of an active mind at work and of the developmentally critical processes of representation and the use of symbols, of the understanding that *this can stand for that.*

Signifiers and the signifieds

DEFERRED IMITATIONS, OBJECT substitutions, and invented spellings are examples of how representational activity is comprised of two components: the *signifier* and the *signified*. The child making believe she is brushing her hair is using the action of her hands (the signifier) to represent the hair brushing (the signified). The young girl pretending to push a car across the floor is using the wooden block (the signifier) as the symbolic representation of the car (the signified). And my daughter used FVBT as the signifier for the idea embodied in the word, EVERYBODY, the signified.

What are some of the things that can signified or symbolically represented? As we have already seen, objects can be represented (the wooden block as the car) and actions can be represented (brushing of hair). It is also possible to represent feelings, emotions, and desires. For example, one day our granddaughter showed us a photograph of a stuffed unicorn that she had seen in the store and wasn't allowed to buy; the downturned corners of her mouth represented her feelings about this situation very clearly. And when I have been taking too many photographs of her, she has communicated her angry feelings with her facial expressions just as clearly. Virtually every aspect of our existence, the animate and inanimate, the tangible and ephemeral, can be represented; it just takes the right *signifier* to stand in for the *signified*.

Signifiers, the ways in which we symbolically represent the objects, actions, people, and emotions in our lives, can take a variety of forms. The master pantomimist, Marcel Marceau, was able to convey entire stories about Bip the clown by just using actions. We knew that Bip was trapped inside a box and trying to get out, and it was crystal clear when Bip was fighting the wind while walking down the street. No words were spoken; Marceau's ability to depict actions and feelings through movement did all the communication.

Dance choreographers also use movement to symbolically represent ideas and stories. George Balanchine, long time director of the

New York City Ballet company, created a dance depicting the story of the Greek god Apollo and the three muses who pay him a visit. The African-American choreographer, Alvin Ailey, used the movement of dance in *Revelation* to tell the story of the African-American journey from slavery to freedom. Again, no words were used - or needed - to convey these stories, just movement.

Music can be another form or vehicle of symbolic representation. The composer Antonio Vivaldi combined musical notes, rhythm, and silence to portray the four seasons that make up a year while Aaron Copeland used the same available pool of notes and rhythms to paint a musical picture of an 'An Appalachian Spring.' And in the world of the visual artist, Vincent Van Gogh used colors and light to represent his idea of a starry night while George Seurat used his vision of colors and light to show us the lives of people spending a Sunday in a park along a Parisian river.

In all of these examples, *signifiers* (movement, musical tones, colors) are combined in unique ways to represent the *signified* (feeling of being trapped in a box, the stars in the nighttime sky, people enjoying a riverside picnic). The ways in which we can symbolically represent our experiences may, in fact, be limitless.

All signifiers, however, are not the same and looking at the differences between and among them is important for understanding how different forms of representation indicate different degrees of *distancing from reality,* and for understanding children's progression through the development of representational competence.

Imagine, for example, that you have a pet dog who is one, allowed to roam free in the house when you are gone, but two, is not allowed to get up on your bed. How might you know whether or not your dog followed the rules while the family was out of the house? If you came home and found black fur on a bunched up bedspread, that would be pretty good evidence that your dog had spent some nap time on the bed. Although your dog may have been smart enough to get down from the bed when he heard the garage door open, he wasn't smart enough to clean up the traces of himself that he had left on the bed - black fur and a bunched up bedspread. You know that the dog had been on the bed because the *this*, the black fur and bunched up spread, stands for the *that*, the guilty dog.

This type of representation, or *signifier*, is called an *index*. An index is a representation that is an actual trace of the original thing being signified. A hunting guide who is an expert tracker, for example, can look at the impressions in the snow and identify the type of animal that left the track and the approximate time the track was made: a deer passed through the ravine about two hours ago. The essential characteristic of index signifiers is that they are actual traces or 'leftovers', if you will, of the signified. I remember hearing about a museum that used the concept of the index as representation to figure out the approximate ages of the people viewing certain exhibits. How did they do this? By looking at the height of the smudges on the glass that encased the displays. They could get a good sense of which exhibits appealed to children by looking at the height of the traces of the hands and noses that the children left on the glass.

An interesting example of the use of index signifiers can be found in the world of criminal justice. Television shows such as *CSI, NCIS*, and *Bones* have portrayed the work of criminalists and forensic scientists. Like the standard 'whodunnit,' these shows depict a crime and the characters on the show then spend the next hour trying to solve that crime. The process of 'cracking the case' includes the standard practices of interviewing neighbors and interrogating subjects, but the characters on these shows also employ the methodology of forensic sciences in determining how certain clues *represented*, or *signified*, the guilty party.

Take the science of fingerprints, for example. Any of us who have watched those television shows would expect to see a police investigator dusting the crime scene for fingerprints. Why is this done? When we touch a surface with a bare hand we are in effect leaving a trace of ourselves on that surface. Since each person has a unique set of fingerprints, that trace can be used to identify a specific person. In other words, our fingerprints are a direct representation, or *signifier*, of ourselves, the *signified*. No one may have actually seen us in the room where the murder took place, but if our fingerprints are found on the surfaces of the room, that is pretty good evidence that we were in fact there; the crime scene can be investigated *as if* we were there.

The smart criminal, however, knows about the power of finger-prints and will wear gloves or will wipe down the surfaces he touched in an effort to not leave his fingerprint trace at the scene. But that doesn't mean he didn't leave other traces of his presence at the crime scene. He may have left a shoe impression in the mud outside the window he broke in order to enter the house, deposited some fibers from his jacket on the window sill as he climbed through the broken window, or perhaps dropped a cigarette butt in the driveway before entering the house, thus providing a sample of his DNA. Once he becomes a suspect, the shoe impression can be matched to a pair of boots found in his closet, the fiber can be matched to the jacket hanging in his closet, and the genetic material from the cigarette can be matched to the genetic material taken from a swab of the inside of his cheek. The shoe impression, the clothing fiber, and the DNA are all traces and representations of the person: they are the signifiers representing the signified, the suspected bad guy.

When all of these types of representational evidence are collect-ed, analyzed and presented in court, what the prosecution is saying to the defendant and jury is something like this: No one saw you commit the crime, and no one saw you at the scene of the crime, but you left enough representations of yourself to leave us no option but to conclude that you were there and that you did, in fact, commit the crime. The moral of the criminal story might be, therefore, that we should be careful of the signifiers we leave behind.

Signifiers, then, are representations that have direct connections to the signified, the black fur of the dog, for example. Now consider a drawing of the dog who left that black fur on the bedspread. The drawing looks like a dog, includes the main features and characteris-tics of a dog - black fur, floppy ears, long tail - and communicates the essence of 'dogness.' But the drawing, the representation of a dog on a piece of paper, never was a dog and wasn't left on the paper by a dog. It is not the trace, or index, of a dog; the drawing is the *symbolic* representation of a dog.

Symbols, a second type of signifiers, can take many forms. There are drawings of dogs and sculptures of dogs. The behaviors and actions of dogs can be symbolically represented by gesture and movement. The key characteristic of *symbols* is that they retain and represent some of the essential aspects of that which is being represented, essential aspects of the *signified*, in this case, essential aspects of 'dogness.' We can see how symbols represent the essence of things in children's early representational drawings. The young scribbler who draws a tree by making one long vertical line covered with squiggly lines on top does so because to him, those shapes approximate the essence of 'treeness.' Children's first representations on paper of people are often basic drawings of hands, legs, bodies and heads, their attempt to capture the essence of 'peopleness.'

Symbols, unlike indices, are created by the person doing the representation as opposed to being left by whatever is being represented. The dog leaves his fur behind but the child creates the drawing or representation of the dog. The symbol, therefore, is one step further removed from reality than the index; there is a little more distance between a symbol and what it represents than between an index and what it represents. Black fur on the bed is actually part of a dog; we relate to the drawing on a piece of paper *as if* it is a dog.

And then there is the word, *dog*, itself.

The third category of signifiers consists of representations that are called *signs*. Unlike *indices* and *symbols*, which have some perceptible connection to the signified, signs are arbitrary representations that have no discernible connection to that which is being signified. Words are the most common example of signs. The word, *dog*, has no apparent connection to the animal it is standing in for; it is an arbitrarily assigned representation. As users of the language, we carry with us some consensual understanding of what that sign means but man's best friend could have just as easily been called a 'perdunkel' and we would all have learned to associate that word, or sign, with what it means to be a dog.

Written numerals are also examples of signs. Consider the numbers one through nine: 1, 2, 3, 4, 5, 6, 7, 8, 9. It is possible that the first numeral, 1, bears some resemblance to what it represents since it is a single, straight line; it is difficult to see, however, how any of the other numerals are anything but arbitrary and agreed upon representations of numerical amounts. Where is 'fiveness' in 5, for example?

A sign, therefore, is any representation that could easily - and arbitrarily - be replaced by a different - and equally arbitrary - representation. The muddy paw print of a dog represents the dog and can't be replaced by the paw print of a bear. Similarly, you can't take a drawing of a bear and decide that it will now represent a dog. But someplace in the etymological development of words, another sign or word for dog could have been attached to the concept of our beloved pet and that would be the word we would be using today; we would all be saying, "You're such a good perdunkle."

Signs, then, are the signifiers that are most distanced from reality, from that which is being represented or signified. The index is an actual trace of the signified; the symbol bears a resemblance to the signified; and the sign is a disconnected, arbitrary representation of the signified. It is no wonder, therefore, that deep philosophical discussions and higher mathematical problem-solving can be challenging for many of us. Those activities live in the world of signs and complex sign usage; representations and the manipulation of representations that can seem to be totally disconnected and distanced from reality.

Children's development of representational competence can be looked at as a journey through the use of the index, symbol, and sign. Although development never proceeds in a definitive straight line, we can see how children's use of the representational *as if*, of their understanding of how *this can stand for that*, demonstrates their understanding of how representations can move further away from the reality of what they are representing. The abbreviated actions of *de-*

ferred imitation are like the trace, or *index*, of the deer track in the snow, while the *object substitution* of a wooden block for a car is an early example of using a *symbol* that bears some resemblance to that which is being represented. Finally, *invented spellings* are the beginning of a child's grappling with *signs*, representations that are arbitrary and have the least resemblance to the signified.

The distancing of representations

IN SOME WAYS the progress of humankind has been marked by the advancements in the ways in which representations can be transmitted and communicated over long distances. Take, for example, the invention of the telegraph in the mid-19th century. It turns out that four-year-old George from the day care center and President Abraham Lincoln shared something in common: the understanding of the power of representation to act across time and space. For George, the representations were marks on a piece of paper; for Lincoln they were electrical impulses across telegraph wires. For George, marks on a piece of paper gave him the power to act *as if* he were in my office telling me what to do; for Lincoln, "The telegraph had given [him] a power not possessed by any other leader in history; to converse with his military leaders in the field as though he were in the tent with them."

The telegraph operates by transmitting pulses of electricity over wires. Wherever these wires could be placed - across town, over the mountain, under the sea - these electrical pulses could be sent. But fundamentally, they are just that, pulses of electricity. The question was how could ideas and words be transmitted via these pulses, over the electrical wires? This was Samuel Morse's mid-19th century contribution to our world , the creation of Morse Code.

The basis for Morse Code is a series of dots and dashes, with the difference between a dot and a dash being the duration of the electrical pulse. The duration of a dot is shorter than that of a dash. Each letter of the alphabet is represented by a particular sequence of dots and dashes. The dots and dashes, then, are the signifiers (the *this*) that represent letters or the signified (the *that*).

A well-known example of a Morse Code representation is the distress call, 'SOS', or 'Save Our Ship'. The Morse Code equivalent for 'SOS' is 'dot dot dot dash dash dash dot dot dot' (...- - -...), with the three dots representing the letter /S/ and three dashes standing in for the letter /O/. Think about the symbolic transformations involved in sending those electrical impulses. First, the actual event or experience, say the approaching enemy ship, is expressed as a series of words, *Save Our Ship!*, which is commonly understood to be a call of distress. So, first of all, the words stand for the need for help. Those words are then transformed into an abbreviation, *SOS*; the abbreviation stands for the words. The abbreviation, in turn, is transformed into a series of dots and dashes which is then transmitted over electrical wires, to be decoded by someone at the other end of the wire. In the end, we have dots and dashes standing in for an abbreviation which stands in for a series of words, which stands for a request, the need for help. They may simply be electrical impulses representing dots and dashes but it's *as if* the person is right there saying, "I need help."

What did people do when threatened by the enemy before the invention of the telegraph and Morse Code? Sometimes written notes were transported by couriers who had to make it through enemy lines in order to deliver the note to its destination. At one point in history, smoke signals were used. And I suppose, at some point in history, perhaps yelling "Help!" at at the top of your lungs was the only possibility. The invention of ways to communicate *this stands for that* over long distances - the printing press, telegraph, telephone, computer and internet - has had an immeasurable impact on civilization's development, which brings us back to Abraham Lincoln.

The telegraph and Morse Code had been invented not long before the Civil War broke out in 1861. Battles between Union and Confederate armies occurred at great distances from the White House in Washington, DC and as Commander-in-Chief, Lincoln needed a way to both know what was happening on those battlefields and to communicate with the generals in the field. Before the invention of the telegraph, "the history of mankind had been controlled by the absolute certainty that distance delayed the delivery of information." With the telegraph came the almost instantaneous communication of information over long distances. Using the representational power of written words, George was able to influence my future behavior *as if* he were with me in my office; using the representational power of code transmitted by electricity, Lincoln was able to influence the behavior of his soldiers in the field *as if* he were right there with them.

> The spirits of leaders past must have looked down on Abraham Lincoln with envy as he transposed the techniques of face-to-face dialog into electronic exchanges that imposed his will onto the decision-making of distant generals as though he was with them in the field.

Codes of all sorts

MORSE CODE IS just one example of an entire category of symbolic representations that falls under the heading of *codes*. The *Oxford American Dictionary* defines a code as a "system of words, figures, or symbols used to represent others, especially for the purposes of secrecy." I remember a childhood game I played with a cousin where we would send letters back and forth to each other, letters that were written in a rudimentary code we had created. (At least we thought it was our invention.) If I remember correctly, we devised a system based on the numerical position of each letter in the alphabet. Our missives to each other were written in sequences of numbers, each number standing in for a particular letter. I do remember that we thought of ourselves as being pretty clever although I'm not sure there was anyone actually interested in reading our letters in the first place. Regardless, the secret code we had created was a form of *this stands for that* and the intention of the code was to keep the *that* (the signified) hidden from anyone other than the intended recipient of the communication.

Our secret code may have been the play of childhood but the use of secret *this stands for that* systems has served a very serious role in the waging of wars. Karen Abbott, in her book about four women who acted as spies during the Civil War, illustrates the use of secret codes during war with two interesting examples. In one case, knitted tapestries were used to communicate the disguised information. Using patterns based on Morse Code, the tapestry was organized according to a "precise vocabulary of stitches and colors," with those stitches and colors carrying - representing - the secret message.

In a second example, a Confederate spy mastered a system of "mysterious looking symbols," with each symbol representing a letter, number, or word. For example, if the information needing to be communicated was about infantry movement, the word infantry was represented by a particular arrangement of parallel lines and circles. If news about President Lincoln was being communicated, he was represented by an upside down triangle with a dashed line running through it.

A more well-known and heralded example of the importance of secret codes in times of war can be found in the work of the Navajo Code Talkers during World War II. Twenty-nine Navajo Marines were chosen to devise a code based on the complex Navajo language, a language that very few non-Navajo people had mastered at the time.

These twenty-nine Marines created a double encryption system that worked in the following way: first, an English word was chosen to represent each letter of the alphabet and then that English word was paired with its Navajo equivalent. When messages were to be communicated, the words were spelled out by using the Navajo code words. Whole words were also transmitted using the same double encryption system. The Navajo Code Talkers created a list of almost 220 words to label and describe various pieces of military equipment. Take, for example, the word battleship. The Code Talkers first paired the concept of battleship with the word, whale. The word, whale, was then paired with its Navajo equivalent, lo-tso. In other words, lo-tso, (this), stands for whale (that), which in turns stands for battleship (a secondary that).

The Navajo Code Talkers were deployed in the South Pacific theater of the war and participated in such well-known operations as the Battle of Guadicanal and the taking of Iwo Jima. Using the code system, they relayed messages and information about troop movements, the need for ammunition and medical supplies, and the locations of the enemy. The code that was developed and used by these Navajo Marines proved to be unbreakable and has been considered a "significant factor hastening the Allied victory in the Pacific." The system created by the Navajo Code Talkers was also used during the Korean and Vietnam wars and because of its value to our country's military efforts was kept classified until 1968. As recognition of their work, the original Navajo Code Talkers were awarded the Congressional Gold Medal in 2000.

SOMETIMES SYMBOLIC REPRESENTATIONS are undecipherable not because they were designed to keep secrets but because the symbolic systems can't be understood. This was the case, and the historical significance, of the Rosetta Stone, which was discovered in 1799.

Originally inscribed around 196 BC, the Rosetta Stone consists of messages written in three different scripts, one of which is Egyptian hieroglyphics. Up until the discovery of the Rosetta Stone, Egyptian hieroglyphics was undecipherable; it was a written language that could not be read and understood. Because the same text was inscribed on the stone in three different languages, two of which able to be read, those two languages were used as keys for figuring out the hieroglyphics system. Once this symbolic system was decoded - once the *this stands for that* of hieroglyphics was figured out - other documents and inscriptions could be read, thus leading to a greater understanding and appreciation of the ancient Egyptian civilization.

A similar discovery was made when the Bisitun Inscription (discovered in Iran) was deciphered by Henry Rawlinson in the mid-19th century. The Bisitun Inscription was created over 2500 years ago, and like the Rosetta Stone, contained messages written in three cuneiform scripts, one of the earliest forms of writing.

The writers of cuneiform scripts were able to use their symbols to encode information about medicine, law and politics of the day but until Rawlinson's breakthrough, that information about their lives and culture was not accessible. Once Rawlinson was able to decipher the scripts, was able to figure out how their *this stands for that* system worked,

> a completely undiscovered and unsuspected dimension of the ancient world [was revealed], not only betraying the long-forgotten secrets of cities like Babylon, Ninevah, and Nimrud, but other civilizations whose very names had been lost long ago.

Metaphors, proverbs, and fables

THERE IS ANOTHER type of code, one that doesn't keep secrets, but one that does use certain words to stand in for the meaning of other words. This is a type of code that doesn't hide meaning as much as reveal meaning. Consider, for example, these words from the Carl Sandburg poem, "Fog."

> The fog comes
> on little cat feet.

Sandburg's poem is about the weather condition of fog. It's not about cats or how cats move on their paws. In the poetic effort to describe the nature of fog, Sandburg found a comparison in the movement of cats and he assumed his readers could, and would, apply their knowledge of cats to what he was trying to say about fog. Sandburg used the movement of cats - and words that described that movement - to represent, to stand for, the movement of fog as it came in over the city. In essence, he asks his readers to think about the movement of fog *as if* it were the movement of a cat, or the movement of a cat *as if* it were the movement of fog.

Sandburg used the figure of speech known as a *metaphor*, and that's what metaphors do; they ask us to consider and understand one thing in light of our knowledge about something else. As the author Wallace Stevens wrote, "Reality is a cliche from which we escape by metaphor." When we hear a newscaster on television describe a particular issue of the day as the 'third rail' of politics, we understand that he is referring to an issue that politicians may try to avoid addressing. The newscaster didn't say that directly but the metaphor used, 'the third rail,' appeals to our knowledge of subway train systems that are powered by electricity; the train's wheels run over the outside two rails and there is a third rail in the middle that provides the power for the train itself. If you are foolhardy enough to want to cross those tracks, you must avoid that middle rail or risk electrocuting yourself. In other words, the newscaster is saying that a politician foolhardy enough to take a position on the particular 'third rail' issue, may lose some votes in the next election. The politician needs to think about the issue *as if* she were crossing the dangerous railroad tracks.

Since this book is at least partially about the development of children, it's interesting to consider how metaphors often have been used to describe how children develop and grow. Saying that a child is just 'blossoming' suggests that like a flower, a child's abilities and talents will emerge according to her own schedule and a child will become what she is destined to become, much like the acorn is destined to become an oak tree. Describing a child's mind as a little 'sponge' suggests that the child soaks up (another metaphor) information from her environment. Likening a child's learning to the act of scientists suggests that children are curious and that they observe, explore, and experiment with the physical and social worlds, testing their theories about how those worlds work. As a way of understanding children and childhood, all of these metaphors ask us to think about children *as if* they are something else. *This* - flower, sponge, scientist - *stands for that*, children. The flowers, sponges, and scientists are the *signifiers* and the development of children is the *signified*.

There are two other examples of words and language used to reveal meaning. When we hear or read the *proverb*, "a stitch in time saves nine", we know that it really isn't a statement about sewing;

someplace in our experiences we were introduced to that proverb as a lesson about the importance of doing the little things now in order to guard against bigger problems developing later. The words, *a stitch in time saves nine*, represent, or stand in for, the lesson and the moral of the story. *Parables* do the same thing just in longer form. The fable from Aesop about the ant and grasshopper is not read in order to learn facts about ants and grasshoppers. The parable is read in order to communicate or teach a lesson about the importance of preparing for the future, whether that be storing food for the long winter or saving money for future emergencies. The fable represents the lesson in such a way that it may be more enjoyable to read and easier to remember than a dry, boring lecture on the importance of preparing for the future. In both cases, the specific words of the proverb and parable stand in for and represent some larger meaning that transcends the specific meanings of the individual words.

The emotional power of symbols

ON THE SURFACE, symbols and signs can be seen as simply scribbles, sketches or letters on pieces of paper. But those scribbles, sketches and letters at time wield such emotional power for people that the use of the symbols or representations can lead to dissension, discord and sometimes violence. During the writing of this book, for example, there was much debate about the place of the Confederate flag in our country's history and in our current sensibilities. Deciding whether or not it would keep its Fighting Sioux mascot was a question that occupied my former teaching home, the University of North Dakota, for years. The drawing of a swastika and the uttering of the 'N-word,' both 'just' symbols, are generally not acceptable actions and if used, can raise very strong reactions. We have also seen how the drawing of a cartoon representation of a revered religious figure led to riots and death. The following example concerning a piece of cloth illustrates this emotional power of symbols.

During the 1984 Republican National Convention in Dallas, Texas, a man by the name of Gregory Lee Johnson set fire to and burned a rectangular piece of cloth. At a very base level, that is all he did; he set fire to and burned a piece of cloth. He engaged in this action as a form of protest against actions of the Reagan presidency with which he did not agree. For these actions, Gregory Lee Johnson was arrested, convicted, and sentenced to one year in prison and fined the amount of $2000.

It was, of course, not just any piece of cloth that he burned. He didn't remove his shirt and set that afire nor did he find a discarded blanket on the street and light a match to it. Johnson burned an American flag and by doing so was found guilty of violating a Texas law that made it a crime to destroy or desecrate certain respected and venerated objects, the American flag being one of those objects.

Johnson appealed his conviction and his case eventually made its way to the United States Supreme Court which handed down a decision in 1989. The Court's decision affirmed Johnson's right to express his First Amendment free speech rights through the burning of the flag, as contemptible as that act may be to many people. This decision effectively invalidated laws that made flag burning a crime in 48 of the 50 states.

At its core, this legal case was about a *symbol*, a piece of cloth that was simply a representation of certain ideas. The cloth itself had negligible monetary value and Johnson had brought it to the demonstration himself; he hadn't stolen it or taken someone else's property. The case wasn't about any intrinsic value or ownership of the object itself. The case was entirely about what the object stood for; what the object signified.

The emotional power of the symbol can be seen in the comments from the four justices who dissented from the majority decision. For example, Justice Rehnquist wrote that,

> *The American flag, then, throughout more than 200 years of our history, has come to be the visible symbol embodying our Nation. It does not represent the views of any political party, and it does not represent any particular political philosophy.*

Similarly, Justice Stevens argued that the flag is,

> More than a proud symbol of the courage, the
> determination, and the gifts of nature that transformed
> 13 fledgling Colonies into a world power. It is a symbol of
> freedom, equal opportunity, or religious tolerance, and of
> good will for other peoples who share our aspirations...
> The value of the flag as a symbol cannot be measured.

These dissenting justices agreed with the State of Texas which had argued that it is in the national interest to protect such an important symbol. The majority of the justices, however, argued that the protection of free speech embodied in the First Amendment superseded whatever values and historical importance might be embodied in the symbol itself, regardless of the emotions that particular symbol represented.

The proverbial blankie

I WILL END this chapter by circling back to children and another way they use the power of *this stands for that* to help them navigate their world and their developmental journey.

People come and go in a child's world. Most of these comings and goings do not really matter or have an impact on a child. The strangers a child sees on the street while being pushed in a stroller or an aunt who visits once a year can enter and exit a child's life with nary a reaction. But if the child's mother or father leaves her field of vision, all 'heck' can break loose.

Why do many infants and toddlers have these strong reactions to the absence of a parent or the person who takes on the role of primary caregiver in the child's life? Children have these strong reactions because they have come to depend on that parent for all of the 'daily doings' of life; the parent feeds them, entertains them, transports them from one place of interest to another, comforts them and in general provides for their safety and security. Children develop intense bonds and attachments with parents. They depend on them and trust them and this trust and dependence helps children see the world as a stable place to be.

But it is inevitable that children will at some point begin to experience separations from these bonds and attachments. Sometimes the separation occurs simply when a parent leaves the room at bedtime and other times the separations occur due to the realities of a family's life. Parents may need to leave for work and have to leave the child at the day care center. And parents sometimes want to socialize with other adults and need to leave their child with a babysitter. Any of these separations can result in a not-so-happy child.

There are also separations that occur due to the child's progress in her developmental journey. As children grow and develop, they can do more and more things for themselves; they do not have to be as dependent on a parent for their needs to be met. As their language develops, children can express their desires and request fulfillment of their needs rather than waiting for an adult to guess what they might want from their cries or gestures. Once a child figures out how to stand upright and take steps across the floor, she can take herself to where she wants to go rather than depend on a parent to carry her to the desired destination. These developments, and more, lead a child to the exercise of independence, to a quest for autonomy, and much to the chagrin of parents, to sometimes (or often) that stage of development known as the 'terrible twos'. This is the stage when obstinance and stubbornness become a major personality trait and a child's favorite word becomes, 'No'. Obstinance, stubbornness, and 'no' are often a child's expression of this quest for independence and autonomy.

Independence and autonomy, however, can sometimes be scary. Venturing out into the world can be, as they say, a mixed bag. Although the child wants to do for herself, the safety and security provided by her parents was also nice; it meant that there were things about which the child didn't have to worry. The child might discover that all verbalized desires expressed to a friend are not fulfilled and that the floor hurts when you fall down trying to get to the desired toy on the other side of the room. It's also not always easy to entertain yourself when you are bored sitting in your carseat in the backseat of the car. A child can feel torn between wanting to do for herself but not wanting to be out there doing for herself all on her own.

Many children find a resolution for this problem, for the tension they feel as they march off into independence. In a sense, the resolution is to bring the parent with them into this new world of autonomy, to carry with them something that will stand in for and represent the parent, to create what the psychologist D. W. Winnicott called, the *transitional object*.

Often a soft toy or blanket, the transitional object, in effect, represents the parent and what that parent stands for: safety, security, and comfort. The transitional object is the signifier for the parent, the signified. Very often the transitional object has been an actual part of the important interactions that have occurred between the child and parent. It may have been the blanket that first wrapped the newborn infant in her crib. Later, this very same blanket was snuggled in the toddler's arms as her parent read a bedtime story. The blanket not only symbolically represents the parent but may actually retain some of the scent of the parent's body, serving as a form of index signifier. The blanket as security object is not just a figment of the child's imagination but a way in which the child can carry the memory and essence of her parent with her, a way in which she can move through the sometimes scary world *as if* her parent is with her. As Susan Linn wrote in her book about the importance of make-believe,

> Transitional objects seem like nothing special to the
> outside world, but their owners invest them with special
> meaning...The baby doesn't create the blanket. But the
> baby does create the blanket's meaning.

Linn's comment echoes what Winnicott wrote about the transitional object: "Not so much the object used as the use of the object."

The toddler, then, walks into a world of independence carrying that blankie or stuffed toy *as if* she is bringing the important part of her parent with her; the part of her parent that protected her, comforted her and provided for her. She takes a representation of her parent with her as she begins to separate (distance herself) from the parent and navigate the world on her own. The strength of her parent as protector, provider and comforter is *represented* by that blanket and supports the child in the development of her own strength. This particular act of *as if*, make-believe, and *this stands for that*, then, helps the child fulfill her destiny as an independent and autonomous human being.

Chapter 3

Standing in the Other Person's Shoes

In his book, *On the Revolution of the Heavenly Spheres*, published in 1543, Nicolaus Copernicus set in motion the beginning of a shift in how we thought about the Earth's position in the universe. Copernicus, a Polish priest, argued that the view which had the Earth as the center of the universe and the stars and other planets revolving around it, was incorrect. In his book, Copernicus "defied common sense and received wisdom to place the Sun at the center of the heavens, then set the Earth in motion around it." Copernicus imagined and posited a heliocentric view; the sun, in fact, was the center of our universe, and the Earth was just one of a number of planets that orbited around the sun. This major paradigm shift in thinking about the universe was not offered lightly nor without some fear; knowing that the Catholic church would not be pleased with his new scientific theory, Copernicus waited to publish the book until he knew his own death was imminent. It then took close to 200 years before his ideas about the earth's position in the universe were fully accepted; in fact, his book was prohibited reading by the Catholic Church for those 200 years.

Children's Copernican Revolution

I WAS VISITING our campus child care center one morning when I stopped by the sand table to chat with Robbie who was pushing a truck around the sand. We were on opposite sides of the table engaged in conversation when he stopped moving the truck and said,

"I can make an exclamation point in the sand. Do you want to see me do it?" I said, "Sure," and he proceeded to make a vertical line in the sand with his finger and then placed a dot, or period, underneath the line. The smile on his face made it clear that he was quite proud of his accomplishment. I then said, "Let me see if I can make one." I also drew a vertical line in the sand with a dot underneath it. Without any hesitation, Robbie said, "No, that's wrong," and reached over to 'erase' the dot underneath my line and reposition the dot so that it was under the vertical line as seen from where he was standing on the other side of the table.

ALLUDING TO THE importance of Copernicus' theory about the universe, the Swiss psychologist, Jean Piaget, wrote that children themselves experience a "miniature Copernican revolution" as they approach the age of two. This "miniature Copernican revolution" is marked by the child's emerging understanding that "he is for all practical purposes but one element or entity among others in a universe that he has gradually constructed for himself." In other words, a child begins to understand that he, like the Earth, isn't the center of the universe; that the way he sees the exclamation point in the sand isn't necessarily the way everyone else sees it. It's all about understanding that your perspective may be just one among many possible perspectives. Like the earth, the child comes to understand that he is just one of a number of planets.

The classic Piagetian experiment for studying the issue of perspective-taking is known as the *mountain-viewing* task. A child is seated at a table and has in front of him a three-dimensional model of a group of mountains; the mountains vary from one another in height and size. The child is then asked to look at a number of photographs, each representing a different view of the mountains; the views differing based on where an observer of the scene might be seated at the table. The basic task for the child is to select the photograph that represents the mountains from where he is seated and to also select the photograph that would represent the view of a doll seated at another position at the table. Generally speaking, up until about the age of four, children tend to choose the photograph that matches their own view of the mountains; they choose that view not only for themselves but also for the doll which is seated at a different position at the table. The child is unable to imagine what the mountains look like to the other observer. Between the ages of four and six, there is a development of an understanding that perspectives might be different depending on your position and by age seven, most children have come to understand that multiple perspectives can exist. This developmental change has been referred to as *decentration* or a *decentering of perspective.*

Coming to understand that people can have different perspectives, that the position of the exclamation point dot depends on where you are standing, is a major aspect of children's social development. The development of friendships, communication skills, and the ability to engage in cooperative activity would be difficult if not impossible without this understanding of multiple perspectives. The ability to understand, and the predisposition to consider, that the world may look different when standing in another person's shoes, and to be able to think about the world *as if* you are in those shoes, is a fundamental piece of our lives as human beings.

Theory of Mind

IMAGINE THE FOLLOWING situation. You are shown a video in which a child, let's call her Mary, watches her mother move a box of cookies from a cabinet in the kitchen to one of the kitchen drawers. Mary's mother then leaves the room. While her mother is out of the room, Mary takes the box of cookies out of the drawer and returns it to the cabinet. Shortly after, Mary's mother returns to the kitchen and at this point the video is stopped. You are then asked the following question: "Mary's mother wants to get a cookie to eat. Where will she look for the box of cookies?" As an adult, you probably think the answer to this question is obvious: Mary's mother will look in the drawer because that is where she put the box of cookies. She didn't see her daughter move the cookies from the drawer to the cabinet so she has no reason to believe that the box isn't where she left it. Her actions in looking for the cookie will be directed by her belief as to where the cookies are; her actions will be directed by her *mental representation* of where she last saw the box of cookies. She will act *as if* the situation and circumstances are exactly as she left them.

The answer, however, isn't so obvious to young children. It wouldn't be unusual for a four-year-old to say that the mother will look for the box in the cabinet. Why? The child answers this way because that's where *she* knows the box of cookies to be. The four-year-old hasn't yet developed the understanding that the mother's *belief* that the box is in the drawer would influence and guide her actions; she hasn't yet developed the understanding that the mother's actions are guided by *her* mental representations of what had happened, even if those representations do not now match the reality of the location of the cookies. This hypothetical situation is commonly referred to as the *false-belief task* (the mother has a false-belief based on her mental representations) and what it is designed to explore, and what the four-year-old hasn't yet developed, is referred to as *theory of mind*.

Sometime around the age of four, children begin to understand that their actions, and the actions of others, are guided by the mind; the beliefs, desires, thoughts, intentions, experiences, etc. that we hold in our minds. And if I have a mind full of my beliefs, desires, thoughts and intentions, and you have a mind full of your beliefs, desires, thoughts and intentions, then our minds could lead to different actions even though we might be seeing or experiencing the same thing. In other words, "an individual has a theory of mind if he imputes mental states to himself and others." This is how a child comes to understand that people can have different, and differing, perspectives, about the same experience; why the exclamation point can look one way from where you are standing and look a different way to the person positioned at the other side of the table. It is also why Mary's mother will look in the kitchen drawer for the cookies even though the child knows that the cookies are in the cabinet.

Understanding that the contents of our minds influence our behaviors is significantly related to much of our lives as social beings. Imagine how difficult it would be to interact with other people if you could not consider what they were thinking or feeling. Without a theory of mind we can't predict what someone might do or explain why they did what they did. How do you persuade someone to change her mind and agree with your point of view if you can't consider what their point of view is in the first place? Without a theory of mind, what would all of those police detectives and prosecuting attorneys do instead of looking for the criminal's *motive* for committing the crime? To look for a motive is to consider the contents of a person's mind and how the contents of the person's mind influenced him or her to take the actions they did. To look for a motive for a crime, in essence, is to think about the reasons for the crime *as if* you were the criminal, *as if* you had the mind of the criminal. To consider motive is nothing less than an act of imagination and putting yourself in the shoes of the criminal.

Considering your audience

THOMAS WAS A four-year-old boy in our campus preschool. He was quite verbal for his age and he loved to read books, both books with words and those known as wordless picture books. One morning he wanted to read Tomie dePaolo's classic wordless picture book, *Pancakes for Breakfast,* to me. He also asked if we could record his reading because we had used a tape recorder previously in our times together. We were sitting side by side at a table and Thomas worked his way through the book, retelling the essence of the story and making comments about the details he focused on in some of the illustrations. When he finished reading, I suggested that he read it again but this time I was going to turn my chair around so that I couldn't see the book while he was doing the reading. Thomas happily agreed to my request and once again quickly immersed himself in the story.

To consider your audience is also an act of imagination and is closely related to the development of a *theory of mind*. Virtually all of our acts of communication - be that speaking, writing, texting - have an intended audience in mind. We are trying to communicate *something* to *someone*. That *someone* is our audience. It might be one person sitting across from us in a coffeeshop, a group of people in a lecture hall, the person who will read the letter we dropped off at the post office, or someone we have never met who is the recipient of our electronic email inquiry. Regardless of the method or mode of communication, if we want our message to be fully and correctly understood, we need to consider the *perspective* of our audience; we need to consider the contents of their minds. We need to think about how our message will be heard and received by our intended audience. As the author Richard Rodriguez stated in his memoir, *Hunger of Memory*, "I write very slowly because I write under the obligation to make myself clear to someone who knows nothing about me."

When I listened to the two tape recordings of Thomas reading *Pancakes for Breakfast*, I was struck by some interesting differences between the two versions of his readings; differences that suggested Thomas was developing a sense of audience. When I had my back turned to the table and the book, Thomas included much more detail about the illustrations and what was happening as the main character of the story went about collecting the ingredients needed for the preparation and cooking of the pancakes. Thomas seemed to be thinking about the reading experience from my perspective; he was able to understand that if I couldn't see the book then I didn't have the same information he did, information he would then need to share with me. Thomas was able to understand the reading experience *as if* he were sitting in my chair, *as if* he were me.

What might we need to take into consideration when we attempt to communicate with a particular audience? Age, background knowledge, interests, life experiences, attention span - all of these factors could be worth noting when attempting to communicate with someone. When we don't take these and other variables into consideration, we might easily, as is often said, lose our audience.

As a university teacher, I was confronted with the question of audience every time I entered the classroom and faced the students. If, for example, I underestimated their background knowledge about the subject matter of the day, I might lose them to boredom. On the other hand, if I overestimated what they already knew and understood about the subject matter, I could lose them because they were unable to connect to the subject matter and couldn't follow what I was talking about. In other words, they might tune me out because the subject matter was too familiar or they might tune me out because the subject matter was too strange. In either case, I could lose my audience. (There were a number of times over the years of teaching when I would stop in mid-lecture and say to the students, "Why do I have the feeling that I am the only one here who finds this interesting?" It was clear from their fidgeting and glazed-over eyes why I had that feeling and it was also clear that I had lost my audience.)

When I was teaching at my best - which unfortunately may not have been as often as I would have hoped - I thought about 'who' my students were. I would think about the courses they had already taken, ask them about their prior experience with young children, encourage them to share their life interests, and inquire about their goals for the course and their futures. When I was teaching at my best, I would try to prepare the course as a whole as well as individual class sessions with that information in mind. I would try to see my course through the eyes of the students; try to see the course, in this case, by imagining myself sitting in their chairs.

Considering cultural differences

IT WAS THE first day of class and after going through introductions and the course syllabus, I shared what for me was an important part of the experience that the students and I would have together during that term. I explained to the students that I valued discussion and that I welcomed challenges to anything they might read in our text materials or anything they might hear me say and espouse during the course. I told them that I genuinely valued their own past experiences and that I didn't believe students came to a course with 'empty' or 'blank' minds. I made an impassioned plea that they shouldn't just accept my viewpoints on the subject matter of the course and that they should respect their own experiences and opinions and bring them to bear on the issues we would be discussing. I shared with them what I once heard the Holocaust writer Elie Wiesel say in a lecture: "You must resist the text."

After the class had ended, one student approached me and asked if she could talk about some of the things I had said regarding the class. She was one of the international students in our program (in this case, from China.) She proceeded to tell me that in her culture, students were raised to respect their teachers and that it would be very difficult for her to disagree or challenge anything I might say. She made it clear that she was uncomfortable with the idea of voicing her own opinion if that opinion conflicted with what I, as the teacher, was stating in class. She made it very clear that her view and my view of what makes a 'good' class were quite different.

I learned over my years of university teaching that one very important aspect of considering your audience relates to the issue of differences in cultural backgrounds. Cultural differences are really differences in perspectives and theory of mind. Cultural differences are more than celebrating different holidays, eating different foods, or wearing different clothes. Some of the most significant cultural differences are the ones that concern world views and the ways in which people understand the dynamics of human relationships. It was this type of difference that my graduate student from China was expressing. From her cultural perspective, the relationship between teacher and student was one built on the respect emanating from the student towards the teacher. From my cultural perspective, I was trying to establish a classroom environment where respect would also flow from the teacher to the student as well. The contents of my mind would lead to one set of actions related to the teacher-student relationship while the contents of her mind could potentially lead to a different set of behaviors.

I had another experience with cultural differences that helped me understand how a conflict between people could occur based on world views. I had been contracted to offer a weekend workshop on language development to teachers from Head Start programs in northern Minnesota. Almost all of these teachers were Native Americans. After almost ten hours of interacting with these teachers over an evening and a day, I left with the distinct feeling that I had 'bored them to death', that I had lost my audience. My evidence for this conclusion? Lack of eye contact. Based on my understanding (i.e., perspective) about good public speaking skills, I did my best to make eye contact with as much of my audience as possible during the weekend but found most of the participants did not make eye contact with me in return. I left the experience believing that I had prepared a pretty good workshop but ultimately was not successful in engaging the teachers.

When I returned back to my university and shared my feelings about the workshop with a colleague, he said that my analysis about the participants' reactions was based on my cultural perspective that making eye contact was a positive approach to social interaction. He told me that from the perspective of many Native American cultures, making eye contact is actually a sign of disrespect. The teachers attending the workshop weren't necessarily bored; they were engaging in the teacher-student interaction based on their view of one aspect of the human relationship dynamic. My actions - making eye contact - were driven by my view while their actions - looking away - were driven by theirs. In order for me to truly understand their perspective, I needed to consider the interactions *as if* I were looking back at *me* from where *they* were sitting.

It is the potential 'clash' of perspectives that can sometimes make dealing with cultural differences a challenge. When I moved to North Dakota to take a faculty position at the university, I began to hear colleagues talking about something they called, "Indian Time." My first reaction was to consider this to be a prejudiced, if not racist, characterization. I then learned from these colleagues that the expression referred to a perceived pattern whereby Native American students would be late for classes and appointments. Again, this pattern of behavior may be a result of cultural differences, in this case, differences related to our relationship to time. (That realization, of course, doesn't mean there weren't prejudicial or racist undertones when the phrase, "Indian Time" was used.)

Western-European cultures tend to have a *linear* view of time; time progresses in a straight line and when a particular moment in that line is passed, the moment is now in the past. There are other cultures that have a more *circular* view of time. If a particular moment in time is passed, since time is progressing around the circle, that moment will come back around again. From the latter perspective, it's possible to understand why being on time for an appointment or class might not be a high priority.

Understanding another culture, then, requires the willingness to *imagine* oneself in the skin of that other person; the willingness to see the world from that perspective and the willingness to consider that their actions are driven by the contents of their minds, just as our actions are driven by the contents of our own minds. This willingness can be of benefit, for example, to people doing business in other countries; as Goleman writes, "Executives good at such perspective-taking...do better at overseas assignments presumably because they can pick up implicit norms quickly as they learn the unique mental models of a given culture."

Empathy and standing in the other person's shoes

DURING IT'S THIRD season, the television show *Star Trek* aired an episode about an alien, named Gem, who could cure people, could perhaps save their lives, by taking on or absorbing their injuries or ailments. In a sense, she was able to relieve people of their suffering by taking on their suffering herself. This being *Star Trek*, in this episode the people she might be able to save were the three main characters of Captain Kirk, Mr. Spock, and the chief medical officer, Dr. McCoy. Unfortunately, Gem wielded her powers at great risk to her own existence. Saving someone else meant that whatever was threatening the life of the other person, once absorbed by Gem, could result in her own death. The title of this *Star Trek* episode was, "The Empath."

According to the Cambridge Dictionary (online version), *empathy* can be defined as "the ability to share someone else's feelings or experiences by imagining what it would be like to be in that person's situation." Note the use of the word *imagining* in that definition. To be empathic (or empathetic), one person comes to appreciate another person's situation by the act of *as if*: I understand your situation and feelings by imagining that I am *you* with those feelings and in that situation. The psychologist Martin Hoffman offers this definition of *empathy*.

> Empathy has been defined by psychologists in two ways: (a) empathy is the cognitive awareness of another person's internal states, that is his thoughts, feelings, perceptions, and intentions...(b) empathy is the vicarious affective response to another person.

For psychologists who study empathy, this distinction between thoughts and feelings is important. In fact, psychologists, like Hoffman, distinguish between *cognitive empathy* and *affective* (or *emotional*) *empathy*. *Cognitive empathy* refers to our ability to understand the thought processes of another person; our thinking can understand and appreciate the other person's thinking. *Affective empathy*, on the other hand, refers to our ability to actually *feel* what another person feels. To experience *affective empathy* is to feel the distress, pain, sadness, or joy that another person may be experiencing. We may cry because we can imagine and feel the same emotions that are causing the other person to cry. The alien Gem, central to that *Star Trek* episode described above, is the fictional embodiment of an extreme example of *affective empathy*.

Precursors to, or versions of, empathy can be seen as early as infancy. Many of us are familiar with and perhaps have had firsthand experience with what is sometimes referred to as 'contagion crying'. One baby crying sets off the crying of other babies who are within hearing range of the first baby. The baby who begins to cry because she hears another infant crying isn't feeling empathy in the adult sense of the concept but there is an affective or mirroring response; there is something about hearing the cries that bring them out in another baby. A couple of months before her third birthday, our granddaughter demonstrated her emerging ability to demonstrate empathy when one of her younger friends at the child care center she attended experienced some difficulty with separating from his parents in the morning. He would cry and not want to physically separate from the parent. Our granddaughter would go to his side and try to comfort him, telling him that everything would be okay. She would also tell him that, "Grown-ups always come back." She was able to take her own experience of morning separations - which didn't always go easily for her either - and use that experience to understand what her friend was feeling. She then told him what perhaps she had heard spoken to her and perhaps what she would tell herself when she was experiencing the same feelings she now saw in her friend.

The toddler of two or three years of age demonstrates some aspects of empathy when she is able to identify representations of faces as expressing happy or sad emotions. She is able to identify what the other person may be feeling. More mature forms of empathy are also based on the representations that people offer and present, whether that be in facial expressions, bodily gestures, or spoken language. We can interpret these representations because we are able to understand what they may be communicating.

There is some evidence that the experience of empathy may actually be hardwired in our brains, that our species could be called *Homo empathic,* for our predilection for understanding the thoughts and feelings of others. For example, Goleman, in his book, *Focus: The Hidden Driver of Intelligence,* discusses a research study where the research subjects listened to depictions of people experiencing physical pain. As they were listening, scans were taken of their brains. Those parts of the brain that register the experience of pain were activated in the brains of the research subjects who were just *hearing* the stories about people experiencing physical pain. They were not feeling the pain themselves but their brains reacted *as if* they were.

The importance of make-believe

IT MAY COME as no surprise, and may even seem to be obvious, that children's engagement in pretend play has a relationship to their development of theory of mind and the understanding of multiple perspectives; that pretend play might be an important activity for the development of an appreciation for audience, cultural differences, and empathy. As one author wrote, "Pretense is important to theory of mind because in pretend play...a child practices at being other people."

As is the case with many aspects of child development, once a developmental construct is identified research begins to emerge that looks at individual differences in the development of the construct and at the antecedent factors that may contribute to the development of the construct itself. In the case of theory of mind, make-believe play, the activity of *as if*, contributes positively to the development of these abilities and the variation of children's experience with make-believe may explain some of the individual differences in the development of the abilities. For example, according to Paul Harris in his book, *The Work of the Imagination,*

> Role play is striking because children temporarily immerse themselves in the part that they create. They frequently start to act on the world and to talk about it as if they were experiencing it from the point of view of the invented person or creature.

If developing a theory of mind is the ability to understand the perspectives of other people, what better way to do that than by pretending to be that other person? The young child who decides to play "Mommy" with her baby dolls will have to interact with those dolls from the *perspective* of what it means to be a mommy; from the *perspective* of what a mommy does. The younger toddler who may simply hold and hug the doll *as if* it were her baby, may just be imitating or mimicking what she has experienced with her own mother. The action being imitated, however, has a reason and purpose behind it; the mother's action of hugging was motivated by some logic or emotion. The toddler may not be conscious of the reason or be able to verbally explain why she is hugging her doll but engaging in the pretend action is the first step towards understanding that there are reasons for the hugging, that there is a mind behind the hugging.

As children's make-believe play becomes more complex, is accompanied by more and more language, and becomes social, there are even more opportunities for children to practice and experience the idea that people's actions are influenced by what is in their minds. When two children are playing mommy and daddy with some dolls, for example, they have the opportunity to hear how someone else interprets the role of parent. For one child, a crying baby may be picked up, wrapped in a blanket and held, while for a second child the response is to leave the child lying in the toy crib and simply rub its back. And perhaps for a third child, the parental response is to do nothing and the let the baby cry. Three different children can 'play' the same event - a crying baby - and respond to that event, *in pretend play*, in three different ways. Three minds experience the same event but have three different perspectives on what to do and each child involved in the play gets to hear and see those differences.

When children engage in social pretend play they inevitably also engage in negotiations with each other about the play itself. Imagine the following scenario.

> Child 1: *"Let's play house with a mommy, daddy,*
> *and baby."*
>
> Child 2: *"OK. I want to be the mommy."*
>
> Child 1: *"I want to be the mommy. The mommy has*
> *more fun."*

At this point, their interest in playing together may be stymied unless they can figure out a way to resolve the common desire - desires that resides in their minds - to take on the role of mommy.

> *Child 2: "You can be the mommy next time. You be the*
> *daddy this time and the mommy next time. The*
> *daddy gets to go to work."*

> *Child 1: "My mommy goes to work."*

> *Child 2: "OK. I'll be the mommy this time and you'll be the*
> *mommy next time and then you can go to work."*

The negotiation between the two children accomplished two major things. One, it allowed the play to actually occur. At the same time, each child heard the desires and perspectives of the other child. Both children had the same desire - to play the mommy - but each child also expressed a differing perspective about what it meant to be a mommy, or daddy, and about what mommies and daddies do. The resolution of the conflict - who gets to play mommy - required both the expression and acceptance of each person's perspective. The psychologist Alan Leslie believes that social pretend play is the

> *First clear sign of children's ability to understand another*
> *person's mental state. This must be so if they can*
> *coordinate their pretending with that of another person,*
> *because they have to link their actions to what the other*
> *person is pretending, not what he or she is actually doing.*

And two other researchers, Judy Dunn and Claire Hughes, echo this sentiment when they write that,

> *To share an imaginary world with another person, to*
> *cooperate and contribute to a shared pretend narrative,*
> *requires an ability to understand what the other is*
> *thinking, feeling, and planning, a grasp of "possible*
> *worlds."*

Now think about another kind of 'social' pretend play; play with an imaginary companion, a type of play that will be explored in more detail in Chapter 5. I will call this type of play 'social' because in some sense it is a child playing with someone else, albeit in this case, the other person is a make-believe person of the child's own creation.

When children play with an imaginary friend by definition they must impute mental states to that friend. In other words, the child is responsible for not only his own mind but for the mind of the imaginary friend as well. As Tracy Gleason, a professor of psychology at Wellesley College writes,

> Imaginary play could encourage social development because children are simultaneously behaving as themselves and as someone else. This gives them a chance to explore the world from different perspectives, and is a feat that requires thinking about two ways of being at once, something that children may have difficulty doing in other circumstances.

It is not unusual for children to create imaginary companions who have definite desires and wishes, perhaps for certain kinds of foods, preferences for where they sit at the dinner table, and whether they want to accompany the family on an outing or not. There are also anecdotes about imaginary companions who are quite willful and ironically not fully under the control of their creators. It is almost as if a child who has invented an imaginary friend is practicing or 'playing' with the concept of theory of mind. Instead of having to figure out the mind of another person, the child creates that other person and creates the other person's mind as well. There is, in fact, some suggestion from research studies that play with an imaginary friend might have a positive effect on the development of theory of mind.

Underlying the relationship between theory of mind and pretend play is the concept of mental representations discussed in Chapter Two. When a child plays mommy and comforts her baby doll, this child is *mentally representing* her understanding of what a mother does when her baby is crying. The doll is a concrete representation of the baby and that toy is then incorporated into the child's experience of the mother-baby relationship, which is then represented by the child's actions. In sociodramatic play, the joint make-believe play of two or more children, we see a coming together of multiple and at times differing mental representations. This dynamic provides each child involved in the play the opportunity to experience that she is not the only one who acts based on mental representations of how some part of the world works. In the case of play with an imaginary friend, now the child is responsible for actually producing and presenting the mental representations offered by two minds. In all of these cases, the pretend play is exercising the idea that how we see our world and then act in that world is a result of mental conception and representation of that world. The connections between make-believe play and theory of mind "are due to the fact that children who engage in more pretense gain more practice at manipulating mental representations of the world and can apply their consequent understanding of mental representation outside of pretense domains."

In other words, practice at creating your own mental representations during pretend play is an antecedent to understanding that the mother will look for the cookies in the kitchen drawer because that action flows from her mental representation of where the cookies are in the kitchen. The young child who has yet to develop theory of mind and answers that the mother will look in the cabinet does so because she hasn't yet developed that understanding. As Lillard wrote, "When children pretend, and when they watch others pretend, they are aware that pretenders are mentally representing the pretend world."

The importance of stories...and how we talk about them

ONE POWERFUL WAY of developing a consideration of other perspectives, theory of mind, audience, cultural differences, and empathy is through the act of reading, particularly the reading of fiction. The psychologist Steven Pinker wrote in his book, *The Better Angels of Our Nature,* that "reading is a technology for perspective-taking." The novelist Julian Barnes, author of such books as *The Sense of An Ending* and *Flaubert's Parrot,* said that "It was through books that I first realized there were other worlds beyond my own; first imagined what it might be like to be another person." And another novelist, Meg Rosoff, muses about the potential consequence for someone who doesn't experience the world of books: "Imagine a person who never reads books...What might it do to your brain, never to be anyone other than yourself, in your own here and now?...Without stories we are trapped in a static version of ourselves." In other words, a "static version of ourselves" without the ability to consider the perspective of others. And as the main character in Lloyd Jones' novel, *Mister Pip* said about reading Dickens' *Great Expectations*, "It taught me you can slip under the skin of another just as easily as your own, even when that skin is white and belongs to a boy alive in Dickens' England. Now, if that isn't an act of magic I don't know what is."

The power of stories to influence the development of perspective-taking begins early in life when young children are introduced to the world of children's literature, when they curl up in a parent's lap and have a story read to them. It turns out that the words and stories of the book being read aren't the only contributors to the development of perspective-taking, theory of mind, and empathy; the language used by the person doing the reading can also have a significant influence on these developments.

Research studies have been conducted that look at the individual differences in children's development of such skills as theory of mind and perspective-taking. One variable that has been identified is the degree to which a parent, the reader, talks about *mental states* during the reading. Parents who focus on *mental states* during reading do such things as drawing the child's attention to what a character in the story might be thinking or feeling. Questions such as "Why do you think he (the character in the story) did that?" or "How do you think she is feeling right now?" These types of questions encourage children to consider what is going on in the minds of the characters and other people in general. In addition, these types of questions can also encourage children to reflect on what is going on in their own minds.

The focus on *mental states* during the parent-child reading interaction is related to a more general aspect of parent-child interaction called *mind-mindness*, which is also thought to have a positive relationship to the development of theory of mind and perspective-taking. *Mind-mindness* has been defined as a "caregiver's proclivity to treat their young children as individuals with minds of their own." This in turn leads the caregiver to such behaviors as: assuming meaning for the preverbal vocalizations of infants and toddler; making note of the *perceived* mental states of their infant; and characterizing their children in general as possessing internal, mental states. In other words, parents act *as if* non-word vocalizations are attempts at communication and act *as if* their children's behavior is motivated and driven by internal and mental desires, ideas, fears, etc. This type of parental pretend can actually have an influence on children's development of theory of mind.

Taking the perspective of others

SOMETIMES WE CAN try and understand another person's thinking or feeling by deliberately trying to see the world from their perspective.

The students in my university classes, most of whom were studying to become preschool, kindergarten or primary grade teachers, would often voice concerns (and sometime complaints) about children in their practicum classrooms who resisted participating in certain activities. They would describe children who refused to be part of a movement activity or children who found it difficult to join in when the class was involved in a group music activity. Some of the students felt a genuine concern for the children and what they were missing while others saw the situation as a classroom management or discipline problem. To help them get a better understanding for what the children might be thinking and feeling, I would take my students through the following *as if* exercise, asking them to *imagine* themselves in the following situation. (You, the reader, might imagine yourself in the same situation.)

You are attending a Saturday evening cocktail party at a friend's house. There are about 15 to 20 people there, some of whom you know and some of whom you are meeting for the first time. There is soft music playing the background, tasty appetizers are being passed around, and you have been engaged in interesting conversations with a number of the other guests. You are enjoying yourself.

Now imagine that the hostess gathers everyone in the living room and announces that the evening's game of charades is about to begin. She has organized everyone into teams and there will be prizes awarded to the winning team at the end of the evening.

After I presented this imaginary scenario to the students, I would ask them to think about what they may be feeling when the the hostess makes the announcement about charades. I introduced this exercise many times over my years of teaching and there was an interesting consistency to the responses of the students. Some said that they would be excited about playing charades; they liked the game and enjoyed performing and being 'on stage'. Other students had a very different reaction. These students expressed a sense of dread at being asked to perform in front of people and said that they would try and find ways of avoiding participation. In fact, some students said that if put in that situation they would make up a reason as to why they had to leave the party. For example, they might say that their babysitter had called to tell them their child was ill and they needed to return home. I remember one student's very succinct response about having to play charades: "I'm out of there."

I used this exercise to make a simple point to the students: If you are allowed to have strong feelings, perhaps strong negative feelings, about being asked to participate in a particular activity, why aren't young children entitled to have their own feelings when asked (or required) to participate in some activity that you, as the teacher, had planned? By asking *my* students to engage in an exercise of the imagination, an *as if* exercise, I was encouraging them to consider life in their classroom from the perspective of the children in that classroom, to think about it *as if* they were the children.

Employing this same 'as if I am in their shoes' approach has helped me understand some of my own daughter's thinking and feeling.

As a young child, our daughter was somewhat shy. She insisted that a parent stay with her when she attended a friend's birthday party and she would agree to attend a sleepover party at a friend's house only to call to come home just as the sleepover portion of the evening was about to begin. They had a phrase for this shyness in North Dakota where we were living at the time - she was, according to local parlance, "making strange."

Our daughter's shyness was on display one day when I had picked her up at the child care center and brought her to see her mother at the elementary school where my wife worked. It was at the end of the day so the children in the school had already left. To get to her mother's office, we had to walk down a long hallway, passing various classrooms on the way. Some of the teachers were still in their classroom at the time and since I had met many of them and they all knew of our daughter, as we would pass a classroom the teacher would say hello, calling our daughter by name. Each time this happened, my daughter moved a bit closer to me and by the third or fourth instance of hearing her name called out, she was tucked behind one of my legs. This behavior led one of the teachers to say, "Oh, she is so shy."

While it may be true that our daughter fit the definition of what it means to be shy, this experience led me to think about the situation from our daughter's point of view, to think about it *as if* I were standing in her shoes. These teachers may have known me and may have known my daughter's name and known about her, but to my daughter, they were strangers. I thought about what it would be like to be on a vacation in some foreign city, say Paris, knowing no one, yet having perfect strangers on the street call me by name. I'm not sure my reaction would be one of being shy; I might actually find the situation quite strange and might even feel afraid. How do these people know my name? They are complete strangers so how do they know who I am?

Did I know for sure that my daughter felt the same way as I might have on the streets of Paris? Of course I couldn't know that for sure but thinking about and comparing her moments in that school hallway to the imagined moments in a Paris street gave me a better appreciation for how those moments might have felt for her.

It's not always easy to stand in the other person's shoes

I WOULD LIKE to close this chapter by reflecting on the fact that the ability to be empathic means that we are also able, if we allow ourselves, to step into the shoes of someone whose ideas and beliefs may be quite antithetical to our own. There may be times when we have to consider the minds of "our enemies - to acknowledge their humanity, individuality, and perspectives."

During the writing of this book, for example, two highly emotional and ultimately divisive examples of differing perspectives made headlines in the news reports of the day. One focused on the battlefields of the Civil War and the second on the 'battlefields' of professional football.

In 2017, a number of cities in primarily southern states were faced with the question of what to do with monuments that memorialized historical figures who had fought on the side of the Confederacy during the Civil War. Like all symbolic imagery, and as was discussed in Chapter 2, these monuments are examples of representations that *stand for* some idea. People on both sides of the issue seemingly agreed that the monuments were *signifiers*; in other words, these monuments of such historical figures as Generals Robert E. Lee and Stonewall Jackson stood for and represented something. The problem was that there was a disagreement as to what that something was; there was a disagreement as to what these *signifiers* actually *signified*.

For some, the monuments represented part of a historical heritage of bravery and loyalty to one's home state and culture. To others, the monuments represented a dark period in our nation's history; one marked by the horrors and atrocities of slavery. And there was also the issue of the Civil War itself. Were the people memorialized by these monuments heroes for defending their rights of self-determination or traitors for engaging in armed and violent rebellion against the nation? Two people could be looking at the very same monument, say a statue of General Robert E. Lee, and see a hero or a traitor; a brave and honorable soldier or a defender of a person's right to own and subjugate another person. It all depended on one's perspective.

At the same time as the controversy about Confederate monuments arose, another controversy emerged on the playing fields of professional football. This controversy actually began during the 2016 football season but grew in intensity during the 2017 season. During the 2016 season, the quarterback for the San Francisco 49s, Colin Kaepernick, decided to make a statement about perceived police brutality towards the African-American community by kneeling during the playing of the National Anthem prior to the start of the game. A few other players joined this symbolic protest during the 2016 season and the number of players kneeling increased during the 2017 season and the act of kneeling spread to some other sports as well.

Like the issue of the Confederate monuments, the issue of kneeling during the National Anthem became a clash of perspectives. For some, the kneeling represented a statement about inequality in our country and was seen as a call for action to address and begin remedying those inequalities. To others, the act of kneeling represented a statement of disrespect for the American flag and all that it stands for and represents. Some people who criticized the players who chose to kneel in protest also believed that the act of kneeling was demonstrating a lack of respect for the American servicemen and women who were risking their lives to protect the ideas represented by the flag. (Living in a world of symbols can get quite complicated. Kneeling in protest is a symbolic act and the American flag itself is a symbol. This was really a clash between the interpretation of *signifiers* and *signifieds*.)

Both of these controversies - the Confederate monuments and the kneeling-in-protest movement - elicited strong and at times heated reactions from people on both sides of the issues. As I said earlier, these controversies were a clash of perspectives. Two people could be standing side-by-side looking at the very same monument or the very same kneeling football player and have two very different responses to what they were seeing. One person might say that the 'offending' monument should be removed from the public space while another would oppose that action, arguing that the monument was an important part of a historical heritage. One person might say that the kneeling football player should be removed from the team while another would argue that it is his constitutional right to express an opinion, and that there might be an opinion worth expressing.

Any one of us could argue that all perspectives aren't created equal; that one perspective is more valid than another. Holding this view doesn't mean that the less valid perspective doesn't exist, however. When four-year-old Robbie changed the position of the dot in the sand, the exclamation point didn't exist anymore *from my perspective* but I was able to understand that it did exist from his perspective. As news reports showed us, the clash of perspectives that arose during the Confederate monument and the kneeling protests were not easily reconciled. But if reconciliation of these heated issues and others like them are ever to be achieved, we first need to acknowledge that the other contrary perspective does exist; we need to look at that monument and the kneeling football player *as if* we were standing in the other person's shoes.

An unwillingness to consider opposing perspectives and the contents of the minds of others can sometimes lead to dire consequences, as Robert Kennedy wrote in his memoir about the thirteen days of the Cuban missile crisis.

There was no question at the time that the Communist regime of the Soviet Union was an enemy of the United States, both in terms of overall ideology and more immediately, in terms of the missiles that the Soviet Union had placed in the island of Cuba, just ninety miles off the shores of the United States. But President Kennedy recognized that in order to solve the crisis peacefully, it was necessary to understand the crisis from the perspective of the Soviet Union, from the perspective of the enemy. As Robert Kennedy wrote,

> The final lesson of the Cuban missile crisis is the
> importance of placing ourselves in the other country's

shoes. During the crisis, President Kennedy spent more time trying to determine the effect of a particular course of action on Khrushchev or the Russians than on any other phase of what he was doing.

Of course there may be times that trying to put yourselves in the shoes of the other person, of the 'enemy' and see the world from his or her perspective can be a difficult, if not impossible, undertaking. No matter how hard I tried after the 2016 presidential election, I could not find the wherewithal to even remotely understand how anyone could have voted for the other candidate. No matter how hard I tried to intellectually understand what would bring someone to make that choice, my emotions prevented me from taking that imaginative leap. I could not see the election choices *as if* I saw the issues from the worldview of the person who made the opposing choice. To me, there could only be one viewpoint, mine. I became that four-year-old at the sand table who could only consider the exclamation point from his side of the table. Just like that four-year-old, all I wanted to say was, "No, that's not right," and reach over and move the dot to the other side of ballot card.

Chapter 4

The Truth Isn't the Only Option

We like to think that telling the truth, or truthfulness itself, is one of the prime virtues of our existence as human beings. Any of us who has watched countless hours of the television show, *Law and Order*, knows that "telling the truth, the whole truth, and nothing but the truth" can be the divider between being a good person and one who is, well, clearly not so good. We may also be familiar with a particular superhero who fights for *truth* and justice because it is the *American* way, and one reason that truth and justice is the American way is because the Declaration of Independence tells us that "we hold these *truths* to be self-evident." And long before the Declaration of Independence was written, Moses came down from the mount with the Ten Commandments, one of which reminds us that it is not a good idea to "bear false witness against thy neighbor." There are times when we have to fill out documents that require us to affirm that all of the information we have provided is accurate and truthful; not providing truthful information can subject us to some serious legal consequences. The laws relating to the act of perjury, for example, suggest that it is a good idea to tell the truth when we have sworn an oath to do so. Telling the truth is so important that there is even a drug, Sodium Pentothal, which purportedly can make us tell the truth when we are inclined not to, and a machine, the polygraph, that supposedly can tell when we are, in fact, choosing to not tell the truth.

And yet, we lie.

There is, then, this paradox. While we may think that telling the truth is one of the better aspects of being human, *if truth be told,* it may actually be the case that the ability to say or profess anything but the truth is what truly makes us human. It is the act of producing a lie and all its variants - fibs, tall tales, white lies, exaggerations - that really makes us special and distinguishes us from the other intelligent and communicative beasts of the animal kingdom. We may think that the act of telling "the truth, the whole truth, and nothing but the truth" is the high watermark of our humanity but a person who is truly unable to lie - to think and act in opposition to what may be real and true - is a person who may not, in fact, have developed his or her full potential as a human being. Part of what makes us human is our ability to say something *as if* it is the truth when we know full well that it is anything but the truth.

We humans, in fact, do lie fairly frequently. A study conducted by the Science Museum of London determined that on average, men in Great Britain produce at least three lies per day; women, the study found, tell the truth a bit more frequently - they averaged only two lies per day. In a research study carried out in the United States, subjects averaged just under three lies during a ten minute conversation. When college students were asked to keep a journal record of their daily interactions, they identified at least two instances of lying each day. The students also concluded that they lied to almost forty percent of the people with whom they interacted during a week's time. Lying is so pervasive that some teenagers believe it is necessary to lie in order to achieve success in life.

It also turns out that some of the people we interact with on a daily basis and perhaps trust the most may very well be lying to us. We might think that our doctor's office, for example, would be one of the last places someone would lie to us but a study of over 1800 doctors in the United States suggests otherwise. The authors of this survey study found some potentially disturbing results, at least from the perspective of the patient. Almost one in three of the doctors surveyed reported that they didn't necessarily agree that a doctor should inform a patient of a serious medical error. Just about one out of every five of the doctors didn't agree with the principle that a doctor should never lie to a patient and one in ten of the doctors did indicate that during the previous year they had been dishonest with a patient. It could be the case, of course, that some of these non-disclosures and lies might be in the best interests of the patient but they would be lies nonetheless.

A 2006 study revealed that nurses are also willing to lie to patients under certain circumstances. The nurses surveyed in this study were all involved in the care of patients with dementia. Of the 112 nurses surveyed, 98% of them indicated that they had lied to a patient at one time or another. One nurse, for example, was caring for a patient who maintained that he had to wait for the bus to take him home. The nurse told him that the bus stop was right by his residential facility when in fact it wasn't. The authors of this study referred to this type of lie as "therapeutic lying," a term that perhaps could also be applied to the types of lies addressed by the survey of doctors.

The researchers conducting the study of nurses also asked seventy-six psychiatrists about their experiences and opinions concerning therapeutic lying. Sixty-nine percent of those psychiatrists responding acknowledged that they had lied when they believed that the lie would be of benefit to the patient. Sixty-six percent of those responding to the survey also indicated that they had sanctioned lying by the people who were responsible for the care of the patients.

In his memoir about his life as a neurosurgeon, Henry Marsh provides a firsthand, insider's account about the lying that can (does) occur within the medical profession.

> It's quite easy to lie if things go wrong with an operation. It would be impossible for anybody to know after the operation in what way it had gone wrong. You can invent plausible excuses...I know of at least one very famous neurosurgeon, now retired, who covered up...[a] major mistake on a very eminent patient with a dishonest operating note.

These reports of medical professionals willing to lie echoes an example that I learned of personally. An acquaintance was diagnosed with a terminal illness and asked the doctors not to reveal the severity of the diagnosis to his wife until absolutely necessary; he wasn't sure that his wife was emotionally strong enough to deal with the real diagnosis and the fact that he didn't have very long to live. The doctors abided by his request and did not tell his wife the truth about his illness until the very end; through a combination of withholding information and providing mis-information, these doctors lied to the man's wife.

We don't need statistics, however, to know that lying is part of the lives we observe and the lives we live. It seems as if there are almost daily news reports of a public figure, be it a politician, celebrity, or sports star, being caught in a lie of some sort. The television personality and author, Martha Stewart, was found guilty of lying to federal investigators about whether or not she had received insider stock trading information and as a result spent almost five months in prison. Esteemed historian and Pulitzer Prize winner, Joseph Ellis, author of *American Sphinx: The Character of Thomas* Jefferson and *Founding Brothers: The Revolutionary Generation*, at one point told his college students that he had served in combat during the Vietnam War and had spent time as a civil rights worker in Mississippi. Neither of those 'autobiographical' statements turned out to be true. President Bill Clinton was impeached by Congress for lying about the relationship he had with "that woman," the White House intern, Monica Lewinsky. The author James Frey was forced to admit that some of the 'facts' in his memoir, *A Million Little Pieces*, were, in fact, not facts at all but fabrications. It turns out that claiming you once spent 87 days in jail when your time behind bars was just a few hours doesn't quite fit the category of non-fiction writing. Financial investor Bernie Madoff bilked his clients out of billions of dollars through what is known as a Ponzi scheme. He promised his clients a return on their investments that he knew was impossible to obtain. He took their money knowing that he ultimately couldn't make good on his promises. He was able to maintain this lie over a number of years before his fabricated financial system came tumbling down; Madoff was given a prison sentence of 150 years for his lies. And the cyclist Lance Armstrong had to finally admit, after many years of denial, that his seven Tour de France victories weren't achieved under the most honest or truthful of circumstances; he had used illegal performance enhancements despite claiming, on multiple occasions, that he hadn't.

Of course public figures aren't the only ones who find reasons to hide or perhaps bend the truth at times. If we are honest with ourselves, we aren't always honest with ourselves. Some of us, for example, have perhaps exaggerated our accomplishments in life a bit while talking to an old classmate at the high school reunion. Those of us who have been university teachers might have written slightly embellished letters of recommendation for students who were applying for teaching positions or admission to graduate school programs. We might not have outright lied about their grades or performance in classes but perhaps did include statements about the quality of their work that might have been somewhat exaggerated. There may also be times when we talk about a book as if we have read it when we actually never made it past the first few chapters. We wouldn't be alone in committing this type of lie. According to a survey of 2000 people conducted by *The Guardian*, lying about the books we have read may be fairly common. For example, 26% of those surveyed said that they had lied about reading George Orwell's, *Nineteen Eighty-Four* and 19% claimed to have made it through Tolstoy's *War and Peace* when they actually hadn't. It turns out that even authors themselves may lie about books read and books never read. In an interview about his reading habits, the novelist Russell Banks, author of such books as, *Affliction* and *Cloud Splitter*, was asked if he was ever guilty of lying about having read a particular book.

> *I have sometimes pretended to a friend or acquaintance who happens to be an author that I have not yet read his or her new book but that I certainly look forward to the chance, when I have absolutely no intention of ever reading it.*

The reasons for our lying

IF WE LIE to ourselves and others as frequently as the statistics and anecdotal evidence suggests and if lying is part of being human, there must be reasons for our lying; lying must fulfill some functions in our lives. Broadly speaking, we lie for one of three reasons: to reap some benefit for ourselves, to benefit another person, or to harm another person. The Bernie Madoffs and Lance Armstrongs of the world tell their lies in an effort to gain some rewards, be it money, fame or both. Harry Truman, before he became president, lied on an application for a staff position at a bank, stating that he had never bet on horse racing when in fact he had. As one of his biographers wrote, "it is the earliest known sign in his own hand that he was capable of telling less than the truth if the occasion warranted, capable of being quite human." Apparently Truman wanted the job, wanted a benefit for himself, and this desire, in his mind, justified the lie.

The 'little white lie' is the classic example of lying for the benefit of another person. Many a husband knows the correct answer to his wife's question, "Does this dress make my hips look heavy?" and many a wife knows the correct answer to her husband's question, "Is my hair thinning in back?" We will lie to protect another person's feelings when we believe that there isn't any real negative consequence to the lie. As parents we are also happy when our children express joy for the gift given by Uncle Bob even if the toy is less than desirable. The lies told by doctors and nurses described earlier were committed for the benefit of the patients. White lies told in consideration of another person's feelings may fall into the category of socially acceptable lies.

Falsely accusing someone of a misdeed is a prime example of a lie told in order to harm another person. Many of us may remember incidents in school when one student falsely 'tattled' on another in order to get him into trouble with the teacher. In a situation with much more serious consequences, false accusations were also at the heart of the 2006 case when charges of rape were brought against a number of lacrosse players at Duke University. (The district attorney who filed the charges against the lacrosse players was later found guilty of criminal contempt for the lies *he* told the court. Apparently swearing to uphold the law doesn't make you immune to lying.)

Sometimes, however, it is hard to understand a person's motives for lying. Take the lies of the historian Joseph Ellis, for example. As an outsider, we might look at his life and think that he had everything a person in his position would want. He had a stellar reputation as a teacher and scholar, and some amount of fame (and perhaps fortune) due to the popularity of his books beyond the university classroom. We might think that he didn't seem to have anything to gain by lying about his military record and yet he did. Ultimately he apologized for his actions but was never really able to offer an explanation for why he had lied in the first place except to say that all people make mistakes.

SO, WE HUMANS profess to value the truth and yet we lie. And at least in the United States, a person's right to lie may actually be protected by law.

In 2005, the Congress of the United States passed a law called the Stolen Valor Act. This law was enacted to deal with a particular kind of liar, one who falsely claims to be a winner of various military medals and honors, including at times the Congressional Medal of Honor. The Stolen Valor Act made it a crime to lie about having been awarded such military medals. In 2012, however, the United States Supreme Court determined that the Stolen Valor Act of 2005 was unconstitutional. In the court's opinion, lying is a form of free speech which is protected by the 1st Amendment to the Constitution. (Not all lying, of course, is protected free speech as the crime of perjury, or lying under oath, demonstrates.) In 2013 Congress once again tried to address the problem of people fraudulently claiming to be medal winners by making it a crime to make money from such lying. In other words, as long as you don't attempt to make money or defraud a person in some way, it is your legal right to claim that you had been awarded the Congressional Medal of Honor; it is your legal right to lie.

What exactly is a lie?

SO, WE HUMANS may be 'natural born liars' and some of our lies may be constitutionally protected but what exactly is the definition of a lie? Do we know a lie when we see (hear) one or is defining a lie a bit more complicated than that? On the surface we might say that a lie is any statement that can be contradicted by facts. If a biographical statement on the back cover of this book described me as tall with thick, wavy, dark hair, the accompanying photograph would quickly contradict those statements and I could be accused of lying. But what if I hadn't submitted the words, "tall with thick, wavy, dark hair" to the publisher of this book? What if the book editor had mixed up some files and included words that were actually meant to be inserted onto another book cover, one that described a different author, one taller and with more hair? In that case we would probably conclude that a *mistake* had been committed, not a lie. And how would we label the following statement uttered by a young boy wearing a cape and boots: "I am Superman and I fly and help people with my super-strength"? Clearly the facts contradict his statement; he can't fly and he doesn't have super-strength. We would probably say he is *pretending* rather than lying. And how would we label the grandfather's statement to his granddaughter that, "I love you so much that I am going to put you into my suitcase and take you home with me"? He can't put her in the suitcase and he is not taking her home with him; the statement can be contradicted by the facts but we would probably say that he was expressing his love for his granddaughter through *exaggeration* and *hyperbole* as opposed to telling a lie.

Most people who have written about the concept of lying - be they philosophers or psychologists - focus on the concept of *intentionality* when attempting to define the term and the act. For example, Sissela Bok, who explored the act of lying in her 1978 book, *Lying: Moral Choice in Public and Private Life,* defines a lie as "any intentionally deceptive message." A lie is different than a mistake, therefore, due to the intention of the person who produced the statement. If I tell you that I had sent the check I owed you on Monday when it really went into the mail on Tuesday, I could be guilty of either making a mistake or committing a lie. If I said Monday because I was confused, I have made a mistake. On the other hand, if I said Monday because I wanted you to think that I was prompt with my payment when I knew full well that I had mailed it on Tuesday, now I have committed a lie. I deliberately made a non-factual statement with the intention to deceive you. Making a false statement, therefore, is not in and of itself an act of lying; deliberately making a false statement in order to have another person believe the false statement is the lie.

We also have to distinguish between lies and other instances when a speaker may be deliberately making a false statement. If I see my wife returning home from the gym in her old, washed-out sweatsuit and with wet, stringy hair and I say to her, "Oh, don't you look lovely," I have uttered a false statement; she really doesn't look lovely and I don't really think she looks lovely. In this case, however, I would be guilty of *sarcasm* not of lying. (Of course, the consequences for me might be the same in either case.) As one article looking at the difference between lying and pretending pointed out:

> Sometimes a speaker says something that is
> not true for the purposes of joking, being ironic,
> being sarcastic, or emphasizing a point by way of
> exaggeration. One distinction between lies and these
> types of false statements concerns the speaker's beliefs
> about the listener's knowledge...In the case of lies,
> the speaker believes that the listener does not know
> the true state of affairs, whereas in the case of jokes,
> sarcasm, and exaggeration, the speaker assumes the
> listener knows the truth.

My wife, in effect, was in on the joke. She knew as well as I did what she looked like after her gym workout. The young granddaughter knew that her grandfather couldn't put her in the suitcase. For an utterance to be a lie, therefore, there needs to be the intent of the speaker to deceive and an assumption on the part of the speaker that the audience for the lie doesn't know the truth. (The latter condition explains why we sometimes are caught in our lies; we may assume that the listener doesn't know the truth when in fact he or she does. It may also explain why sometimes young children can become frightened by our exaggerations of love; they might not know that you can't really be put into a suitcase.) Bernie Madoff, Lance Armstrong, and President Clinton weren't joking, being ironic or sarcastic, or making a mistake; they were banking on the fact that their 'audiences' didn't know the truth and therefore would believe the lies being told.

So, despite all the fables and admonitions not to lie, despite all of the emphasis on the importance and virtues of honesty, we lie. Intentionally trying to deceive someone, either for personal gain, or the harm or benefit of another person, is so endemic to the human condition that according to David Livingstone Smith, author of the book, *Why We Lie*, "Human beings are the grandmasters of mendacity. It would not have been out or place to name our species *Homo fallax* (deceptive man) instead of *Homo sapiens* (wise man)." And given that lying seems to be part of human nature, it should come as no surprise, then, that the youngest members of our species, children, also lie.

The emerging liar

IT'S REALLY NOT a question of *if* a child will lie but rather *when* a child will utter a deliberate untruth. When do children tell their first lie? Paul Ekman suggests that it may be sooner than we might think is possible: "Some people think that young children are too innocent to lie. Others think that they would [lie] if they could but lack the ability. The evidence suggests that kids are capable of lying at an earlier age than most adults give them credit for." And according to Robert Feldman, many three-year-olds are quite capable of telling a lie and even some two-year-olds are able to make a deliberately false statement.

Children lie despite our best efforts as parents and a culture to teach them the importance of honesty. Fables and parables about the evils of lying and the importance of truthfulness have long been a staple of the stories we tell and read to our children. Tell a lie and your nose may grow longer like Pinocchio. Continually tell lies and no one will believe you when you are telling the truth; at least that is what happened to the boy who cried wolf. The idea that "bad" people tell lies is portrayed by the actions of two well-known "villains" in children's literature: the witch in *Hansel and Gretel*, and the wolf in *Little Red Riding Hood*. The notion of honesty as a virtue is embodied in the story of a chopped down cherry tree, and the young George Washington's inability to lie about his misdeed. (According to historians, however, George Washington didn't really chop down a cherry tree as a young boy and didn't proclaim that he couldn't tell a lie. The truth of the matter is that the first person to write a biography of Washington, Parson Mason Weems, made the story up. Written just a few years after Washington's death in 1799, Weems' tribute to Washington didn't restrict itself to just the facts. It seems that Weems created a myth - told a lie - about a man who couldn't tell a lie.)

And, of course, there is the simple yet oft-repeated maxim offered by parents to their children that, "honesty is the best policy."

Thinking about how parents try to help their children understand that "honesty is the best policy" reveals another paradox about this emphasis on truth-telling: parents are human and therefore engage in a fair amount of lie-telling on their own. As a result, many parents regularly lie to their children, the very same children they are trying to raise as honest tellers of the truth. The use of lies in raising children is so common that it has been referred to as *parenting by lying*. One study surveyed parents in the United States and China to see how common parental lying actually was. The subjects of the study were given a list of statements representing an assortment of lies and were asked whether or not they had said something similar to their own children sometime in the past. One of the most common parental lies - admitted to by two-thirds of the parents in both countries

- was threatening to leave a child behind when the child was resisting the parent's directive to move along in a public space. Another common lie involved false promises made by parents. In China, for example, better than two-thirds of the parents said that they had told a child that a toy that couldn't be purchased today would be given to them sometime in the future, all the while knowing that the parent was not going to make good on that promise. All told, 84% of the parents in the United States admitted to lying in ways represented by the sixteen examples that comprised the survey, while in China the percentage was just short of 100%.

Why do parents lie to their children? Parents very frequently use lies as an attempt to control the behavior and emotions of their children. There are the lies, for example, that explain to a child that his mother has no money to buy the piece of candy in the supermarket; the mother has the money but the speaking of the lie is easier than dealing with a potential temper tantrum when the child's request is denied. Parents in the Tzeltal-speaking Mayan culture attempt to control behavior with even more ominous lies; they tell their children that wasp stings or dog bites or being kidnapped are all possibilities if they don't conform their behavior to parental expectations. And as one mother reported, "I have said the police will get my son in trouble in some instances when the threat of mom is not intimidating." As the authors of the study looking at the lying behavior of parents in the US and in China wrote, "Taken together, our findings suggest that the vast majority of parents in the US and China lie to their children to obtain behavior compliance."

Finally, parents may also lie for reasons that may be related to their own psychological needs. The author, Christopher Buckley, learned about this type of lying from his mother, who had told stories about how the king and queen of England had been her houseguests - his mother told these stories *as if* they were true; she wasn't telling them as 'tall tales' for the sake of entertainment. The stories were not true and Buckley had a bit of an epiphany about his own future as a liar when he realized his mother's stories were works of fiction.

*I looked at Mum and realized - twang! - That she was
telling an untruth. A big untruth. And I remember
thinking in that instant how thrilling and grown-up
it must be to say something so completely untrue, as
opposed to the little amateur fibs I was already practiced
at - horrid little apprentice sinner that I was - like the
ones how you'd already said your prayers or washed
under your fingernails. Yes, I was impressed. This was my
introduction to a lifetime of mendacity. I too must learn
to say these gorgeous untruths. Imaginary kings and
queens would be my houseguests when I was older!*

So why do children begin to lie, other than the fact that the predisposition and ability may be part of the human condition (and the fact that they have parental role models for lying)? The first lies of young children are generally produced in response to their own misdeeds; essentially the lie is usually offered as a preventative strike against anticipated punishment for a misbehavior of some sort. The earliest lies of children are frequently the 'I didn't do it' type of lie. This denial of culpability sometimes carries with it the shifting of blame to someone else, perhaps a sibling or the pet cat. The lie, therefore, takes the form of claiming that younger sister Susie or Jasper the kitty was the one to knock the plate of cookies to the floor, not me.

It doesn't take very long before children expand their reasons for lying and the *white lie* or the socially acceptable lie, becomes part of their repertoire. Children begin telling white lies as early as three-years of age and their predisposition to tell a white lie and their ability to do so increases with age. Perhaps children's ability to tell white lies develops as they listen to their parents exercise *their* abilities at white-lie telling.

And just as an adult might exaggerate the size of the fish reeled in during the fishing trip, children begin to bend the truth in order to gain standing among their peers. As Feldman writes in his book, *The Liar in Your Life: The Way to Truthful Relationships,*

*As children begin preschool and have greater peer
interaction, the need for lies that ingratiate or boost a*

fragile ego increases. Again, in their early forms such lying is crude, but it often serves the same psychological needs as adult lying. Whereas an adult may brag about exaggerated success at work, a child may brag about the trip he took to hunt down the Loch Ness monster.

The 'As If' of lying

HOW DOES CHILDREN'S emerging ability to tell lies relate to make-believe play, the main topic of this book? There is perhaps no clearer act of *as if* than the telling of a lie. In its most basic sense, when we lie we are offering a statement *as if* it is true; *as if* what we are stating is a fact. The telling of a lie is also an example of the previously discussed idea that when children play, reality isn't the only option; in the case of lying, it is clear that we are acting *as if* the truth isn't the only option. When that two- or -three-year-old child utters her first lie, she is expanding on the ability and disposition to transform reality, a disposition that is part of the object substitutions, use of symbols, and make-believe play that were discussed in earlier chapters. The ability to lie, therefore, doesn't emerge in a child's developmental life as a discrete ability but is related to the fundamental human capacity for imagining, pretending, representing, and transforming reality.

Just like philosophers and psychologists, the understanding of intention plays a role in how children define the concept of lying as well. Up until the age of six or seven, children tend to define any statement that is untrue as a lie; they base their judgment on the facts of the situation and don't take into consideration the intention or knowledge base of the speaker of the lie. This reliance on a purely objective view of the situation - as opposed to considering subjective knowledge or intent - leads the young child to view mistakes, pretend, and irony, for example, as lies. As children get older they, too, begin to understand that a definition of lying must include the intent of the speaker and the perspective and knowledge base of the audience to whom the lie is directed.

If we consider the defining characteristics of a lie and the act of lying, we quickly can see how much skill it takes to be able to lie and how these developmental abilities relate to the fundamental ability of *as if*. Object substitutions, the use of symbols, and the personal creation of transitional objects are all examples of how a child is able to create a reality in which an object or symbol stands for something else; the block represents an airplane, the ratty old blanket stands in for the absent mother, and the scribble on the page represents a word or an idea. The ability to tell a lie is built on this same foundation, in this case the foundation of making a statement *as if* it were true; in other words, the lie stands in for the truth.

What skills does it take to tell a lie or to deceive someone into thinking something is true when, in fact, it isn't? And how do these skills relate to the play of *as if*? If we think about the forms of lies and deception that are based in language, either oral or written, then the ability to use symbols to represent and communicate is perhaps the most fundamental of skills needed. In general, a person doing the lying needs some form of representation - gestures, spoken words, written language - to offer a statement that contradicts reality or the facts of the situation.

But representational competence and communication skills are necessary but not sufficient. The liar needs to have developed other cognitive and social skills in order to attempt to deceive another person with the lie. These skills include those discussed in earlier chapters: social-perspective taking, distancing and decontextualization, and the control of one's own behavior and actions, all skills that a child practices in her make-believe play, in her *as if* stance towards reality.

As we saw in Chapter 3, the act of *as if* is related to what is called the development of *theory of mind*. Developing a theory of mind, in turn, is important for a person's ability to tell a lie. Theory of mind refers to an understanding that our actions, and the actions of others, are influenced and guided by our beliefs and intentions. Lying requires the liar to 1), know what the truth is ("I know I was the one who knocked the plate of cookies off of the counter. It happened when I climbed up on the stool which I know I wasn't supposed to do."); and 2) have the desire to deceive another person by planting a false statement in the other person's mind. ("I don't want to be punished so I will tell my mother that the kitty knocked the plate off of the counter.") As you can see, the liar is taking into consideration two minds: his own and the mind of the person to be deceived, in this case, his mother.

The liar, then, is able to consider multiple perspectives. First, there is his own perspective of the situation. He knows what really happened; he knows that in the past he has been warned about using a stool to get to the counter and he has been warned not to take any cookies without first asking permission. He also knows that he is likely to be scolded and perhaps punished for his misdeed. The child/liar is also aware that in the past the cat has jumped up and walked across the kitchen counter. That is one perspective the child holds in his mind. The child is also able to imagine the perspective of his mother, the person he is attempting to deceive; the child is able to think about the situation *as if* he were standing in his mother's shoes. He believes that from his mother's perspective, his taking the stool to the counter would be considered a misdeed and she might be angry about what he had done. But he also knows that his mother has at times been angry with the cat for walking on the kitchen counter. The child is able to *imagine* that the truth will result in one outcome (mother's anger and perhaps his being punished) and that the lie will hopefully result in a different, and more pleasing outcome (his mother being exasperated by the cat and not angry with him). He lies to see if he can produce the second outcome and avoid the first. But that's just the beginning of being able to say, "I didn't do it. The cat did."

The second requisite skill is the ability to not let your actions be bound by context; to be able to *distance* yourself from the specific aspects of the situation in the here and now. Context consists of place, time, and circumstances. Most animals (other than humans) respond to the specific stimuli of the context in which they find themselves, i.e., they can't help but respond to the circumstances of place and time. The chameleon lizard that changes color does so in response to temperature, color of the surroundings, and perhaps perceived threat from a predator. Looking like and blending into the surrounding foliage may be a form of deception but it's not an action that is consciously chosen. Given the confluence of stimuli, the lizard has no choice but to change colors; in reality, there are no choices for the lizard to make. Our family had a golden retriever who seemed to have the ability to tell time; sometime between 4:30 and 5 o'clock in the afternoon she would stand in front of us and stare, letting us know that it was time to be fed. Her timing was uncanny. She was unable, of course, to tell time by reading the clock but again due to a confluence of circumstances - physiological feelings in her stomach, the arrival home of family members from school or work, perhaps the position of the sun - she performed her staring routine and was fed. What she couldn't do, however, was distance herself from the context and circumstances and lie; she couldn't stare and stare at 2 o'clock in the afternoon, watch us fill her food dish, and then laugh because she really wasn't hungry and was just playing a joke.

We human beings, on the other hand, are able to distance our behavior from the immediate stimuli that are part of the circumstances we find ourselves in the here and now. We aren't always successful at this - I still have anxiety reactions just from the smell of a dentist's office even if I am not the one who has the appointment - but we are at least potentially capable of producing behavior that is not tied to and controlled by the immediate context. And this ability is necessary if we want to tell a lie. To say that the cat knocked over the plate of cookies when you know full well that you were the one who did it requires that you are able to utter words that contradict the reality or truth of the situation. To say that you loved the pie your Aunt Mary baked even though the uneasiness in your stomach is suggesting otherwise requires the ability to respond based on factors other than the immediate physiological feelings unleashed by the undercooked dessert. A desire to not hurt Aunt Mary's feelings outweighs our response to the taste of the pie and motivates the telling of a little white lie. We can do what the lizard can't; change our colors when we want to and not just when the circumstances force us to. We don't have to wait until we are chased by a predator in order to change our colors; we can change our colors *as if* there is a predator nearby. We can change our colors just for the fun of it. The chameleon doesn't decide to change his colors; we do decide to lie.

The third skill needed for lie telling is the ability to control our own behavior. This is closely related to the aforementioned ability of distancing oneself from the immediate context but it merits its own discussion. Telling a lie requires a conscious decision to produce a representation that is contrary to reality and a set of facts. It may be true that for some people the telling of lies is so second-nature and automatic that they aren't always aware of what they are doing but if asked, even these habitual liars would probably be able to acknowledge, upon reflection, that they had told a lie. (There may be pathological liars who are so out of touch with reality that they don't know when they are lying; these people may, in fact, not believe that they are lying.) If intention, as discussed earlier, is the essence of lying, then by definition, the liar is intentionally controlling what he or she is doing. This requires what is known as *executive function*, or the ability to regulate, guide, and shape one's own behavior and actions, an ability that is practiced and developed during make-believe play. It turns out, however, that the young, emerging liar isn't always very good at this type of control but does get better at it with age and practice.

When children lie they in effect are producing statements that are inconsistent with the facts of the situation as they know them to be. In order to be a good liar, children (and we more grown-up liars), also have to be consistent with the inconsistencies. (This is why police detectives and prosecuting attorneys will often ask the accused criminal the same question repeated times; they are trying to see if his story stays consistent, i.e. will he be able to stay consistent with his lies.) It turns out that although children may produce lies early in life, that doesn't mean they are able to manage the necessary inconsistencies very well. Young children are prone to what has been called *semantic leakage,* a term used to refer to the situation when children produce a lie but then are unable to continue acting in ways that remain consistent with the lie; they are unable to "conceal verbal and nonverbal behaviors that are consistent with their true beliefs but incongruent with the false statement." The ability to remain consistent is referred to as *semantic leakage control.*

Semantic leakage, and semantic leakage control, has been studied using one of the classic research approaches to exploring children's lying, the *temptation resistance paradigm.* The experimental situation goes something like this: A child is left alone for a few minutes in a research room after being instructed not to peek to see what is under a cloth or in a box that is sitting on the table in front of him. Researchers on the other side of a one-way mirror then watch to see what the child does. Upon returning, the experimenter asks the child whether or not he had peeked under the cloth or looked inside the box. It is quite common for children to peek under the cloth or look inside the box. In one study, for example, 82% of the more than 100 three- to seven-year-olds had peeked even though they were instructed not to. Most of the children who had peeked then lied about doing so when asked by the experimenter.

The child's ability to demonstrate *semantic leakage control* is teased out by asking a follow-up question after the child has denied peeking: "So, you didn't see what was in the box (or under the cloth)?" Children who have not yet mastered semantic leakage control might answer, "No, I didn't see the toy car in the box." The child has lied about the act of peeking but is unable to keep her statements about her actions consistent with the lie. She was at first able to produce the lie but was unable to manage her subsequent actions to keep them in line with the original lie.

It has been suggested that the development of semantic leakage control is related to the development of theory of mind. In order to maintain the lie successfully, the child, or any liar, needs to maintain a consistent understanding of what the audience for the lie knows and doesn't know, or at least what the child presumes the listener knows or doesn't know. In the temptation research experiment, the child begins by presuming that since the experimenter was out of the room, the adult could not have seen the peeking into the box that had occurred. Based on that presumption, claiming that you had not peeked is a potentially viable lie. But in order to maintain the lie, the child needs to maintain that presumption and realize that all future statements about what had occurred need to be consistent with that presumption. The liar must be "aware of his listener's knowledge" and be "aware of what information would best convince his listener." In order to be an effective liar, the child "Must be able to have an appropriate assessment of their own and recipients' mental states." And semantic leakage control also requires the executive function characteristics of self-control and willpower; in order to maintain the lie, you must reflect on the situation, consider the knowledge and perspectives of your audience, and control what may be an immediate impulse to blurt out the truth.

Children, therefore, become better at lying as they become better at understanding the perspectives of others, get better at distancing themselves from the here and now, and better at reflecting on and controlling their own thinking and actions. As we have seen, one of the ways in which children practice all of these skills is through pretend and make-believe play. What happens, then, if children don't engage in pretend and make-believe play? Would their ability to lie be affected?

There is interesting evidence of the relationship between the ability to lie and the ability to pretend in the study of children with autism. In general, children with autism show a deficit in the production of spontaneous pretend play. Paul Harris, in his book, *The Work of the Imagination*, for example, notes that children with autism "appear to understand the logic of pretense...However, unless prompted to do so, [they] rarely engage in pretend play themselves."

Harris then goes on to suggest that a predictor for a subsequent diagnosis of autism might be the lack of make-believe play by the time a child reaches the age of 18 months. For Harris, "the study of early pathology shows that it is the absence of early imagination, and not its presence, that is pathological."

Since pretend play is considered an activity that is closely related to the development of theory of mind, it's not surprising to find suggestions in the literature that children with autism experience difficulties with this particular aspect of development, as evidenced by Baron-Cohen's concept of *mindblindness* and Wolfberg's suggestion that "a defining characteristic of people with autism is their difficulty in taking into account other people's social perspectives."

If children with autism have difficulty engaging in pretend play and difficulty with tasks requiring an understanding of theory of mind, or considering the perspectives of other people, it would seem logical that they would have difficulty lying and this turns out to be the case. Feldman goes as far as saying that for children with autism, "the inability to lie can be viewed as a symptom of the disorder." He also notes that parents of children with autism frequently state that their children are not capable of lying. Clara Claiborne Park, who has written two books about her daughter's life with autism, confirms this point when she writes that "Autistic children don't know about cheating" and "The inability to lie convincingly could pass as a diagnostic indicator of autism."

The development of the ability to lie in children with autism reveals one more paradox concerning the relationship between truthfulness and lying. It turns out that as children with autism improve developmentally, their ability at producing lies may increase. Feldman notes the irony of this situation when he writes "Honesty in children with autism is viewed as a manifestation of their disorder. Subsequently, autistic children who were originally unfailingly honest but have begun to show signs of lying effectively are considered to be showing improvement in their condition." In other words, learning how to lie may be a mark of developmental progress.

Lying and morality

SOME YEARS BACK I gave a presentation at a professional conference that discussed many of the same issues and topics contained in this chapter: as human beings we place a great deal of emphasis on honesty and yet we lie with some frequency and for a variety of reasons, and children as human beings do the same. Lying, I concluded, was closely related to our ability to pretend, distance ourselves from reality, and engage in *as if* thinking. After my talk was over, one member of the audience challenged me somewhat on my view that lying was natural, part of a developmental progression, and to some degree, acceptable. The questioner worked in a school and said that part of the school's philosophy and curriculum was to emphasize honesty. Did I really believe, he was asking, that lying by children was okay, that it was an acceptable behavior?

Despite our efforts as parents to teach our children that 'honesty is the best policy' I do believe that lying is an *inevitable* behavior and in some instances also an *acceptable* behavior. Most parents do want their children to master the ability to tell the 'little white lie' so that Aunt Mary's feelings aren't hurt after she spent all that time baking the pie that upset our stomachs. And don't we actually instruct our children *how* to lie when they are home alone for the first time and the phone rings with a strange voice asking if a mother or father is in the house? Don't we tell them to respond with something like, "My mother is taking care of the baby in the other room and can't come to the phone right now." There is no way of describing that behavior other than saying the child is lying. If our child is incapable of telling that lie, we might decide that she is not developmentally mature enough to stay at home by herself. She may need more practice at lying.

Acceptable - and sometimes necessary - lying is part of our adult lives as well. We, too, tell the white lie to spare a friend's feelings and as we saw earlier, doctors may lie when the lie benefits their patients. Another example of 'necessary lying' can be seen in how nations engage in warfare. Sun Tzu, in his book *The Art of War*, wrote that, "All war is based on deception." The Greeks built a massive wooden horse, hid men inside of it, sailed away, and convinced the Trojans that they were disengaging from the conflict. The Trojans pulled the horse into the city as some sort of trophy and then during the night, the hidden Greeks emerged, opened the gates of the city to let in other Greek forces, and proceeded to overtake the city of Troy, essentially bringing what has come to be known as the Trojan War to an end. (Not only is this event one of the earliest examples of deception in warfare but it also serves as the origin of the expression, 'Beware of Greeks bearing gifts'.)

Spies have also long been part of the waging of war and almost by definition, a spy is a play actor and a liar; a spy is someone who acts *as if* he is loyal to one side of the conflict while in fact is working for the other. Whether we value the lying spy will depend upon whose side the lying serves. Benedict Arnold, whose name has almost become synonymous with the word, *traitor*, was a general for the Continental Army during the American Revolutionary War. He rose to the command of the fort at West Point, New York, but by that time was secretly working as a spy for the British. Like the young child who can act *as if* he is a doctor or superhero, Arnold was able to act *as if* he were a loyal supporter of the revolutionary cause when in fact he was plotting to turn the fort at West Point over to the British.

But the British weren't the only ones to employ spies. James Armistead was a slave on a Virginia plantation. After getting permission from his owner, Armistead volunteered in 1781 to serve in the Continental Army and did so under the leadership of General Marquis de Lafayette. Armistead's task was to pose as a runaway slave - to lie and act *as if* he were a runaway slave - and infiltrate the British forces. His 'play acting' skills were such that he was able to win the confidence of British officers including Lord Cornwallis and, ironically, Benedict Arnold. Armistead became privy to conversations that provided important information about British troop movements, information that he relayed back to the Continental Army and Lafayette. Some of this information turned out to be vital to the Continental Army's victory at Yorktown, which led to the surrender of the British forces and the end of the war.

The tale of these two spies, Benedict Arnold and James Armistead, demonstrates how the issue of morality and lying is a tricky question. From the perspective of a country fighting for its independence, Benedict Arnold was a traitor and James Armistead was a hero, although they were both liars. We are grateful for our child's ability to spare another person's feelings by telling the socially acceptable white lie but at the same time we will try to teach him that the lying of people like Lance Armstrong and Bernie Madoff is wrong. It is perhaps inevitable that as parents we will raise our children to be capable of lying but at the same time hope that we are raising children who know the difference between lies that harm and lies that don't.

In the end, telling our lies, our deliberate untruths, is just another form of *as if,* and springs from the same well as object substitutions, transitional objects, pretend play, and the transformation of reality. Children lie to escape punishment and to behave *as if* they are not guilty of the behavioral transgression. The Bernie Madoffs of the world lie in order to reap financial rewards and the commanders of armies lie to win wars. Kind and considerate people lie to avoid hurting the feelings of friends. It may all come down to the fact that sometimes we don't like reality as it is and we lie to create an alternative one.

Lying, then, is just another example of our human ability to transform and create alternate realities, an ability that is closely related to the *as if* quality of make-believe and imaginary play. A child needs an airplane in order to act out her make-believe story, so she picks up a block and transforms its identity, using the block *as if* it were an airplane. A child needs to feel strong and capable so she ties a towel around her neck and acts *as if* she is a superhero with super powers. A child is feeling a little insecure about stepping out into the world so she acts *as if her* mother is with her by carrying around her blankie. And a child who doesn't want to get into trouble offers the statement that 'cat did it' *as if* those words represent the truth. We might not always like it when children lie, but the *truth* is, they are just being human, just like the rest of us.

Chapter 5

Real Friends Aren't the Only Option

His name was William Martin. He was born in 1907 to a Roman Catholic family in Cardiff, Wales. His mother, Antonia, had died but his father, John, was still alive and would come to William's rescue when his son's sometimes exuberant lifestyle got him into trouble. When World War II engulfed Britain and Europe, William joined the Royal Marines, a branch of the British Royal Navy, and rose relatively quickly to the rank of Acting Major. And when Major Martin embarked on what turned out to be his final, and life ending, war mission, he left a fiancée, Pam, behind. Their final evening together included attending a theater production of "Strike a New Note." The historical record of World War II recognizes that this final mission of Acting Major William Martin made a significant contribution to the defeat of the Nazis and the ultimate ending of the war.

The most interesting aspect of William Martin's existence, however, is that he never actually existed. He didn't exist, his family didn't exist, his fiancée Pam didn't exist, and his enlistment in the Royal Navy never happened. Although his contribution to the defeat of the Nazis was real, the life of Acting Major William Martin was a total fabrication and a product of adult make-believe, of adults, in effect, engaging in a game of *as if*.

Using a real body, British intelligence created a fictional person, one to stand in for an officer in the British navy. The body was dumped at sea so that it would wash up on the shores of Spain. Knowing that the Spanish authorities in that particular geographi-

cal area were friendly to the German forces, the British rightly assumed that the Germans would be informed of the discovery of the
major's body. Papers and letters were planted on the body with the
intention of providing disinformation about the impending Allied
invasion of Southern Europe from Northern Africa. To make sure
the Germans believed the information they would discover, details
about Major Martin, who would later be memorialized as the "man
who never was", were carefully and meticulously planned. For example, in addition to military documents, the body contained a photo
of his fiancée, love letters to this fictitious fiancée, and a bill for the
engagement ring the dead officer had purchased for his wife-to-be.
There were also ticket stubs from the theater show he had attended
and the store receipt for a shirt he had purchased. One of the smallest
details considered had to do with the fact that this fictional man was
an officer in the British navy; he was, therefore, wearing high quality
underwear befitting someone of his rank.

All of this pretending produced the intended results; the Germans
were led to believe that Allied forces were going to invade Southern
Europe through Greece and Sardinia and the Germans redirected
many of their forces and resources to those geographical locations.
The Allies, however, mounted the invasion via Sicily; an invasion that
was as successful as it was because of an elaborate game of make-believe, one that included an adult version of a child's imaginary friend.
The intelligence agents "dreamed up the most unlikely concatena-
tion of events, rendered them believable, and sent them off to war,
changing reality through lateral thinking, and proving it is possible
to win a battle fought in the mind...[it] was pure make-believe, and
it made Hitler believe something that changed the course of history."

The imaginary friends of childhood

IMAGINARY FRIENDS ARE a fairly common occurrence in childhood. Research studies have found that somewhere between 30 and
60% of young children have had imaginary friends. Why the wide
range? The percentage of children identified as having imaginary

companions will vary depending on how the definition of the concept is determined. Some researchers stick to a fairly narrow definition and reserve the concept to apply only to the classic invisible friend. The percentages at the lower end of the range come from those types of studies. Other researchers include in their calculations those imaginary friends that take the form of what are called *personified objects*. The child whose imaginary friend is embodied in the form of his stuffed rabbit is said to have a personified object. The higher percentages result when both invisible friends and personified objects are included in the category of imaginary companions.

How do the researchers determine if a child has an imaginary playmate? Typically, they ask the child and the child's parents. Ideally, they look for parental report of the imaginary friend to corroborate what they learn from the child herself. A researcher can be quite certain of the existence of an imaginary friend when child and parent both offer similar descriptions of the imaginary companion and similar depictions of how the imaginary friend plays a part in the life of the child and the family. This corroboration doesn't always exist, however, for essentially one of two reasons (or perhaps both). First, some children are reluctant to admit that they have imaginary friends. They may feel self-conscious about their friend's existence and they may feel that other people might make fun of them for having an imaginary friend. For their part, parents can be unaware of the imaginary friend's existence. It is sometimes the case that parents first learn of their child's imaginary companion when they are participating in the research study that asks them if their child has an imaginary companion.

It was once believed that imaginary friends were most prevalent among children in the three-year-old age range. It was thought that after about the age of three or four the incidence of imaginary friends declined and by the time children were in the early school years, imaginary friends were a rare occurrence. It turns out, however, that a good number of six- and seven-year-old children, perhaps as many as 30%, continue to create and build relationships with imaginary companions.

It has also been found that once created, an imaginary companion can have a reasonably long life expectancy. For some children, their imaginary friends can be with them for up to three years. One study found that the characteristics of the imaginary friend - as described by the child - stayed fairly constant over a three-year time period. What this suggests is that children aren't making up these friends at the moment they are being asked about them; as much as it may sound like an oxymoron, for the children who create them, there can be real substance to these imaginary companions.

Who are the creators of imaginary friends?

THE ARTIST FRIDA Kahlo wrote the following in a 1950 entry in her diary: "Thirty-four years have passed since I experienced this magic friendship and every time I remember it, it revives and becomes larger and larger inside of my world." She was describing the origins of her largest and perhaps most well-known painting, "The Two Fridas." Completed in 1939, this painting depicts two images of the adult Frida. Painted at about the time she was becoming divorced from the artist Diego Rivera, at a surface level the painting portrays one Frida with a broken heart, symbolizing the dissolution of her marriage, and one with an intact heart. In the diary entry, however, Kahlo was linking the painting to a particular childhood memory.

Kahlo contracted polio at the age of six. As a result, she essentially stayed in her room for about nine months. As was sometimes the case with polio, one of her legs withered and remained thin and weak for her entire life. Being out of school, isolated from her peer group for nine months, led to feelings of loneliness and made her the subject of teasing by other children. A childhood friend of Kahlo's remembers the teasing that Kahlo endured: "We were quite cruel about her leg. When she was riding her bicycle we would yell at her: Frida, para de palo (Frida, peg leg), and she would respond furiously with lots of curses."

From her diary, we learn that Kahlo had another reaction to the loneliness and teasing: she created an imaginary friend, one who came into her life at about the age of six. She would encounter this friend by entering another world.

> On the glass window of what at that time was my
> room...I breathed vapor onto one of the first panes. I
> let out a breath and with a finger drew a 'door'...Full of
> great joy and urgency, I went out in my imagination
> through this 'door'...and I went down in great haste into
> the interior of the earth where 'my imaginary friend' was
> always waiting for me.

Kahlo writes that she doesn't remember what this friend looked like, but she did remember that the friend laughed easily and danced and "while she danced I told her my secret problems. Which ones? I do not remember. But from my voice she knew everything about me."

Kahlo also remembered how it felt to visit this friend.

> When I returned to the window I entered through the
> same door drawn on the glass pane...I was happy. I
> blurred the 'door' with my hand and it 'disappeared'...I
> ran with my secret and my joy...I cried out and laughed,
> surprised at being alone with my great happiness and
> with the so vivid memory of this little girl.

WHO ARE THE children who create imaginary friends? Are they special in some way? Are they significantly different from children who don't have imaginary companions? The short answer is no, not really. Children who like to play with an invisible friend, like to act and talk *as if* their friend is real, are normal, regular kids. On average, they are well-adjusted, sociable, and understand the difference between reality and fantasy. They are not troubled, psychotic, or confused about what is real and what is not. On the other hand, the longer answer is that there are some characteristics about children who create imaginary friends that are interesting and worth noting.

There is some evidence, for example, that birth order relates to the creation of imaginary companions. Imaginary friends seem to be created more by first-born and only children than children who are later born and have siblings. In one research study, for example, not a single child who was a middle-born child reported having an imaginary companion.

What about the differences between children who create imaginary companions and those who don't? There is some suggestion that children with imaginary companions may involve themselves in imaginary play in general to a greater extent than children who do not have an imaginary companion. Some researchers have also suggested that the pretend play of children with invisible friends may be of a higher and more mature level than the play of children who don't have an imaginary friend. There is also a research finding that children without imaginary friends - those children who have not found a reason to create an invisible companion - may watch more television and read more books than those children who do create imaginary friends. This may be the case because "Children who were immersed in someone else's imaginary world seemed less likely to create such a world themselves."

In a study looking at the storytelling skills of children with and without imaginary friends, the study's authors found that children with imaginary friends generally told richer stories and their stories included more dialogue and employed more specific vocabulary terms when discussing past events in the stories. These differences may develop because "children with imaginary companions...gain practice in decontextualized conversations both during interactions with their imaginary companions, and when they tell others about their imaginary companions." (The idea of "decontextualized conversations" relates to the concept of *distancing* discussed in Chapter 1.) It is also possible that the creation and maintenance of an imaginary friend exercises the perspective-taking and consideration of audience discussed in Chapter 3 because "children have sole knowledge of their imaginary companions [and] adults may be required to ask a greater number of questions about imaginary companions than they ask when conversing about topics which both adult and child share knowledge."

There are also gender differences among children who create imaginary friends. First, imaginary companions are more likely to be created by girls than they are by boys. Furthermore, boys tend to create companions who are like themselves, i.e., boys tend to create male imaginary friends. Girls, on the other hand, are more likely than boys to have an imaginary companion of either gender. In terms of human and non-human companions, girls are more likely to create a human invisible friend while boys are almost as likely to create a non-human friend as a human one.

What is perhaps most interesting in terms of gender differences are the nature of the relationships between the child and his or her imaginary friend. Boys often establish a relationship where they see themselves as more competent than their imaginary friend; as a result, boys make such comments as "He doesn't have a bike, I go much faster then him" and "I run faster than him because I have faster shoes. His shoes are a little worn out." For their part, girls might also create a friend who they view as less competent but not from the perspective of being competitive with the friend; girls establish relationships where they can be the nurturer. This type of relationship produces such comments as "He is not good at puzzles. I have to help him"; "She needs me to push her on the swing"; and "She only has me as a friend." It has been suggested that these relationship dynamics may be influenced by how children understand sex-role stereotypes, a view that the psychologist Alison Gopnik finds somewhat depressing because "little boys seem to have a penchant for becoming super creatures of enormous power, while little girls are more likely to invent small animals to pity and take care of."

Why do children create imaginary friends?

WHY DO CHILDREN conjure up an imaginary friend that is visible to only themselves? What functions do imaginary friends serve children in their lives? Of course the answers to these questions are always idiosyncratic to the individual children doing the creating, but there seem to be some general reasons why children choose to populate their worlds with imaginary beings.

A common reason for the existence of an imaginary friend in a child's life is companionship. This desire for a playmate might suggest that the child is lonely (and may explain why more first-born and only children have imaginary friends) but it may also be the case that a perfectly social child, one who has a full complement of real friends in real life, just wants to have a playmate when those real friends are not available. Marjorie Taylor, who has conducted extensive research on imaginary friends believes that since "children who create imaginary companions enjoy social interaction - makes sense that they would invent companions when no one else is around and they want something interesting to do."

It can also come in handy to have a friend under your control at times, particularly if you want to blame that companion for something that you have done. Children have been known to use their imaginary friend as a scapegoat. One child, whose imaginary friend was named Whisper, denied responsibility for the spilling of a glass of milk and blamed his imaginary companion. This scapegoating and blaming also relates to the concept of distancing discussed earlier. Children can use the existence of an imaginary friend to create a sense of distance from their own feelings and emotions, helping them "distance themselves from 'Bad me' percepts as well as hold onto 'Good me' percepts...By warehousing these forbidden characteristics in the imaginary companion, children earn safe emotional distance." The novelist Anthony Marra captures this function of imaginary friends when he describes the play of two sisters in his novel, *A Constellation of Vital Phenomena*.

> When they were children they had pretended to have a third sister, a black-haired girl named Lidiya...the ghost sister was never around, and in her absence, they had teased, chided, scorned, blamed, and hated Lidiya so they could love each other more simply.

This distance that results from the *as if* play of and with imaginary friends can help children reflect on their feelings and emotions and perhaps help get their emotions under control. The imaginary companion can provide a vehicle for the expression of emotions that the child may not feel comfortable sharing as himself. The child who blamed his imaginary friend, Whisper, for the spilt milk, also let his father know that, "Whisper is so angry with you, Daddy." It is quite likely that it was the child himself, not Whisper, who was angry with the father. As Marjorie Taylor notes, "Interactions with imaginary companions often include elements from the real lives of children. It is as if play with an imaginary companion provides a forum for mulling over or thinking about things that catch their attention."

This function of control is another example of Erik Erikson's construct of *microcosms* and is characteristic of children's play and engagement with *as if* in general. When a child creates an imaginary friend she is, in effect, carving out a small portion of the world that is (usually) under her control. Within this world she can express feelings and try out ideas that may not be possible or allowable in the 'real' world of friends and companions. Imaginary friends "allow children to explore issues of control, discipline, and power without the anxiety attached to interactions with real authority figures." It is true that at times imaginary friends seem to develop a mind of their own but for the most part,

> The child doesn't have to worry about an imaginary
> companion getting cranky and threatening to take his
> or her toys and go home. On the other hand, the child
> can walk out on the imaginary companion at any point
> without repercussion - the companion will be cheerfully be
> ready to start up again at a moment's notice.

CONSIDER THIS REFLECTION of an adult looking back on her fictional childhood friend:

> I created an imaginary Laura who, like my doll and the
> other girls I saw in school and in stores, wore a short-
> sleeved white blouse with a lace collar, blue skirt, white
> socks and shoes, and had curls.

The young girl who created the imaginary Laura was also named Laura. Why did she feel the need to create an imaginary friend with the same name? Real Laura was raised in a Mennonite family and following Mennonite culture and practices her family valued the principle of plainness. A practice of plainness meant that, among other things, clothing didn't have decorations, jewelry wasn't worn, shirts didn't have collars, and hair wasn't cut nor was it worn in curls. As Laura writes, "To insiders, such plainness constitutes normality; the fanciness in the dominant culture constitutes abnormality." But as Laura also recognized, "As a result of our plain dress, we were - in public schools, bus stations, and stores, - immediately identified as minority people."

Accepting her culture's practices didn't inhibit Laura from dreaming about alternative ways of living; she noted that, "As a Mennonite child, I outwardly accepted plainness. But I found ways to fulfill inner desires for prohibited items." And Laura wasn't alone in employing make-believe to create an alternative experience for herself: "Some of us children began to wish for the prohibited things and for a life in a less censored group. This need we tried to satisfy by creating imaginary characters and objects, by trying out substitutes in the privacy of our rooms, and by fantasizing escapes."

For the young Laura quoted above, one of the substitutes and means of escape was the invention of her imaginary namesake, Laura. This Laura was able to have curly hair, tie ribbons in that hair, adorn herself with jewelry, and wear fancy clothes. This Laura was able to be what the real Laura was not outwardly able, or allowed, to be.

Later in life, real Laura saw a connection between who she was as adult and who she was as a child and the role imaginary Laura played in her life. As an adult, Laura "no longer dresses 'plain' and reflecting on her childhood she has come to understand that "My adult distress at that lack of versatility [of clothing, hairstyle, etc.] was clearly anticipated by my having created a Laura who looked as I wished her to." In other words, through her imaginary friend, she was able to consider life *as if* she were someone else.

Living with imaginary friends

ONE OF THE most well-known imaginary friends in all of literature is Harvey, a six-foot, three and half-inch rabbit. Harvey, the title character of Mary Chase's play, is Elwood Dowd's best friend and his prime drinking companion. Listen to Veta, Dowd's niece, describe what it is like to live with Harvey.

> Well, yes, I say definitely Elwood drinks and I want him committed out here permanently because I cannot stand another day of that Harvey. Myrtle and I have to set a place at the table for Harvey. We have to move over on the sofa and make room for Harvey. We have to answer the telephone when Elwood calls and asks to speak to Harvey.

Living with imaginary companions isn't always easy, not for the family and not always for the child herself, the actual creator of the invisible friend. Families sometimes have to make real life accommodations for the imaginary friend: the imaginary companion may require a seat at the family dinner table or at a restaurant; televisions may need to be left on to entertain the friend while the family is out of the house; and if a seatbelt must be fastened around the real child in a car then certainly the child's imaginary friend needs to be buckled in as well.

Imaginary friends can also prove to be difficult because even though they are the invented creations of the child, they don't always cooperate or behave as their creators would like them to. Marjorie Taylor, for example, tells the story of a 3-year-old who was taken to a horse show. His parents thought this would have been an exciting outing for the child because his imaginary companion was a pony. Unfortunately, when the child arrived at the horse show he learned that his pony, his imaginary friend, "had made other plans and was not there." The child was not pleased.

I once witnessed a fairly serious conflict occur between a child and his imaginary playmate. The child was out on his front lawn, tree branch in hand, fighting an imaginary sword battle with an imaginary opponent. All was well until this imaginary opponent got the upper hand and was pushing the child into retreat. The boy was chased across the lawn, up the front steps of his house, and into the front door, at which point he screamed for his mother's help. The opponent was imaginary, the swordplay was imaginary, but to my ears at least, his scream for help was very real.

Ironically, it can sometimes be the case that an imaginary friend doesn't have enough time to play with his or her creator. The writer, Adam Gopnik, tells the story of Charlie Ravioli, the imaginary friend created by his three-year-old daughter, Olivia. Olivia and her family lived in New York City and her imaginary friend Charlie Ravioli took on many of the characteristics one would imagine a young professional living in Manhattan might possess. He lived in an apartment on Madison and Lexington Avenues, enjoyed grilled chicken and fruit, and drank bottled water. He exercised at a gym and vacationed on the beach during the summer. (Remember, we are talking here about the imaginary friend.) But as Gopnik, the father, points out, perhaps the most interesting characteristic of this imaginary friend, and one that again might be associated with young, urban professionals, is that Charlie Ravioli was too busy to play with Olivia, his creator.

> She holds her toy cell phone up to her ear, and we hear
> her talk into it: "Ravioli? It's Olivia...It's Olivia. Come and
> play? O.K. Call me. Bye." Then she snaps it shut, and
> shakes her head. "I always get his machine," she says.
> Or she will say, "I spoke to Ravioli today." "Did you have
> fun?" my wife and I ask. "No. He was busy working."

At some point, another name begins to enter Olivia's play with her imaginary friend. Her parents begin to hear their daughter referring to someone by the name of Laurie. They hear Olivia talking with Laurie about Charlie Ravioli. It was as if Olivia had created an imaginary friend with whom she could talk about the other imaginary friend. But Gopnik and his wife discovered that this wasn't what was happening.

And then it came to us, with sickening clarity: Laurie
was not the patient friend who consoled you for
Charlie's absence. Laurie was the bright-toned person
who answered Ravioli's phone and told you that
unfortunately Mr. Ravioli was in a meeting. "Laurie says
that Ravioli is too busy to play," Olivia announced sadly
one morning. Things seemed to be deteriorating; now
Ravioli was too busy to say he was too busy.

It doesn't seem fair that our own creations wouldn't want to play with us but sometimes they apparently just have minds of their own.

Parents and the 'reality' of imaginary friends

When the character Chandler, on the television show,
"Friends", was asked if he were an only child and
therefore escaped some of the challenging dynamics
that occurs among siblings, he wistfully answered,
"I had an imaginary friend, who my parents actually
preferred."

WHAT DO PARENTS think about their children's imaginary companions? As noted earlier, apparently a good number of parents aren't even aware that their children have an imaginary friend. Some parents learn about their child's imaginary companion while participating in a research study about imaginary companions. Other parents come to understand that the friend they keep hearing about from their child isn't real after asking a teacher about the friend at their child's preschool.

When parents do know about the imaginary friend (or become aware of its existence), reactions can be mixed. Many parents are accepting of their children's creations. In one study, for example, only one of the parents participating said that she had attempted to discourage her child's involvement with the imaginary companion; all of the other parents at least tolerated the invisible friend's existence. In her book, *Imaginary Companions and the Children Who Create Them,*

Marjorie Taylor writes that parents often report that while they are "comfortable with their children having pretend friends, they don't actively encourage this type of play." The parents are willing to "allow their children to 'do their own thing,' but they don't ask about pretend friends or participate in the pretense."

On the other hand, some parents are less than thrilled about the idea of their children talking and playing with an invisible friend. These imaginary companions may "throw some parents for a loop" and cause parents to wonder if their child has "lost her grip on reality." Parents may wonder if their child's relationship with an imaginary friend represents a confusion between reality and fantasy or whether it is the same as lying. There also may be some cultural differences regarding the value of fantasy play in general and play with imaginary friends in particular. Marjorie Taylor reported that when compared with parents in the United States, Mexican parents were less comfortable with the imaginary friends created by their children. Taylor and her colleague Anne Mannering quote a Mexican parent expressing the concern that, "I was afraid it was something supernatural. Their [the child's] reassurance that they could see it [the imaginary friend] frightened me." Taylor and Mannering also found that more Mexican parents saw a relationship between pretending and lying than did parents in the United States.

In terms of participating with children in their imaginary friend play, some parents do and some don't. And the phenomenon of imaginary friends can illustrate how parents aren't always necessary: children can create their friends and maintain the friendships without any help from their parents. When parents do attempt to discourage the existence of an imaginary friend, their efforts usually don't meet with success. It is possible, however, for parents to sometimes 'exploit' the existence of the imaginary friend for their own benefit: as Marjorie Taylor writes, "If you want to know how your child feels about a sensitive topic, you might try asking about the imaginary companion's feelings."

The developmental importance of imaginary friends

A NUMBER OF researchers have found that children who have invented imaginary companions for themselves show greater facility at understanding the beliefs of others, a greater ability to see the world *as if* they are standing in the shoes of the other person.

If you think about it, it makes sense that engaging in the *as if* activity of living with imaginary playmates would exercise the ability to understand and consider the perspectives of other people. In some ways, interacting with imaginary friends may exercise these abilities better than play with real friends because when playing with an imaginary friend, the child has to assume the mental beliefs of *both* players, himself and the imaginary friend. With a real friend it is easy to fall into what is called *parallel play. Parallel play* is a term used to describe the play of children where they are playing in physical proximity of each other; they might be playing with the same materials, for example blocks, but each child is 'doing his or her own thing'. The children are playing *with* each other only by virtue of sharing the same physical space and the same materials. The children are not playing with each other in terms of the give and take of cooperation and negotiated activity; one child's play is not constrained or influenced by what another child is thinking or believing. To play with an imaginary friend, almost by definition, requires a consideration of what that friend is thinking and believing; after all, you have created the friend and you are responsible for what that friend is thinking and believing. Play with an imaginary companion often involves a good deal of negotiation between what the child is pretending and the real world. For children with imaginary companions, this negotiation involves integrating the companion into everyday activities, such as having an extra place set at the table and keeping others informed about the companion's behavior and mental states.

In real life, a child can ignore what someone else may be thinking; he can choose to not consider the other person's perspective. That is much harder to do in the world of imaginary companions because you have given the imaginary friend a perspective in the first place.

The creation of paracosms

SOME CHILDREN AREN'T satisfied with creating just one imaginary friend. There are children who feel the need for two or more imaginary companions and then there are children who create not just imaginary beings but entire imaginary worlds. There is even a technical term for these worlds: *paracosms*. A *paracosm* might have a particular geography, its own language and its own set of laws. *Paracosms* are populated with imaginary people and the lives and interactions of these figments of the imagination take place within the characteristics and constraints of the imagined world, worlds that are "invented universes with distinctive languages, geography, and history." Think Harry Potter and his friends navigating the world of the Hogwarts School.

The creation of paracosms is most often found in the play of older children, those between the years of nine and adolescence. Once children have 'mastered' the imaginary companion, "The shift...to paracosms may...reflect shifts in children's causal knowledge of other people. Older children, who already understand how individual minds work, become more interested in what happens when minds interact in socially complex ways." It is important to note, however, that just because a child invents an imaginary friend that doesn't mean she will also create an imaginary world populated with multiple imaginary beings; fewer children create paracosms than those who bring a single imaginary friend into their lives.

An example of a paracosm can be seen in the life of Woodrow Wilson, the 28th president of the United States. As a teenager, Wilson was fascinated with the ocean and lives related to the sea and "became consumed with knights and pirates and then naval stories." In addition to learning facts and histories, he "began imagining that he was an admiral of his own navy, about which he wrote daily reports... For several years he continued issuing orders, granting promotions, and 'decorating' himself with knighthoods of the Garter and the Star of India." These imaginary musings were part of Wilson's creation of an elaborate paracosm.

He fantasized once again about what he dubbed 'the Royal United Kingdom Yacht Club.' He even composed a constitution for his mythical flotilla, and elaborate lists of rules and regulations for his make-believe organization, complete with details of officers' duties, times of meetings, fees for entrance, fines for absences, and requirements for bills and resolutions, which demanded the signature of the Commodore - himself.

We see in Wilson's creation one of the interesting characteristics of paracosms - they can exist and evolve over a number of years. The Bronte siblings (Emily, Charlotte, Anne, and Branwell), for example, authors of such classic books as *Jane Eyre* (Charlotte) and *Wuthering Heights* (Emily), used their imaginations to create stories about an empire located on the coast of Africa and a kingdom called Gondol that was ruled by a not so pleasant Queen. Ann McGreevy who wrote about the early years of the Brontes noted that these creations were, "virtual universes...consisting of histories, philosophies, generations of families, maps, and illustrations." McGreevy also notes that the involvement with these worlds lasted a long time as evidenced by birthday notes shared between sisters Emily and Anne in their twenties that referred to some of the characters from the kingdom of Gondol.

According to one study, which referred to the creation of paracosms as *worldplay*, the motivation and skills required to imagine elaborate and complex fictional worlds may be related to the development of creativity in general. The authors of the study suggest that *worldplay* appears to provide an early apprenticeship in absorption and persistence, discovery, synthesis, and modeling. Paracosms, or *worldplay*, may exercise some specific skills related to the creative mind: the capacity to imagine, empathize, and model; the capacity for problem-solving; the ability to imagine solutions to challenges; and the ability to make a connection between 'virtual imagination' and creativity. As a 'test' of their hypothesis that the creation of childhood paracosms is related to later creativity, the authors surveyed 90 winners of the prestigious Macarthur Fellowships, a program that, according to the Foundation's website, "celebrates and inspires the creative potential of individuals"; these fellowships are referred to as the Macarthur Genius Awards. They found that of the 90 fellows who participated in the survey, between 20% and 26% had created a paracosm, had engaged in *worldplay,* sometime during their childhoods.

But sometimes paracosms aren't created simply for the purpose of entertainment and play; sometimes paracosms are created by adults for very serious purposes, as the story of Juan Pujol Garcia will attest.

Juan Pujol Garcia was a Spaniard who despised Adolf Hitler and the fascism that Nazi Germany was attempting to impose upon Europe. He decided that he wanted to be a double agent spy; he would convince the authorities in Germany that he was spying for them against the Allies while in fact he would be working for the Allies against Germany. At first Britain turned down his offer (they would later see how valuable he could be) so he set out to put into place the first step of his plan - convince Germany that he was on their side by pretending to spy on Britain.

In 1941, he began his ruse by informing Germany that he had made his way to Britain. This was his first step in what would become an elaborate world of make-believe. Garcia didn't actually go to England; he was in Portugal. By using maps, tour books, etc., he provided detailed descriptions of where he supposedly was 'in England' and what he observed there - *as if* he were actually there. He then began to create an entire network of spies and sub-agents who worked for and reported to him. All of these spies and sub-agents, however, were imaginary. His imaginary agents "began recruiting their own sub-agents. The network began to self-replicate and metastasize until [his] work...came to resemble a limitless, multi-character, ever-expanding novel." And like the characters of a novel, these agents and sub-agents were all fictional creations of the author, Juan Pujol Garcia.

Who were these imaginary spies? Over time Garcia's imaginary beings included someone who worked at an airline, a student from

Venezuela, a waiter from Scotland, a deserter from the Greek armed forces, a sergeant in the American army, and a group of Welshman who were very much in support of Nazi anti-Semitism. At one point, Garcia's stable of agents and sub-agents numbered twenty-four, a number which included Garcia himself. In other words, Germany was relying on receiving information from a network of twenty-four spies, twenty-three of whom were imaginary and didn't exist.

What did these imaginary spies do? Basically they provided Germany with information. Sometimes what was communicated to Germany was mis- or dis-information; for example, information that was designed to mislead the German powers about Allied troop strength and movements. Sometimes true or accurate information was given to the Germans - information of no great significance - in order to establish the 'credibility' of the fictional spies. Regardless of whether the information was true or not, it was always information that the Allies wanted the Germans to have. Over a three year period, Garcia transmitted almost 1800 messages and letters to his German contacts.

Sometimes one of Garcia's spies had to be eliminated or terminated. In one case, one of his agents was "simply too well placed for [his] own good." This fictional agent was living in Liverpool, England and since Allied ships and troops were in the area preparing for the invasion of Africa, it would only be logical that he would have observed this activity and therefore should have been able to provide the information to Germany. Once the invasion occurred, Germany would have questioned why this agent hadn't communicated the information about the Allied preparations. The way out of this dilemma was to arrange for the death of the spy from some undisclosed illness. A death notice was actually printed in a local newspaper, a copy of which Garcia sent to the Germans, who then followed up with a letter expressing their sympathy for the agent's death. So in the end, there was a real death notice and a real letter of sympathy for an imaginary spy. And the web of imagination regarding this particular spy didn't end there - the imaginary spy was replaced in Garcia's network of spies by the deceased, imaginary, spy's imaginary wife.

As suggested earlier, children may create imaginary friends because these friends may be more 'controllable' than the real people in their lives. The same has been said about imaginary spies. John Masterman, one of the main players in Great Britain's espionage apparatus, wrote that, "for deception...imaginary agents were on the whole preferable to living ones." Ben Mcintyre, an author of a number of books on the world of spycraft, agrees with Masterman: "Real agents tended to become truculent and demanding; they needed feeding, pampering, and paying. An imaginary agent, however, was infinitely pliable and willing to do the bidding of his German handlers at once and without question."

Imaginary friends aren't just for children

HAVING THE PREDISPOSITION and wherewithal to create an imaginary friend is not just the province of the young. Perfectly normal and sane adults may create an imaginary person when a particular need arises. Jason Collins was the first professional basketball player to announce that he was gay. He has talked about needing to avoid some social situations before he was open about his sexual orientation. When his teammates would be going out to spend time in the city, Collins would say that he couldn't join them because he was meeting up with some friends, and as he wrote, "Sometimes those friends were real. Sometimes I made them up and would sit alone in the hotel room watching TV while the guys went out to enjoy the nightlife." Another example of an adult needing to create imaginary people for very pragmatic reasons comes from the life of Jacqueline Kennedy, wife of the president. There was a time in her life as First Lady when some people were invited to stay in the White House and she wasn't very happy with the prospect of their presence in her home. She came up with the plan to make the potential guest rooms look as if they were being decorated. Collaborating with her on this ruse was the head White House usher, J. B. West: "West had the furniture covered with drop cloths, the rugs rolled up, and buckets of white paint and dirty brushes set out. As a finishing touch, he scattered around ashtrays, filled with butts left by the imaginary work-men." In other words, Jackie Kennedy put imaginary people to work as a way of discouraging the presence of real people.

Adults, particularly creative types, have been known to hang out with, or at least want to hang out with, a particular kind of imaginary creation: the muse. Both the early Greeks and Romans believed that there was some inspiring spirit that resided outside of the mind and body of the painter, poet, or musician.

> The Greeks had called her daemon (who inhabits artists
> and stoked them with fires of outrageous invention), the
> Romans called her genius for they believed not that one
> was a genius but that one had a genius, a patron saint of
> inspiration, that must be fed with brilliance of mind, lest it
> move on to a more spritely host.

In other words, the artist might be the one who physically puts the paint to canvas or words to blank page but the idea or inspiration for what is painted or written comes from the imaginary muse. The muse, most often thought of as female in form, is known to be a fickle sort of friend; a friend who doesn't always come when needed or bidden. The muse most often has a mind of her own.

Albert Brooks wrote, directed and starred in a 1999 movie, titled, *The Muse*, that portrayed the sometimes tortured relationship between the artist and his muse. Brooks plays a Hollywood screenwriter who is suffering from the proverbial writer's block; it has been a while since he was able to produce a hit or even sellable screenplay. Through a friend he is introduced to a woman, played by Sharon Stone, who, the friend can attest to through personal experience, will provide the inspiration to 'unblock' him. The problem, and the source of much of the humor of the film, is that this woman, this muse, is somewhat demanding. She requires an increasing amount of care and feeding in order to provide this inspiration; this care and feeding takes the form of attention and at times expensive gifts. These demands become more and more difficult for Brooks to satisfy. A secondary challenge for Brooks is that in addition to her demands,

Stone's character also winds up inspiring Brooks' wife to fulfill her own passion for baking and her dream of opening up a bakery. For Brooks, the life forces of these two women, one imagined and one real, require him to make some difficult adjustments in his life.

Like Brooks' character, artists frequently have a challenging relationship with the imagined muse. Most artists will say that you just can't wait around for the muse, *your muse*, to show up. You have to put yourself in the chair in front of the computer, or you have to stand in front of the easel, and be ready. When the muse does show up, the rewards can be most gratifying, and like the imaginary friends of childhood, she can play a very important role in your life.

> Which is why I like waiting for what we call The Muse.
> She's the one I pay attention to when I'm writing. She's
> like the best friend you can imagine. If I'm willing to listen,
> she's always got something very interesting to say. She has
> her own language, of course, and so I have to translate
> what she says so other people can understand it. That's
> my job in this arrangement.

The demise of imaginary friends

WHAT HAPPENS TO an imaginary friend after a child no longer needs it? (Him? Her?) One answer to this question was provided by the Cartoon Network which between 2004 and 2009 produced 79 episodes of a show titled, *Foster's Home for Imaginary Friends*. The premise of the show was simple: after a child no longer needs her imaginary friend, that friend retreats to *Foster's Home* and adopts one of the 'residents' for herself. As the creator of the show Craig McCracken wrote, 'They [the imaginary friend] have this history. They were created by a kid for a purpose. That defined their personality, and now they are leading this second life in the foster home."

Another imagined answer to what happens to no longer needed imaginary friends is offered by Matthew Dicks in his lovely novel, *Memoirs of an Imaginary Friend*. Dicks is considering the same question - what happens to imaginary friends when their creators, the children, no longer need them - but his answer is not quite as 'warm and fuzzy' as the one embodied in the Cartoon Network show. For Dicks, imaginary friends who have outlived their usefulness simply fade away...or worse. School, for example, can hasten the demise of an imaginary friend.

> A school is full of kids, but most of them leave their imaginary friends home because it is hard to talk or play with an imaginary friend when teachers or other kids are around. They might bring them to school on the first day of kindergarten, [but]...the kids figure out fast that talking to someone who no one else can see is not a good way to make friends.

Dicks goes on to write, "This is time when most imaginary friends stop existing...Kindergarten kills them."

Although she might not use the term, 'kill,' researcher Marjorie Taylor concurs that for most children the life expectancy of an imaginary friend is limited.

> Not much is known about how these fantasies end, but the available evidence suggests that children simply move on to other things. In most cases, no well-marked event leads to the imaginary companion's disappearance - it simply fades away.

Just being human

IT IS CERTAINLY true that in some cases living with imaginary beings might be considered a sign of pathology or underlying illness. People suffering from schizophrenia may have the experience of hearing voices and in some cases engage in conversation with those voices. Some people diagnosed with dementia may suffer from hallucinations during which time they may believe that a person is in their presence and sometimes they will describe this person with a good amount of detail. The typical child who creates an imaginary friend, however, is not evidencing some pathology nor is the emergence of the imaginary companion a symptom of any illness. Studies have shown that the creation of imaginary friends is not linked to any emotional illnesses or significant emotional difficulties in the lives of the children who create them.

On the contrary, "contemporary wisdom is that imaginary companion play may even offer some developmental benefits for children." It has been suggested, for example, that children who have imaginary companions demonstrate more mature levels of pretend play, more advanced language and social skills, and are better able to understand the perspectives and beliefs of other people. Children who have imaginary friends have been found to be less shy and more outgoing than children without imaginary friends. As mentioned earlier in the chapter, it has been suggested that having an imaginary companion is related to the development of creativity and theory of mind. As parents it may be easy to be resistant to our child's attachment to this unreal being but as the psychologist Alison Gopnik wrote, "There's no getting around the fact that, from the adult point of view, there's something spooky about imaginary friends. But in fact, as far as children go, they're not only commonplace, they're a sign of social competence."

It may be that the creation of imaginary friends is just the manifestation of some basic human abilities and urges. The creation of imaginary friends may be a prime example of children's engagement with *as if* play; the child is acting *as if* this friend exists. The imaginary friend is just one more example of how a child uses the power of pretend to distance herself from reality in order to create other options for herself. It may also be that a child's creation of an imaginary companion is evidence that "Human beings have a unique capacity to love, share our lives, and even bare our souls to imaginary others."

Chapter 6

Superheroes, Tales of Fairies, and Monsters

Jonathan Gottschall writes in his book, *The Storytelling Animal: How Stories Make Us Human*, that, "Children's play is clearly about many things, mommies and babies, monsters and heroes, spaceships and unicorns. And it is also about one thing: trouble." In his book he likens children's stories to fiction in general and suggests that, "There is a universal grammar in world fiction, a deep pattern of heroes confronting trouble and struggling to overcome."

The stories children love are often stories about dark forests, children in danger, good guys and bad guys, and giants needing to be vanquished through daring and trickery. Many children will want to return to these forests, escape the dangers, and do battle with the giants over and over again. The parents of these daring children might not always understand their children's fascination with these forms of *as if* play, but despite the parents' best efforts to redirect the children away from the dark woods and scary giants, return they will. As Stephen Sondheim wrote in his musical, *Into the Woods:*

> *So it's*
> *Into the woods*
> *You go again*
> *You have to*
> *Every now and then.*
> *Into the woods,*
> *No telling when,*
> *Be ready for the journey*

So where do children find 'trouble' in their playworlds? Three prime examples where children grapple with 'trouble' are superhero play, fairy tales and and stories that bring them face to face with monsters. Most children will involve themselves in these types of play at one time or another and for some children, the play of superheroes, fairy tales or monsters may dominate their play lives at some point in their childhood. Children's fascination with trouble includes such themes as power, the grappling with good and evil, overcoming adversity, and confronting the monsters, real and imaginary, in your world.

Capes, masks, and superheroes

But don't underestimate me
I'm seven years old
And all I need is a cape and a mask
So I can fly out of here

IN JUNE OF 1938, DC Comics published the first issue of a new comic book with the title, *Action Comics No. 1*. The significance of this publication wasn't that it was the first ever comic book; that event took place about five years earlier. What made this publication historically significant is that within *Action Comics No. 1* there appeared a brand new comic book character, who some eighty years later is such a part of the fabric of our culture that it's hard to imagine he never existed. His image can today be found in comic books, movies, and television shows, and on lunch boxes, Halloween costumes and children's underwear. He is, of course, the 'man of steel,' the man with the big letter S on his chest. He is Superman.

But then sometime after Superman appeared in full color in that 1938 comic book, another type of superhero was born. Unlike the original Superman, we don't know his exact date of birth, where this new superhero was born, or who his parents were. We do know that somewhere and someplace, a young child tied a towel - or some other suitable *object substitution* for Superman's cape - around his neck, bent his knees and jumped. This leap into the air of imagination may have started from a chair or stool, or may have simply been a small hop from one spot on the floor to another. Regardless of the trajectory or distance of the jump, the intent was the same: this was a leap of transformation from being 'just' a young child to now being that man of steel who was fighting injustice wherever it may be found. This was the transformation from being 'just' a child to becoming a superhero.

Although we don't know who that first pretend superhero was, we do have evidence that this child must have existed because we see his descendants among us today, capes flowing and imaginary muscles flexing, flying around our early childhood classrooms, our playgrounds, and our living rooms. These superheroes may go by the name of Superman or Batman or Wonder Woman or Iron Man or Power Ranger or the Green Lantern but their secret identity is always the same: a young child who has set reality aside for the moment, stepped into the play frame of *as if*, and transformed him or herself into someone larger than life, transformed himself into a superhero.

In our culture at least, it's not a question of *if* a child will cross paths with the idea of a superhero, it's only a question of *when* and *how*. At times it seems as if superheroes are everywhere. The superhero may be "as much a part of our communal DNA as Paul Bunyan or Huckleberry Finn" or, as one author put it, "You'd have to live in a cave to escape the current superhero craze."

And most parents and teachers would agree that children do not escape the superhero craze. To one degree or another, and in one way or another, most children are introduced to the concept of superheroes. The introduction may come from comic books, movies, television shows or other children. If an individual child doesn't incorporate superheroes into her own *as if* play, she could very likely, at one time or another, be the audience for some other child's superhero imagination. The results of one research study, for example, indicated that just over 68% of the parents surveyed said that their children engaged in some kind of superhero play at home. More than 50% of the parents also said that their children would rather watch a television show based on superheroes than other television offerings.

Superheroes have also found their way into schoolrooms across the country. In fact "the findings from the school culture and teachers' perspectives highlights how superheroes and superhero play became part of almost every aspect of school routines and activities." Dealing with the sometimes boisterous aspects of superhero play has become a fairly common challenge facing teachers, particularly in the preschool and primary grades. Teachers may be responsible for introducing what *they* may think are the important subjects and activities of the curriculum but children have their own ideas about what those subjects and activities could - or should - be; and the escapades and dramas of superheroes are right up at the top of their list. And one of the challenges for teachers is that "Children usually know more than their teachers do about Batman and Superman, Ninjas and Star Wars, the Incredible Hulk and Spiderman. The cast of superheroes keeps changing, while teachers just get older."

We shouldn't think, however, that the passionate interest children have in superheroes is a recent phenomena, witness this statement from over seventy years ago about the popularity of comic books and the superhero characters who populated their pages.

> Nobody urges children to read about Superman or Dick
> Tracy or Mandrake the magician, yet twenty million copies
> of the comic magazines are circulated every month.
> Parents keep protesting, educators back them up, and
> the comics go rolling along, the major reading interest of
> American boys and girls.

It's been over eighty years since Superman first entered our consciousness and it's hard to argue with the evidence that superheroes are as popular as ever. Comic books about superheroes are still published and read. Movies about superheroes are still produced and attract large audiences, raking in millions of dollars in ticket sales. Superhero costumes are still big sellers when Halloween rolls around each year and young children are still flying around living rooms and classrooms with towels tied around their necks. So why are superheroes so popular, particularly for young children?

To begin to answer that question, it helps to think about the essential nature of a superhero, be that a Superman, Batman, Wonder Woman, or Power Ranger. A superhero is clearly someone different than the usual 'other' a child encounters in her experience. We all meet people who are different than we are in a variety of ways; some are taller or shorter, others have different color hair or skin, and others can (or can't) beat us in a footrace or climb higher than we can on the monkeybars. But a superhero is something else altogether, different from us in ways that we have never encountered in our daily experience; different in ways we will *never* encounter in our daily experience. The difference is all about those powers.

The common defining denominator for superheroes is the possession of some particular strength or power. As I learned from all those hours in front of the television set as a child in the 1950s, Superman, for example, was able to "leap tall buildings in a single bound," was "faster that a speeding bullet." and was "more powerful than a locomotive." Spider-Man, a la his name, is able to climb straight up vertical walls and can use his web spinning powers to leap between buildings. Wonder Woman has bracelets that protect her from harm and a lasso that forces other people to speak the truth. We can all probably imagine a time in our lives when having any one of those powers would have come in handy.

Another characteristic of superheroes that has an appeal for children is the concept of *transformation*. A superhero is often a 'regular' person who transforms him or herself into someone with special powers. Listen to novelist Michael Chabon describe how that experience of transformation felt to him as a child.

> We had begun the journey that day, through the street-melting, shimmering green Maryland summer morning, as a pair of lonely boys with nothing in common but that loneliness, which we shared with Superman and Batman...a fundamental loneliness and wild aptitude for transformation. But with every step we became Darklord and Aztec a little more surely, a little more irrevocably, transformed by the green-lantern rays of fancy, by the

spider bite of inspiration, by the story we were telling each
other and ourselves about two costumed superheroes, about
the new selves that had been revealed by our secret skin.

In addition, once transformed, the superhero often wears a disguise of sorts to keep that 'regular' identity hidden. The 'mild-mannered' reporter Clark Kent is transformed into Superman. The wealthy recluse Bruce Wayne becomes Batman. The quiet and gentle scientist Bruce Banner is transformed into the muscle-bound and green-with-anger Incredible Hulk. And who would think that the not-quite-adult Peter Parker could be the superhero known as Spider-Man?

The sociodramatic pretend play of young children is frequently about transformations. Young children have a good deal of practice adopting other personas through the help of costumes and props. It is likely that before transforming himself into Superman, for example, a child has already become a parent or doctor or shopkeeper in his imaginary play. Each of these transformations is helped by a prop or costume, e.g., grown-up shoes, a long white shirt, or a toy cash register. Becoming a superhero hero by using a towel for a cape is a similar transformation except this one brings with it the particular power of the particular superhero. As much fun as it may be to pretend that you are a parent or doctor, becoming a superhero is a transformation into the *extraordinary*.

Children are also attracted to superhero play because of a main theme that characterizes many (if not all) of the superhero storylines: a good guy, the superhero, chasing after a bad guy, the villain. In many of the original worlds of superheroes, each superhero typically had an arch enemy, one who tormented the superhero and was pursued by the superhero on a regular basis. Superman had his Lex Luthor and Batman his Joker and Riddler. To the degree that children are learning about superheroes from the media and popular culture, they would also be learning about these 'bad guys' who were in some way inextricably connected to their favorite superhero character.

The existence of the 'bad guy,' leads to another common characteristic of superhero play: chase and capture play. It may be that the primary purpose of bad guys is to be the object of the good guy's pursuit. Once captured, however, there is always the possibility that the bad guy can escape which means that the chase-overpower-submit-capture cycle can begin again. In fact, having the bad guy escape is what allows the play to continue. The balance between the superhero's ability to chase and capture and the villain's ability to flee and avoid being captured can ebb and flow within and across the play episodes. And sometimes it's more fun to be the one being chased.

> Think about the universal pleasure of chasing games. The three-year-old girl squeals with almost unbearable joy as she flees from the terrible monster, in the form of her father or big brother, who threatens to catch her and eat her for breakfast. In every human chasing game I can think of the preferred position is that of being chased. In nightmares and in real life, nothing is more terrifying than being chased by a predator or monster. But in play, nothing is more delightful.

This repetition of chase and capture is a common aspect of children's superhero play and one educator noted that the "children seemed to be obsessed with repeating the same actions over and over again." This obsessive repetition might be a result of the fact that superheroes often (if not always) are identified by a particular action or attribute. In other words, Superman is Superman because he is "faster than a speeding bullet" and Batman is Batman because he uses his Batmobile to pursue the bad guys. And can you really be a Teenage Mutant Ninja Turtle if you don't karate kick and chop your opponent? The repetition seen in children's superhero play may exist because the actions being repeated are seen as the essence and identifiers of the superheroes being imitated. It may be that "no matter how creative and analytical they might be, superheroes follow routines. Spider-Man still shoots webs, Wonder Woman runs in a swimsuit, and Batman throws batarangs, works out of a cave, and drives a big black car."

It is this repetition of the sometimes aggressive superhero play that concerns some teachers and parents. At times a young child can't seem to get beyond the action of Superman jumping down and overpowering the bad guy; the child's play can become a continual looping of these actions. Gerard Jones, in his book, *Killing Monsters: Why Children Need Fantasy, Super Heroes, and Make-Believe Violence*, acknowledges this concern when he writes that, "We are troubled by the idea of repetition. We fear that if kids do something over and over again in play they're more likely to replicate it in real life." But Jones then goes on to suggest that the repetition seen in children's play may actually have a positive, growth-producing effect: "But the evidence suggests that repeated play is usually a good tool to diminish the power of their thoughts and feelings, not to strengthen them."

In many ways, the reasons why superhero play is attractive to children are the same reasons why play, particularly dramatic pretend play in general, is attractive and beneficial for children. Play provides children with the opportunity to control some aspect of their experience when so much of their lives is controlled by other people and circumstances. Children are also able to set aside the known reality in order to try on alternatives to that reality by transforming themselves, their environment, and their life circumstances through the act of *as if*. And all of this takes place in the 'safe' *as if* world of play because, after all, it's just pretend.

The pretend dramas of superhero play also provide children with the opportunity to try on roles, negotiate play scripts with other players, and work out their ideas about how the world works. But superhero play can provide children with one particular *sense of* that other types of dramatic play don't or can't: a sense of *power*.

As suggested above, superheroes are special imaginary characters because of the powers they possess: Superman can fly and is incredibly strong and Spider-Man can crawl up buildings. Children are attracted to these powers because in their real day-to-day lives they can often feel fairly powerless. Parents, siblings, teachers and classmates may all be exerting power over them in ways that can range from simply frustrating or annoying to menacing.

Here is an example of a child specifically using the symbolic representation of a superhero in her play in order to help her cope with family circumstances that were beyond her control in 'real life'. In pretend play, as opposed to her real life, she could control and exert some power over those circumstances. The story was told by the therapist who was working with the young girl.

> *A 5-year-old girl spent numerous sessions on the floor of my clinical playroom, carefully assigning superhero action figures to either the 'bad side' or 'good side.' The violence and destructiveness in her weekly superhero battles mirrored the painful and often aggressive battles between her warring parents. As tensions between the parents ebbed and flowed, so did the violence in the superhero play. When finally the parents reconciled, the child's play began to contain themes of helping and healing. The savagery in her battles gave way to detente and friendship.*

Here the therapist provided the child with time and space to play and also provided the child with some props to be used in that play. The child, for her part, brought to that time and space her knowledge of what those superhero props could represent and perhaps most importantly, brought with her some ongoing life experiences that apparently were of high emotional importance. When all of these components were mixed together - the time, space, materials, knowledge of superheroes, life circumstances and emotions - the child started playing in a way that helped her sort through those life experiences.

What was happening in this play? As the therapist described, the girl took the superhero action figures and incorporated them into her play as representations of power and aggression. They were symbolic *stand ins* for her parents and the tensions between her parents that she had been experiencing in her home. Playing out violent and aggressive scenes between these action figures may have been her way of expressing what she was witnessing at home. It is possible that she didn't have the linguistic and/or cognitive skills to express those experiences in words and it may also have been possible that the emotional component of those experiences was too strong and scary to let her express them in words. But there is safety in play; those action figures really aren't her parents and their violent actions are only pretend. And perhaps most importantly, those violent actions are under her control. She can't control the actions of her parents but she can control the actions of the superheroes.

It's important to note the role that these action figures play in this story. It is possible, or even likely, that the young girl would not have engaged in the same type of aggressive and violent play if the only toys she had to use were two teddybears or baby dolls. The power, action, and aggressive scripts that are associated with superhero characters were understood by this child and became the vehicle through which she could 'play out' the emotionally charged experiences from home. The therapist was wise enough to understand that soft, cuddly teddybears were not what this child needed at this moment in time.

CHILDREN'S FASCINATION WITH superheroes and the powers that they represent can also be used by others to help children through some of the difficulties that life unfortunately throws at them from time to time. There are a number of examples of how adults have capitalized on children's love of superheroes and their desire for superhero power and used these feelings as a means for helping children who are experiencing serious medical issues.

In Philadelphia, for example, workers whose 'day job' was the washing of windows on hospital buildings, "donned the colorful tights and masks and became Power Rangers, rappelling down he side of Children's Hospital of Philadelphia and thrilling the young patients."

At a children's medical center in Austin, Texas, members of the local police department help put on a superhero day. On this day, police officers dress up as some of the children's favorite superheroes, rappel down the walls of the hospital chasing after the 'bad guys' and then meet and greet the children for conversation and autographs.

In 2013, nursing students at Baylor University in Texas believed that acting *as if* you were a superhero might help hospitalized children fight their diseases. Out of this belief grew a project where volunteers came together once a month to make superhero capes for hospitalized children. Anywheres from 40 to 100 people gathered to create these capes and the volunteers, dressed as superheroes themselves, brought the capes to the children.

A cancer center in Brazil established a program with the goal of drawing "parallels between the [superhero's] battle against evil and the child's own battle against cancer." The program used what it called the "invincibility suggestion" in an effort to convince children that "like the superhero, they, too, have power on which they can draw." They were asking the children to act *as if* they had the power to overcome the cancer that had invaded their bodies.

A final example comes from a professional photographer in Los Angeles. Josh Rossi set up a photo shoot for children with illnesses and disabilities. Using professional costumes, he transformed each of the children into a superhero character: transforming a 3-year-old with cancer into Wonder Woman, a 5-year-old with cancer into Batman, and a child who had already endured three open heart surgeries, into Superman. As Rossi said

> The kids that my team and I chose have been through hell and back and have real superhuman strengths... The whole idea was to take the things that are weaknesses for the kids such as cancer and other diseases and turn them into strengths.

The attraction of fairy tales

CHILDREN ALSO GRAVITATE toward fairy tales, both classic and new, because of the stories of trouble that characterize many of the tales. It may arguably be said that fairy tales have been around forever. The history of fairy tales traces back better than a thousand years; there is some evidence that the origins of the Jack and the Beanstalk story, for example, goes back more than 5,000 years. And although there is a strong tradition of fairy tales that is closely associated with Europe, many cultures around the world also have generated stories that have the feel of what we know as the fairy tale. These stories have their own ogres and trolls and people facing all sorts of challenges.

What is the essential nature of the fairy tale, these stories by which "Generations of children [have been] soothed to sleep with the witch-torturing, limb-severing, child-devouring horror"? In other words, soothed to sleep by tales of trouble.

Marina Warner writes in her book, *Once Upon a Time: A Short History of Fairy Tale*, that fairy tales are relatively short, emphasize the imagination, depict particular kinds of characters such as stepmothers and giants, and are often built around "recurrent motifs" such as keys, apples, mirrors, rings, and toads. And as mentioned earlier, fairy tales can often portray some gruesome and frightening events. One tally found that the gruesomeness included eight murders, two choking deaths, one decapitation, several instances of severed limbs, and four instances of broken bones.

But fairy tales are attractive to children because children understand that they are not real, that they are fantasy. The play frame of 'this is not-real' is based on the distance from the here and now that the fairy tale establishes in a number of ways. First and perhaps most directly, the fairy tale establishes that the story is set in the frame of 'once upon a time' (distance from the *now*) and 'in a land far, far away' (distance from the *here*). Furthermore, the ways in which the characters of the story are portrayed reinforce the 'not here and not now' aspect of the story as well. Most often, for example, the characters are dressed in clothing styles that a child would not see in his day-to-day life. In fact, the clothes of fairy tale characters are seen as costumes that a child could wear for his own pretend dress-up play.

Another way in which the characters of the fairy tale signify the 'not real' is the fact that at times characters are animals or non-human. For example, there are the pigs of "Three Little Pigs," the wolf in "Little Red Riding Hood," the giant in "Jack in the Beanstalk," and the troll in "Three Billy Goats Gruff." In the fairy tale, these animals and non-humans speak, have intentions, and carry out actions that don't reflect what children know of animals in their real life experience. In terms of trolls and giants, we can also assume that the average child doesn't cross paths with such entities in real life either.

The final, essential characteristic of the fairy tale concerns the typical story line or plot of the tale. Fairy tales often involve danger of some kind, a danger that is often experienced by the child or children in the story. Little Red Riding Hood may be eaten by the wolf and Hansel and Gretel may find themselves baked in an oven. It's also not unusual for the danger a child is facing to be perpetrated by a mean parent, step-parent or sibling. As Bruno Bettelheim wrote,

> *Though the fairy tale offers fantastic symbolic images*
> *for the solution of problems, the problems represented in*
> *them are ordinary ones: a child's suffering from jealousy*
> *and discrimination of his siblings, as is true for Cinderella;*
> *a child being thought incompetent by his parents, as*
> *happens in many fairy tales - for example, in the Brothers*
> *Grimm's story, 'The Spirit in the Bottle.'*

But fairy tales almost always have happy endings. The protagonist of the fairy tale - Little Red Riding Hood, Hansel and Gretel, Cinderella - almost always prevails, often by outwitting the nefarious plans of the mean adult, wolf, or giant. In addition to "once upon a time, in a land far, far away," fairy tales are also the embodiment of "happily ever after." Again, Bettleheim has something to say about this aspect of the fairy tale: "In the traditional fairy tale, the hero is rewarded and the evil person meets his well-deserved fate, thus satisfying the child's deep need for justice to prevail." In other words, trouble is overcome in a satisfying way.

Bruno Bettelheim put forward his theory on the importance of fairy tales in what is arguably the best known book on the subject, *The Uses of Enchantment*. In this book Bettleheim, who was steeped in the psychoanalytical traditions of Freud and Jung, argued that fairy tales are at their core symbolic representations of some of Freud's classic psychological constructs: id, ego, superego and the Oedipal conflict. According to Bettleheim, the child is pulled towards fairy tales because she sees in the fairy tale some of the inner conflicts, the inner troubles, she is feeling within herself: "The child is unaware of his inner processes, which is why these are externalized in the fairy tale and symbolically represented by actions for inner and outer struggles." In other words, the trouble the child sees in the fairy tale, the trouble she is experiencing in her own life, isn't necessarily a conscious trouble.

Not only does the child see her inner conflicts and struggles in some sense mirrored in the characters and plot of the fairy tale but the child also gets to see how these characters, often children like herself, cope and most often triumph over the conflicts and adversity. This speaks to what Bettleheim says is the therapeutic nature of fairy tales; the fairy tale is therapeutic because the child "finds his own solutions, through contemplating what the story seems to imply about him and his inner conflicts at this moment in his life." Bettelheim goes on to write that "As he listens to the fairy tale, the child gets ideas about how he may create order out of the chaos which is his inner life."

Bettleheim maintains that the very fact that fairy tales have been around for thousands of years, cross cultural boundaries, and depict common stories and themes speaks to their universal nature. But he also points out that fairy tales are the products of human beings and the developmental conditions in which they find themselves. Children, he posits, see themselves and their inner feelings in fairy tales precisely because fairy tales were created by humans in the first place.

Superheroes, fairy tales, and cultural capital

> Superhero stories were Sammy's fruitcakes, so to speak, a means of entry into a social world beyond his sisters, his caring mother, his supportive teacher. In that social world, mediated as it was by a superhero tale...he was able to overcome what may be the worst 'terror' of all, isolation.

IN ADDITION TO providing an outlet for expressing emotions and feelings, learning the stories of superheroes and fairy tales also provides children with what one author called, "cultural capital." Knowing the story of Superman or Cinderella gives children the tools for entering into social relationships with other children. Just like the adult bringing the fruitcake to the party, a child who knows what a Power Ranger does or how Jack tricks the giant has a 'ticket,' if you will, into the activity of an ongoing play group of her peers and into the ongoing peer conversation.

Conversely, children who don't know the stories and the characters may be at a disadvantage. Rebecca Kantor and her colleagues at Ohio State University observed this in an interesting ethnographic study they conducted; a study which was designed to look at how children created their own peer cultures in the early childhood classroom.

The researchers observed that superhero play was a significant form of play for the children. It occurred frequently and was initiated and self-directed by the children themselves; it wasn't a type of play that was organized and directed by the teachers. The researchers saw how the participants in the superhero play brought their knowledge of superheroes to their social engagement with their peers.

And what they also observed were the consequences of what happens if a child doesn't possess this cultural capital. One of the children in the classroom didn't have a television at home and therefore was not familiar with the genre of superheroes and the characters that populate those stories. As a result, this child had a difficult time entering ongoing playgroups when the theme of the sociodramatic play was based on superheroes. In other words, the child didn't have the requisite fruitcake needed to greet the hostess and step into the party.

Getting scared every now and then

ONE OF THE interesting things about fairy tales and superhero play is that on some objective level they can be downright scary. Hansel and Gretel are going to be baked in an oven. Little Red Riding Hood is going to be eaten by a wolf. The step-sisters in Cinderella get their eyes pecked out by birds. Some parents and teachers question the value of fairy tales precisely because of the violence and at times goriness that many of them contain. And as has been often noted, many fairy tales have been sanitized or "Disneyfied" over the years to eliminate some of the scary factors. And yet many children love the scary tales, find them fascinating and perhaps even comforting. And they don't mind hearing the stories over and over again or watching the movies over and over again.

Many children also are attracted to monsters of various sorts, those that may reside in fairy tales and those that come their way through other media. The fierce, huge and menacing Tyrannosaurus Rex, for example, is a favorite play companion for many children. And there are children who are fascinated by sharks; the bigger and the 'toothier' the better. These are frightening creatures and children love them. As the author Neal Gaiman said, "Fear is a wonderful thing, in small doses."

So why do children like and even search out scary stories and frightening creatures? Why do they like to hear the creepy fairy tale over and over again and why do they like to imitate the roaring T-Rex (or be chased by their friend imitating the roaring T-Rex) over and over again? The reasons can be found in all of the previous discussions in this book about *as if* and how the *as if* play frame offers children the opportunity to exercise feelings of control, mastery, and power in safe contexts. Children know that the characters in fairy tales are not real; these stories of long ago and far away are safe distances from the real here and now. The scary idea of Hansel and Gretel being baked in the oven is only an idea in a story; it's not something that happens in real life. But since it is in a story, is just pretend, the child feels good about surviving the experience and coming out the other side. In the end, Hansel and Gretel come out on top and don't get baked in the oven. As Susan Linn wrote,

The darker side of childhood - that enthusiastic embrace

*of gruesome and violent fantasy often so shocking to
adults - can emerge even in the play of children whose life
experiences are relatively trauma free. It's a way of gaining
a sense of mastery over feeling small and helpless in a
large, confusing, and sometime frightening world.*

As noted a number of times in this book's discussion about the importance of make-believe, for young children much of the world and their experience is outside of their control. The time of play is the time in which they can carve out some space - and time - to control that experience. They do so by setting aside reality for a moment and imagining alternative possibilities in a safe context. Stephen Asma, in his book titled, *On Monsters*, says this about monsters: "Monsters of demonic possession are imaginative expressions of this loss of control." Reading about the monster, imitating the monster, and subduing the monster are all ways that the child regains that control.

In some ways, playing with the ogres of fairy tales, the bad guys of superhero play, and with T-Rexes and sharks provides children with the opportunity - in the non-realistic and safe context of play - to prepare themselves for the scary things they actually may encounter in real life. Hearing how Hansel and Gretel and Little Red Riding Hood overcome the troublesome obstacles in their lives can give children the confidence that they will overcome their obstacles as well. Neal Gaiman talked about this aspect of fiction in general when he answered the question of why people enjoy being scared.

*It is one of the places that horror and scary fiction work.
You're giving people little rehearsals. Back in the 17th
century, back when poisoning used to happen a lot more
than it happens now, people would ingest poisons regularly
in tiny amounts to build up immunity, so that if someone
tried to poison them, they would be O.K...Fiction allows us
to go safely behind other eyes and allows us to look out at
the world. We take our little bits of poison and safely ingest
them, so when the real thing happens, we're prepared.*

Stephen Asma goes even further and argues that our encountering of monsters in tales and literature is fundamental to the development of a moral imagination; it is through these encounters that we develop our understanding of good versus evil.

> In a significant sense, monsters are part of our attempt to envision the good life or at least the secure life. Our ethical convictions do not spring fully grown in our heads but must be developed in the context of real or imagined challenges. In order to discover our values, we have to face trials and tribulations, and monsters help us imaginatively rehearse.

Christopher Golden reflected on how he learned some moral principles not from his father but from the superheroes who filled up the pages of the comic books his mother allowed him to read.

> He [his father] taught me to shave, but never thought a moment about what he might be teaching me about being a man or husband, about being a responsible member of my community. I learned these things from Captain America. From Iron Man. From Spider-Man. From Ben Grimm and Reed Richards of the Fantastic Four.

The author of *Killing Monsters*, Gerard Jones, echoes this sentiment when he writes that,

> For young people to develop selves that serve them well in life, they need modeling, mentoring, guidance, communication, and limitations. But they also need to fantasize and play, and lose themselves in stories. That's how they reorganize the world into forms they can manipulate. That's how they explore and take some control over their own thoughts and emotions. That's how they kill their monsters.

Finally, the biologist E. O Wilson actually argues that we may in fact be in love with our monsters.

> We're not just afraid of predators, we're transfixed by them, prone to weave stories and fables and chatter endlessly about them, because fascination creates preparedness, and preparedness, survival. In a deeply tribal sense, we love our monsters.

There are, of course, some parents and teachers who believe that the content of many fairy tales and superhero storylines are too scary or violent or aggressive or upsetting for children, particularly young children. The argument is that children don't need to be exposed to stories about kidnapping, being devoured by wolves, being baked in ovens, or about bad guys with their evil ways. The argument may also be made that children shouldn't be introduced to the possibilities that parents (and step-parents) or older siblings or adults in the neighborhood may be mean and desire to do children harm. The argument may be made that real life can be potentially traumatizing to children so why introduce them to - and inflict upon them - pretend stories about potential trauma.

There is, then, this interesting paradox: a parent doesn't want her child exposed to the scary or violent story but once exposed, the child can't seem to get enough of it. Why else do children want the same story told or read to them over and over again?

Jane Katch, in her book *Under Deadman's Skin: Discovering the Meaning of Children's Violent Play*, offers one answer to this question by talking about a young boy's love and fascination with scary movies. Katch first presents the child's experience in the child's own words.

> Partly it's like if you think enough about it, it starts not
> being scary anymore. Like I saw this movie at my friend's
> house and I thought it was really very scary. And I went
> over to his house again and we saw it again, and it wasn't
> that scary that time, but it was still pretty scary, and we
> watched it again and again and little by little it started
> getting less scary until it wasn't scary at all.

This is a very reflective child, discussing how the movie progressed from "really very scary" to "still pretty scary" and finally to not "scary at all." In some ways, watching the movie is a form of *as if* play, during which the child begins to master and gain control over the experience. Katch does point out that this mastery and control can emerge only if the experience, in this case the movie, is 'scary enough' but not so scary that it is beyond the child's control: "Jason's use of movies to master his fears works only when the movie is scary enough to satisfy his sense of mastery without being so frightening that it 'resets the button' and brings on a new set of anxieties."

Since the scary and at times gruesome aspects of fairy tales and the out-of-this-world characters and adventures of superhero stories are embedded in fantasy and full of fantastic elements, children understand that what they are hearing or reading is not *really* real. I use the phrase, *really real,* to emphasize Bruno Bettleheim's thesis that fairy tales are real to the extent that they symbolically represent the issues and conflicts that may in fact be part of children's normal developmental journey. What are some of those issues and conflicts? Sibling rivalry, fear of abandonment, and striving for independence from controlling (well-meaning and otherwise) parents are some examples.

> Many adults today tend to take literally the things said
> in fairy tales, whereas they should be viewed as symbolic
> renderings of crucial life experiences. The child understands
> this intuitively, though he does not 'know' it explicitly.

Seeing these issues played out in stories of superheroes, fairies, and monsters reassures children that they are not alone in experiencing the conflicts and the attending feelings and emotions that may accompany them. And since one of the main characteristics of fairy tales is that the 'stars' of the tales live happily every after, children are presented with reassurance that the conflicts and issues can be resolved, overcome and conquered.

> This is exactly the message that fairy tales get across to
> the child in manifold form: that a struggle against severe
> difficulties in life is unavoidable, is an intrinsic part of
> human existence - but that if one does not shy away, but
> steadfastly meets unexpected and often unjust hardships,
> one masters all obstacles and at the end emerges
> victorious.

It's all about the power

IN THE END, it might all be about the power; power over our adversaries, our fears, and the monsters in our lives. As has been discussed in earlier chapters, pretend play provides young children with the opportunity, and in some sense the sanction, to experiment with power and the feeling of being powerful in the safe context of make-believe. This is perhaps most true with superhero play and the engagement with fairy tales and monsters. What is most interesting to consider is how superhero play and fairy tales illustrate both side of the 'power coin.'

In the case of both superhero stories and fairy tales, children are exposed to and confronted by images of power. There are the various powers of the superheroes themselves and the powers of the evil step-parents, ogres, trolls, and monsters of fairy tales. There are also the powers wielded by the villains of superhero stories and the powers exhibited and embodied in the fierce dinosaurs and sharks that some children love so much. All of these are powers that can be scary and threatening and the stories that describe these powers may suggest and portend dangers for the story-listener herself.

But that leads to the second type of power that is part of this play, to the other side of the 'power coin.' By taking on the *as if* stance towards these stories and dangers, children can assume their own feelings of power. You are not frightened by the bellowing Tyrannosaurus Rex if you yourself are pretending to be the Rex and you are the one bellowing. And you can feel even more powerful if one of your playmates runs away from your T-Rex bellowing in a fit of make-believe fright (or in some cases, real fright). You don't have to be afraid of the man-eating shark if you are the man-eating shark swimming in the waters of the playroom.

The same assumption of power can be seen in the reading of fairy tales. Yes, it can be frightening to think that as a child you might be baked in an oven by mean adults or eaten by a menacing wolf. But think about how powerful it feels, in the end, to outwit the adults and the wolf. In the happily-ever-after worlds of the fairy tale, the protagonist or hero wins out in the end and overcomes the power wielded against her. In the end, the main character is more powerful than her adversaries, be they human or animal or giant; in the end, she is more powerful than the trouble.

The feeling of power is perhaps most obvious in superhero play. Playing Superman means you can fly and exhibit extraordinary strength. Playing Wonder Woman means that you can make people tell the truth and protect yourself from the literal 'slings and arrows' of conflict. By definition, being a superhero means that you are powerful.

And the powers of superheroes are used to overcome the powers of the villains. So just like the heroes of fairy tales, pretending to be a superhero means that you can overcome and triumph over powers mounted against you. Lex Luthor, the Riddler, and any manner of 'bad guy' can be defeated.

For children, the power that they may feel when engaged in *as if* is the power that they often would like to possess in real life. Listen to Anthony Doerr, the author of the novel, *All the Light You Cannot See,* describe how his 10 year old son wished for power.

> Here's my 10-year-old son, Owen, last week, as he stared grim-faced at another math worksheet: "I got them all wrong! I hate long division. I wish there were superpowers. I wish I didn't have to work."

And listen to this mother describe her son's use of pretend power.

> My son always used power fantasies to help himself through anxiety-provoking transitions. At the beginning of every school year from preschool through first grade, he became a dinosaur - no docile plant eater either, but the biggest and most savage carnivore he could think of. He'd want to play dinosaur fights with his friends and family, if no one wanted to play he'd go off by himself and fight invisible enemies...After the jitters of the first few weeks, the dinosaurs would yield to fish, frogs, and the other creatures of his imagination.

The esteemed neurologist and author, Oliver Sacks, also captured this youthful desire for power as he thought about his feelings when he had been sent away to school by his parents.

> When I was at boarding school, sent away during the
> war as a little boy, I had a sense of imprisonment and
> powerlessness, and I longed for movement and power, ease
> of movement and superhuman powers.

Playing with power, then, both overcoming it and wielding it, are part and parcel of children's interactions with the world of superheroes and fairy tales, and part and parcel of defeating the monsters in our lives. On the one hand, it might be just plain fun to tie the towel around your neck and make-believe that you are Superman; and it might be just plain fun to spend time within the fairy tale and see how a little child just like you can turn the tables on a mean adult or looming giant and escape from danger. But in addition to just plain fun, the *as if* power may also be where children can escape the feelings of powerlessness that comes with being young, dependent, and controlled by the world around them. As one little boy said,

> I feel like I'm a real kinda superhero. I feel sort of like I'm
> powerful and brave and strong and stuff, I can do lots of
> stuff, like I'm actually not a regular kid. I am special and
> can do powerful things like Underdog and Spider-Man...I
> like all superheroes because they do good things and
> help. I smile every time, it makes me happy, it's fun to play
> superheroes.

Chapter 7

The Simulation of Reality (and the Reality of Simulation)

When I was teaching at the University of North Dakota, there was a fairly large air force base about ten miles or so outside of the city. It wasn't unusual for people stationed at the base to be taking courses at the university but it wasn't that common for them to be taking classes in my field of early childhood education. One year I did have a captain from the base in my graduate seminar that focused on the theory of Jean Piaget and the implications of his theory for early childhood education. The captain's main responsibility on the base was the training of missile launch operators - those personnel who spent time underground in concrete capsules with the job of being ready to launch intercontinental ballistic missiles if given the command to do so.

My student, the air force captain, became very interested in Piaget's four stages of cognitive development and began to wonder if this developmental progression could be mapped onto the stages his students went through as they learned to assume the role of missile launch operators. His interest developed into a desire to conduct a small research study investigating this question. In order to help me understand the nature of the training, and then be able to help him with the study, he arranged for me to come onto the base (which included some level of security clearance) and engage in a portion of the training to become a missile launch operator.

Of course, I didn't get anywhere near the real process of launching missiles. The part of the training that I did experience involved a room set up to look like a missile launch command; a mock up of what could be found in those underground capsules. The room was used to present certain scenarios to trainees to both help them understand what their job entailed and to train and test them on their abilities to carry out that job.

My experience that day consisted of getting an overview of the training process and then being positioned at the mock launch console which had a large array of lights. I was given a manual that provided instructions about what to do when I saw a particular configuration of those lights on the console. These configurations of lights provided information regarding individual missile silos, including such variables as the temperature in the silo and the security of the silo itself; the information indicated by the lights was pertinent to the readiness of the missile inside the silo for launching. My student then retreated to a back room where he would control the types of situations that would be presented to me on the console's light display. My task was to look at the lights, find the corresponding pattern in the manual, and then take the appropriate actions as detailed in the manual, *as if* I were a missile launch operator.

How did I do? After the first array of lights appeared, I sat there looking at them, analyzing them, trying to figure out what I was supposed to do; trying to figure out the correct response. After about a minute or so passed by, I heard the captain say over the speaker, "What are you doing?" My response to him was: "I'm trying to figure out what to do." His response back to me was direct and to the point: "You are not supposed to figure out what to do. Look for the light array in the manual and do what it tells you to do."

Fortunately for the world, this was only make-believe.

The 'As If' of simulation

MY EXPERIENCE IN that room on that Saturday morning falls into a category of pretend known as a *simulation*. Simulation activities can take a number of forms: role-playing, board games, video games, and increasingly with the rapid development of technology, virtual and augmented reality simulations (VR and AR). According to the online version of the Merriam-Webster dictionary, the word *simulation* is defined as: "the imitative representation of the functioning of one system or process by means of functioning of another." In other words, the physical space on the air force base was representing the real launch control capsule and I was imitating the actions of a missile launch operator (or at least trying to).

Based on that definition, young children have been practicing their skills in their own simulation labs for as long as there has been this thing called childhood. In essence, much (if not all) of pretend play, of *as if* activity, is a form of simulation. Children can "enact what people might do in a given situation by a process of simulation; they imagine themselves in that same situation and act *vis-a-vis* that imaginary situation." This is not much different from me trying to enact what people might do in a missile launch situation (with admittedly much higher stakes). The pretense activity of children is fundamentally "a theoretical construct defined as behavior in a simulative, or 'as if' mode."

In pretend play, children are able to simulate the behaviors of people and the circumstances in which those behaviors occur, much like I was doing in the missile launch simulator. The child can simulate what the worker does at the post office, what the baker does when selling pies, and what the doctor does when examining a patient. Just like a model of the missile launch center was constructed on the air force base, the child constructs a model of the kitchen in which the pies are baked and a model of what a baker does when making those pies. The child doesn't use the real materials to build her model; she just uses cardboard boxes, make-believe utensils, her knowledge of pie making (however limited it might be), and her imagination.

An interesting example of pretend as simulation is the creation of the imaginary companion since "pretense involving an imaginary companion is a simulation of reality - including performance of behaviors that imitate real interactions." The child's creation of an imaginary friend, and the sustaining of interactions with that creation, can be looked at as a form of practice, and "this extra practice, albeit imagined and only a simulation of reality, might help children develop the social skills and relationship-related cognitive abilities necessary for successful adaptation in adulthood." The air force trainee practices and develops her skills in the simulation lab while a child "practices at being other people" in the laboratory of make-believe and imagination.

Forms of simulation

THE USE OF simulation in the world of games, both board and video, has been around for a long time. It's believed by some, for example, that the game of chess began as a simulation of warfare. The board game, *Monopoly*, can be seen as a simulation of the world of big business and real estate. In 1974, the computer game *The Oregon Trail* was released as a simulation of 19th century pioneer life. In the game, players took on the role of wagon leaders shepherding a wagon train of settlers from Missouri to Oregon in 1848. Teachers expanded on the game by bringing the simulation out from the computer and into the classroom itself, as described by a fifth-grade teacher on the National Education Association website.

> We end the year with a simulation game of the Oregon Trail. The kids dress in 19th-century style clothes and play pioneer games, cook Johnny Cake, and sew period quilts as we make the journey on the Oregon Trail. The students work in groups of 4-6 with each person representing a wagon within the wagon train. They decide on the supplies needed for the 2,000-mile trip. They are responsible for making trail decisions that may affect the entire train. There is journal writing and trail mishaps several times a day in which the team must work cooperatively in order to survive. The room is noisy and full of activity and a favorite for my fifth-graders.

With advances in technology, the complexity of simulations found in computer applications, video games, and on the internet has grown exponentially. *SimCity*, a series of video games, is a prime example. The Wikipedia entry for *SimCity* offers this description of the game.

> In the SimCity games, the player develops a city from a patch of undeveloped land. The player controls where to place development zones, infrastructure like roads and power plants, landmarks, and public services such as schools, parks, hospitals and fire stations. The player also determines the tax rate, the budget, and social policy. The city is populated by "Sims," simulated persons who live in the city created by the player.

Perhaps the most technologically complex video game simulation is *Second Life*. The game was introduced in 2003 and within a decade had as many as one million users. According to Wikipedia,

> Second Life users (also called residents) create virtual representations of themselves, called avatars, are able to interact with places, objects, and other avatars. They can explore the world (known as the grid), meet other residents, socialize, participate in both individual and group activities, build, create, shop and trade virtual property and services with one another.

There is much more to the *Second Life* experience and in fact businesses and educational institutions have adopted the platform as a way in which they can engage their constituencies in various communication, problem solving, education and training experiences.

Specifically designed and dedicated forms of simulation have also become widely used as training and educational devices. Just the other day I watched a television commercial for a drug company that referenced a "joint damage simulation" that could be accessed on their website. The company markets a drug for different forms of arthritis and after answering a few questions, the "joint damage simulation" shows you what the joints in your hands or feet look like as a result of the disease.

Like my experience on the air force base learning how to be a missile launch operator, flight simulators have become an almost required component of aviation training. Like so many other types of *as if* activity, a flight simulator provides the opportunity for someone to learn the skills related to flying an aircraft within a risk-free environment. As one commentator said, "There is one major thing that separates simulators from real life. If you crash in a simulator, then you can reset it and start again." Children learn how to build bridges out of blocks without risking the lives of people who drive cars over them; pilots learn to fly airplanes without risking the lives of real passengers.

The simulation of war

> A lot of soldiers enter the training sessions thinking they're gonna be fun, just a chance to play around on video games...And I've seen how shocked they are when they're killed in VBS2, when they just can't reboot. I've seen them start to make connections between what they're doing in the simulation and what they'll be doing in Afghanistan. For a lot of these kids, playing VBS2 is the first time that they realize they might die.

MAKE-BELIEVE WAR HAS long been a staple of video games that are popular with millions of people. Some of the settings for these games have been real wars, both historical and more recent, and some have been fictional battlefields, those that could have existed in the past, present or some future time. These video games are full of weapons, small and large, teammates and enemies, and often not a small amount of mayhem, destruction, and death.

In 2002, perhaps in a 'can't beat 'em, join 'em' effort, the United States Army created a video game of its own, titled, *America's Army*. With the need to add better than 70,000 new recruits to their forces, the Army's goal for this video game was to introduce potential recruits to both the nature of Army life and the activities of the Army as a force for military defense. One press story about the video game said this about *America's Army*: "It's a video game created by the U. S. Army to win over the hearts and minds of American Teenagers." The Army's own website describes the player's experience this way.

> Players will experience the type of positional tactical training that U.S. Soldiers encounter at a real Army MOUT (Military Operations on Urban Terrain) site. Set in a fictional country, The Republic of Ostregals, players take the role of an 11B Infantryman practicing combat maneuvers at the JTC Griffin, a fabricated training environment created by Conex modular containers and found materials.

Working with professionals from the world of virtual reality, the Army set out to create an experience that was as realistic as possible. A *New York Times* article about the game wrote that "Everything from the direction and velocity of shell ejection to the way soldiers high crawl when carrying a rifle is based on the way the Army really operates." The article goes on to elaborate on the realism of the simulation.

> The designers, primarily the Modeling, Virtual Environments and Simulation Institute at the Naval Postgraduate School in Monterey, Calif., say they have modeled each weapon accurately. A player's aim will be affected by his stance, breathing and movement. A player who charges an enemy trench, wildly firing his rifle, is unlikely to hit very much.

The game was initially created for PC computers and was available as a free download. Less than three years after it was released, there were more than 4 million registered players and the game was being played more than 1 million times each day.

The success of the game led the Army to take it 'on the road,' so to speak. In 2007, the Army rolled out what was called the *Virtual Army Experience* (VAE). The VAE was a "mobile mission simulator" that could be set up at public events such as NASCAR races and air shows. People would enter the inflatable structure and experience

America's Army on steroids, if you will. A participant would enter a Humvee and through an immersive, virtual environment, experience the sights, sounds, and physical feelings of battle; as "the camera goes into the Humvee, bringing everyone a first-person perspective, as if they are viewing the action from their vehicle. Although there is no actual driver, the vehicle starts moving on-screen, and a physical rumbling from the vehicle simulates movement." One of the developers of VAE described it this way.

> It has kinetic hammers that, when an explosion goes off, rock the Humvee. And gas action weighted recoil mechanisms of the weapon. So you get this kinetic integration. You know, when you're trying to physically control the muzzle climb of a weapon, shooting in a simulation allows you to suspend disbelief more. Suddenly that physical integration into the virtual environment takes you in and creates a greater sense of presence, which is really cool.

The Army, however, doesn't just use virtual reality and simulation games for the recruitment of soldiers into its ranks. The Army also created a video game called, *Virtual Battle Space (VBS)*, to train those new recruits.

VBS is a first-person simulation game designed to prepare recruits for the Army's basic combat training. Using the idea of progressing from crawl to walk to run, *VBS* moves the recruit through the crawl and walk stages of training. Some of the tasks that the recruit can practice in a realistic simulated environment include: breaching an obstacle, conducting an attack, entering and clearing a building, and establishing an observation post.

Like children at play, this *as if* activity allows the player (the new recruit) to practice, try out, and develop his or her skills in a safe and low (or no) consequence context. One soldier using the simulation activity described the experience this way: "She said it's easier to get lost in the computer than in the woods...but she knew she wouldn't be hurt, afraid or scared. And, when she gets into the woods, it would help her navigate better." And as one Army captain said, "You get a chance to work out the bugs and kinks and rehearse before you go out."

This practice and rehearsal in a non-literal, simulative context has benefits for the Army as well as the individual soldier. The simulation game lets soldiers "rehearse what they would be doing out there, but they're not out there, burning gas, wasting Soldiers' time figuring out how they're going to do it because they can do it [in the game]." Or as an Army captain said, "And you don't go out there and waste fuel and ammo messing things up."

The *Virtual Battle Space* game is now in its third version and one of the improvements is that the game allows the Army to more closely personalize the avatar to the individual soldier. Data pertaining to the soldier's physical makeup (height and weight), gender, and test results from physical training and marksmanship testing can be entered into the program. An individual's avatar will be as good as the individual soldier but won't perform better in the game than the real-life data suggests. If a soldier is not qualified to use a particular weapon in real-life, he or she can't use the weapon in the game. If the soldier is overweight in real-life, his or her avatar will be overweight as well. If the data suggests that the 'real' soldier would get fatigued at a certain point in a mission, the avatar will experience fatigue at that point in the simulated mission. Unlike many video games where you adopt a persona with particular powers or strengths (sometimes superhuman powers and strengths), in *VBS*, you are not playing *as if* you are *someone else,* you are playing *as if* you are *yourself,* warts and all.

Medicine and simulation

The greatest power of virtual reality is the ability to try and fail without consequence to animal or patient. It is only through failure - and the learning the cause of failure - that the true pathway to success lies.

A FASCINATING (AND heartwarming) story made the news while I was writing this book. It was the story of a 9-year-old girl who had experienced a serious medical trauma: blood vessels had burst in her brain, which then filled with blood and as a result, she lapsed into a coma. She was transported to Boston Children's Hospital and underwent complicated and intricate surgery that saved her life.

In addition to the fact that the young child's life had been saved, what made this story newsworthy was that the surgeons at Boston Children's had practiced the surgery before the child had arrived at the hospital. They hadn't practiced, however, by just going through the general motions of what the surgery would entail. These surgeons had practiced, had rehearsed, going through this surgery with this specific patient, even though the patient hadn't yet arrived at the hospital. They underwent this practice in the hospital's simulation center. This center was designed for situations just like this one; to provide a place where the medical team could run through procedures with as close to a real-life, specific patient, as possible. The simulation center was where the doctors could rehearse *as if* they were operating on the real patient.

One way in which the rehearsal involved the specific patient was through the use of 3-D printing. Using imaging data from the real child, the staff of the simulation center was able to print, i.e., construct, a 3-D model of her brain. With that model, the doctors were able to rehearse the surgery and "see which tools can fit down which corridors" of this particular child's brain. As one news report of the successful surgery noted, "Like flight simulators for pilots, the idea is that medical procedures will go more smoothly if the medical team gets to practice them first."

A point that could have been added - and should have been added - to that last sentence is that a simulation center like the one at Boston Children's Hospital lets the medical team practice procedures under risk-free circumstances; no patient's life is at risk while the team is practicing. The potential stakes of this practice are much higher and no one would call this practice play, but just like the young child playing truck driver, superhero, or doctor, for that matter, the *as if* nature of the activity is the same. The doctors in the simulation center were going through the surgical procedure *as if* the patient were real, and as if they were performing the surgery for real.

Simulation centers like the one at Boston Children's Hospital may be the newest and most technologically advanced form of simulation used in medical education and training but they certainly aren't the first use of medical make-believe. Whenever you hear of someone administering or receiving CPR (cardio-pulmonary resuscitation), you might give thanks to a doll named Resucci Annie. This doll was created over fifty years ago, by a toymaker, for the sole purpose of simulating a person whose heart has stopped beating and thus providing the opportunity for people to be trained in the process of CPR. In other words, if you were being trained in CRP you would learn how to breathe into the doll's mouth and administer chest compressions *as if* she were a real person, *as if* her heart had stopped, and *as if* you were attempting to save her life.

High-tech simulation centers and life-like mannequins like Resucci Annie are just two types of simulation processes used in medical education and training. Real people are used for medical simulation as well. It is not uncommon for actors, amateur and professional, to be hired (or work as volunteers) to portray patients in medical education settings. These actors would be given scripts to frame their portrayal of a patient, a patient presenting particular symptoms and backgrounds. The simulation activity itself would entail the doctor-in-training interviewing and examining this pretend patient. The purpose of this role play is more serious but it is essentially the same *as if* play of two preschool friends acting out the roles of doctor and patient. (Leslie Jamison has written a very interesting book, *The Empathy Exams*, that in part describes her experience working as a make-believe patient.)

AS IF SIMULATION is not only used in the training of doctors but has also found its way into the actual treatment of patients. For example, people who suffer from what is known as phantom limb pain have found some relief through the use of *as if* treatment approaches.

It has long been known that people who have lost limbs through accident or medically necessitated amputation can experience pain in those missing limbs. Sometimes the pain is just 'there' and sometimes the pain is a result of the sensation that the missing limb is frozen in a particular position, for example, a clenched hand that may dig fingernails into the hand or cause muscle spasms. This phantom limb pain is real; people who experience it are not imagining the pain and are not suffering from some psychological issue. The pain is real and can be excruciating at times and be quite debilitating.

There have been a number of theoretical explanations for why the pain exists, ranging from the existence of irritated nerve endings at the site of the amputation to a reorganization of the neural pathways in the brain. There have also been a number of different approaches to the treatment of phantom limb pain including the use drugs, stimulation of the spinal cord, and hypnosis. The treatment approach relevant to our discussion is called Mirror Visual Feedback or Mirror Box Therapy. It is an approach that uses the power of *as if* to, in effect, trick the mind into thinking that the missing limb is no longer missing.

V. S. Ramachandran is the neuroscientist who has pioneered this approach to treating phantom limb pain. He posited that the origin of the pain might be related to the problem of visual feedback. Ramachandran's model works something like this: the brain, acting on the existence of past links between it and the now missing limb, sends a signal down to that limb, for example, to unclench the hand. Where there is an intact limb, the hand would unclench and through the visual feedback of the action, the brain would know that the hand was unclenched and no further signal or instruction would be needed. In the case of the missing limb, however, there is no visual feedback and the brain then sends the signal again and again, resulting in both pain and frustration.

The idea behind the Mirror Box Therapy approach is that perhaps the brain can be 'tricked' into thinking that it is receiving the visual feedback. The Mirror Box is a fairly simple apparatus: it is a four-sided box without a top. There are two holes cut into one side of the box and a mirror is placed down the middle of the box, dividing the box into two sections. The patient puts his or her intact limb in the side of the box with the mirror and the missing limb is imagined placed in the other side. The patient is then asked to move the intact limb in various ways while watching the reflection of that limb in the mirror.

The first person who tried Ramachandran's Mirror Box was a young man who had his left arm amputated as a result of an automobile accident. Ramachandran met him ten years after the amputation and during those ten years the man had experienced significant pain in his phantom limb, specifically in his elbow, fingers, and wrist. In addition, although he was aware of the phantom limb he was never able to move it; the phantom limb was frozen in one position and this contributed to the pain. Ramachandran had him slide his right hand (the intact hand) into the hole on the right side of the box and then imagine placing his missing left hand in the hole on the left side of the box. Ramachandran then instructed him to move his right and left arms at the same time. The patient replied that he couldn't but Ramachandran asked him to try to move them anyway. After looking into the mirror, the patient cried out, "It's like it's plugged back in!"

Ramachandran sent the Mirror Box home with the patient and asked him to use it for about five or ten minutes a day. Two weeks later, the patient reported that he had relief from the pain when he used the Mirror Box but the pain returned in between the times he used the box. A week later, however, the patient reported that the phantom limb itself was gone, along with the pain.

Since that first patient, Ramachandran and others report that some people do get relief after experiencing Mirror Visual Feedback. It doesn't provide relief for all people suffering from phantom limb pain but research results do suggest that it is a viable approach to try along with some of the other approaches mentioned earlier. What might be happening when it does work? Ramachandran hypothesizes that it works by "restoring the congruence between motor output and sensory input." The brain sends the signal for motor output (e.g., move the hand) and now the mirror provides some sensory input back to the brain that the hand is moving (albeit the mirror image of the intact hand). Ramachandran calls this process an "optical trick." The missing limb is in reality not there but the mirror provides the circumstances in which the brain responds *as if* it is there and moving.

SIMULATION HAS ALSO been used to help people understand what patients and families experience when faced with illness and disease and, unfortunately, what it may feel like to experience the tragic consequences of those illnesses and diseases.

Joel Green was a young boy who was diagnosed with cancer not long after turning one-year of age. He died from that cancer when he was five. It's not difficult for any of us to imagine what those four years must have been like for the Green family, beginning with hearing the diagnosis, through all of the treatments, hospital stays, and ending with death of their son. But Ryan Green, Joel's father, didn't want to leave it just up to our imagination. In 2012, he created an immersive computer application called, *That Dragon, Cancer.* The application "mixes animation and magical realism to convey the Green's emotional state during Joel's illness. There is one dragon, but much of the game consists of re-enactments of mundanities like phone messages and hospital visits." The simulated experience,

> places the player as Ryan, a distraught father standing
> in an intensive care unit while his child lies in a hospital
> bed suffering from the side effects of cancer treatment.
> The player moves about the room, interacts with physical
> elements, experiences Ryan's thoughts through monologue
> and poetry, but also hears the dreadful sounds of the ICU,
> of the suffering child.

Unlike many video games, entering the simulated world of *That Dragon, Cancer,* does not provide you with powers and 'things' that lead to the conquering of something. It doesn't matter what you do in this world, the ending is always the same. And sometimes what you can do doesn't have positive outcomes.

> *Players found themselves in a hospital room with Ryan, clicking the walls and furniture in search of some way to relieve Joel's suffering and quiet his screams.. Yet every action - rock him, bounce him, feed him - only caused the crying to intensify.*

Much of the experience in *That Dragon, Cancer*, focuses on the very act of standing in another person's shoes that was discussed in Chapter 3. Sometimes the shoes belong to the dying child's father and at other times, "In a stark hospital scene, the player can switch between the perspective of two medical staff trying to hold themselves together while delivering terrible news." This stepping into another person's shoes, this experience of empathy, is the real power of Ryan Green's creation.

> *Scenarios such as these can be overwhelming. Even virtually, it is agonizing being in that room, and it's one of several occasions where TDC [That Dragon, Cancer] had me in tears. But the game's real power is in teasing out your own reflections on those loved, and lost...That Dragon, Cancer shows how video games can create empathy, both through the simple method of allowing the player to experience unfamiliar situations - and by twisting what is real and not-real within them.*

I think Ryan Green, the creator of the game and the father of Joel whose story is told in the game, captured the empathy producing power of the simulation that is *That Dragon, Cancer* when he said, "We went from caring for Joel to making everybody care about Joel."

Simulation and self-development

WHAT MIGHT HAPPEN if we were able to see the effect of current decisions on our future selves? Would that *as if* experience alter those decisions? Two interesting research studies offer provocative clues about how simulation and virtual reality can potentially affect some areas of personal development. One study focused on the saving of money for the future and the second study looked at decisions to exercise and lose weight. Both of these studies were based on the idea that if individuals were able to 'see' through a simulated experience, their future selves, then they might be more likely and more motivated to make changes in their present day behaviors. In some sense, the premise of these studies was that, "Neglect of the future self can arise from a failure of imagination."

In the first study, participants were asked to make decisions concerning how much money to designate towards a savings account. Through the use of avatars and virtual reality, participants experienced the simulation of the aging process and saw a "visual analog of a 70-year-old version of a current college student." The researchers hypothesized that "the participants who saw the age-morphed version of their future selves would be more likely to allocate money to a hypothetical savings account after exposure than those who saw a current version of themselves." The participants who did experience this simulated, virtual reality version of their future selves chose to save twice as much money as did the participants who did not experience future versions of themselves. In other words, seeing the *as if* self in the future led to a decision to save more money *now* for that future.

These studies focusing on saving money for some future self reminded me of an experience my wife and I had during the writing of this book.

Like most people approaching and then entering the retirement years, my wife and I had questions - and worries - about our financial future. Would our pensions and modest investments be enough to support us if we were fortunate to live to a reasonably old age? Could we maintain the lifestyle to which we had become accustomed? And like many people, we sought the assistance of a financial professional to help us get a handle on that question.

The conversations with the financial professional led us to the experience of another kind of simulation activity, another kind of *as if* engagement. Based on our life expectancy, required and desired spending levels, predictable pensions, projections about inflation, and historical data regarding the ups and downs of the stock market, our financial future was subjected to what the adviser called a *financial stress test*. A computer program ran those variables through 1000 simulations of what could happen in the coming years. The result of this stress test, of these 1000 simulations, was a 'best guess' as to whether or not our financial foundation would be enough to support us in the years to come. For example, the test might state that for 900 out of 1000 scenarios (90% confidence level), our financial resources would last for our expected lifetimes. The test can be run more than once to see how changes to variables such as spending levels and stock market projections change the outcome (e.g., buy that yacht now and the money runs out five years earlier).

The financial stress test, in essence, plays out 1000 different future scenarios; each of these scenarios is an *as if* simulation. Each of the simulations is a depiction of how life will turn out under these particular conditions. For example, let's pretend you spend five percent of your portfolio each year instead of four percent and see what happens to your future self.

TURNING FROM FINANCIAL health to physical health, in the second set of studies, virtual reality was used to influence the degree to which individuals would engage in physical exercise. In these studies, virtual self-models of participants were created through a process called "immersive virtual environment technology," which is defined as the "replacement of natural sensory information with digital information and the ability to track and respond to users' movements in order to tailor that digital information." Participants then observed these virtual selves "performing health-related behaviors from a third person point of view." In other words, individuals watched digital versions of themselves exercising.

Just as young children create make-believe worlds in which they can do things not possible in their 'real worlds' (e.g., drive a truck, fly like Superman, be a mommy), the researchers were, in effect, creating pretend worlds for the participants, worlds in which "virtual humans [serve as] models [that] can be manipulated to portray a range of desirable behaviors that may be difficult to enact in the real world." The participants in these studies also saw virtual representations - mapped onto their own bodies - of the consequences of exercising or not exercising: "Participants witnessed [their virtual self] gain or lose weight in immediate accordance with his or her physical exercise behaviors." In other words, participants were able to see what they would look like in the future *as if* they had made a decision to exercise (or not) in the present. Being given the opportunity to "imagine the future self" had a positive affect on the exercise behaviors of the participants in their actual, not virtual, lives. It turns out that "exposure to virtual cause-and-effect actions can change actual behavior."

One of the more interesting and intriguing studies employing simulation to improve personal well-being was conducted by the psychologist Ellen Langer and her associates. The participants in this study were a group of people who fell into the category of 'senior citizens,' people in their seventies and eighties. These were basically healthy people who nonetheless had experienced the normal effects of aging in terms of strength, flexibility, stamina and emotional well-being. Ellen Langer described her study this way.

> My students and I devised a study - which we would later come to call the "counter-clockwise study" - to look at what effects turning back the clock psychologically would have on people's physiological state. We would re-create the world of 1959 and ask subjects to live as though it were twenty years earlier.

In other words, Langer and her co-researchers asked their subjects to live in this simulated world *as if* they were twenty years younger.

To create this simulated world, the researchers created an environment that tried to reflect what things were like in 1959 and they requested that participants not bring anything with them, e.g., current magazines or family photos, that were part of their lives since

1959. The participants were asked to provide photos of their younger selves, from 1959 and earlier. They then proceeded to live for a week *as if* that year, 1959, were the present year.

The result of the study were quite provocative. Compared to a control group - comparably aged people who did not experience living through the simulated 1959 - the experimental group registered greater improvement on such measurements as flexibility, manual dexterity, and reduction of arthritis symptoms as measured by their ability to straighten their fingers. There were positive changes in regard to height and weight, and observations of gait and posture also suggested that the experimental group showed greater improvement than the control group. On measures of intelligence, better than 60% of the subjects in the experimental group showed improvement while less than 50% of the control group did the same.

The results of this study suggest that intelligence, physical flexibility, and even height (probably a result of standing up straighter) can be positively affected by simply pretending to be younger than you are. Langer might quibble with my last statement because she noted that her study was not asking participants "to 'act as if it is 1959' but to let yourself be just who you were in 1959." I think I understand the distinction she is trying to make but I would argue that an 80 year old can't literally be transformed into a 60 year old but can act *as if* he or she is 60 years old, and apparently, by doing so, can grow taller.

AS I DISCUSSED in Chapter 1, a major characteristic of *as if* is the idea of *transformation*. In their pretend play children transform objects (a cardboard box can become a car, a crib, a mailbox); they can transform their life circumstances (in play I can have two parents while in real life I have only a father); and they can transform themselves (I can pretend I am a doctor or that I have superpowers). In effect these transformation are simulations; when my granddaughter announced that I was the patient and proceeded to listen to my heart, give me medicine, and administer an injection, she was simulating the activity and behavior of a doctor. My granddaughter was also very definite as to how I, the simulated patient, was to behave. In this case and many role playing cases like it, the child uses props, language, and scripts to simulate the people being portrayed in the make-believe drama.

There have been some interesting research studies that take the simulation beyond props, language, and scripts and demonstrate the power of simulation to perhaps change subjects' attitude towards people who are different than they are in some way; in other words, these simulations can lead to a change in your current self. One of these simulation approaches utilizes something called the Rubber Hand Illusion, which is related to the Mirror Box therapy discussed earlier.

You can find videos on the internet of the Rubber Hand Illusion used as a form of a 'parlor trick' but researchers have also brought it into the realm of scientific research. The illusion works like this: the subject is sitting at a table where he can see one of his own hands but his second hand is cloaked and not visible. In its place is a rubber hand. The experimenter then strokes or taps the visible hand and the rubber hand at the same time and with the same rhythm and intensity. For most people, what soon happens is the sensation that the rubber hand belongs to your body. In effect, the brain processes the visual feedback of the seeing the rubber hand being tapped and the sensory feedback of feeling the other hand being tapped and concludes that the hand I see (the rubber hand) belongs to my body. When used as a 'parlor trick,' the feeling might seem funny and weird; when used in the research lab, the Rubber Hand Illusion provides some interesting secondary consequences.

One of the effects studied involved people's implicit racial bias. The researchers wondered what would happen to a person's attitude if the rubber hand being used was of a different skin color than the subject's skin color. In other words, if I, a Caucasian, am presented with the illusion and the hand is dark-skinned, would that have any effect on my racial attitudes? The answer was, yes; sitting there *as if* one of my hands were dark-skinned could, based on a pre- and post-test of racial bias, change my attitudes towards people of the other race. The researchers summarized their study in the following way.

> Using the rubber hand illusion, we induced light-skinned Caucasian participants to feel that a dark-skinned rubber hand was part of their bodies, and measured whether this could change their implicit biases against people with dark skin. We found that the more intense the participants' illusion of ownership over the dark-skinned rubber hand, the more positive attitudes became, and that this effect was specific to the 'outgroup.'

The make-believe of simulation

ALL OF THE simulation activities discussed in this chapter demonstrate the characteristics that define children's pretend play as described in earlier chapters of this book. Children enter the *play frame* by putting on a costume or announcing "Let's play..." In terms of simulation activities, the *play frame* is identified by pulling out the board game, loading up the computer application, clicking on the video game, or entering the simulation lab. As noted above, the idea of *transformations* are very much a part of many simulation activities. The creation of an *avatar* is a form of transformation as is the assumption of the role of a wagon train leader in the computer game, *The Oregon Trail.*

The use of symbols and the concept of *this stands for that* could be seen as almost a defining characteristic of simulation activities in general. Resucci Annie, the CPR training doll, represents and stands for a real person. In the game of *Second Life*, when I create an *avatar* I am creating a symbolic character that represents and stands in for me. I may not be able to literally walk around the properties represented on the *Monopoly* board but I can figuratively visit those properties by moving the stand-in playing piece around the board, *as if* I am inspecting real properties.

In Chapter 5, we saw that in the playful world of imaginary companions, children sometimes create *paracosms*, entire worlds in which their companions reside and interact with other imaginary characters. These worlds often have their own geographies, laws, governing principles, and sometimes languages. Simulation games like *SimCity* and *Second Life* at their cores are complex and intricate paracosms, filled with interrelating characters and governed by rules and principles.

A fundamental similarity between children's pretend play and adult simulation activity is the idea that the play and the simulation are both relatively risk-free activities. The young child who acts meanly towards a baby doll can do that in play whereas acting meanly towards a real baby sister might incur the wrath of a parent. In a similar way, the surgeon can practice the intricate surgical procedure without risking the actual life of a patient, and the Army recruits can practice storming a terrorist stronghold without risking the lives of the actual soldiers. One of the powers of play is the ability to try things out without worrying about the consequences of failure. I was willing to sit in front of that computer console on the air force base (and the captain was willing to let me sit there) because no matter what I did, no missiles were going to be launched that Saturday morning.

And finally, make-believe play of young children and the simulation activity of army recruits, surgeons, and virtual reality gamers are both an engagement with the act of *as if*. I will operate on this model of a brain *as if* it belongs to a real patient. I will fire this military automatic rifle *as if* it is a real gun firing real bullets. I will make decisions about the dangerous trip undertaken by these 19th century pioneers *as if* they are really undertaking the journey. I will work the controls of this cockpit *as if* I am lifting this airplane into the sky. Sometimes the stakes are higher but all of these *as if* transformations are not all that different from the four-year-old wrapping the towel around her neck *as if* it were a cape and using her superpowers to fly around the room *as if* she were Supergirl.

Is it all just a simulation?

I WILL FINISH this chapter with a discussion of one more type of simulation, one that I must admit, I do not fully understand.

There is, I have learned, a theory called the *simulation hypothesis*. This hypothesis suggests that reality as we know it is really just a simulation. As the Wikipedia entry states,

> The simulation hypothesis proposes that all of reality, including the earth and the universe, is in fact an artificial simulation, most likely a computer simulation. Some versions rely on the development of a simulated reality, a proposed technology that would seem realistic enough to convince its inhabitants the simulation was real.

In other words, all that we believe to be real might only be the *as if* play and simulation of some entity, existing in some other place or dimension; an entity that is way smarter than we are.

Lest we think that such a theory is only held and espoused by crackpots and science fiction fans, Neil deGrasse Tyson, who holds a doctorate in astrophysics from Columbia University and is, as of the writing of this book, director of the Hayden Planetarium in New York City, believes that the simulation hypothesis *could* be true; that "he wouldn't be surprised if we were to find out somehow that someone else is responsible for our universe." DeGrasse himself said that "it is easy for me to imagine that everything in our lives is just the creation of some other entity for their entertainment."

As I read about the simulation hypothesis, the idea that our universe might be someone else's plaything or toy, reminded me of the final scene from the television series *St. Elsewhere*. An hourlong drama set in a hospital, *St. Elsewhere* aired for six seasons between 1982 and 1988. It featured a large cast of doctors, nurses and other hospital personnel and portrayed the workings of the hospital and the interpersonal dynamics of the staff.

The final scene of the last episode of the last season is considered by many to be a classic in the annals of television series' endings. This scene takes place in an apartment and two of the people in the scene appear to be two of the senior doctors from the hospital but judging by their clothing and the setting, they seem not to be doctors. There is also a young boy in the apartment who is the son of one of the men and the grandson of the other. It turns out that the young boy has been diagnosed with autism, a set of behaviors and a diagnosis that confuses the father and grandfather. In the scene, the young boy is playing with a snow globe. When the boy leaves the room to join his father and grandfather for dinner, he sets the snow globe on the television set. A camera closeup of the snow globe reveals that inside the globe is a model of the very hospital which was the setting for the television series.

I remember watching that last episode and I came away believing, as did many other viewers, that this last scene was telling us that all that we watched for those past six years emerged from the imagination of this young boy. The hospital, the doctors, the stories were all part of a simulated universe created by, and in, the mind of this young boy. Perhaps the simulation hypothesis discussed above is simply saying that we are all living in someone else's snow globe.

Chapter 8

Making It Through
the Dark and Stormy Night

The *Oxford Learner's Dictionary* offers the following definition for the word, play: "To do things for pleasure, as children do; to enjoy yourself, rather than work." As for synonyms for the term, the following words are then listed in the dictionary entry: fun, recreation, pleasure, and amusement. It's probably safe to say that most of us would find both the definition and the list of synonyms to be reasonable representations of the nature of children's play, or even play in general. Most of us would probably associate play with leisure, free time and perhaps frivolity. We might even consider play to be something of a luxury, an activity that is only allowed to occur *after* your homework is finished, your chores completed, or the workday has ended. In fact, it's not unusual for the idea of play to be viewed as the opposite of work; as President Theodore Roosevelt wrote, "When you play, play hard; when you work, don't play at all."

But if play is enjoyable, a form of amusement, and takes place in a leisurely fashion, why then does it continue to exist even during what one author has called some very "startling circumstances"? We know that life isn't always kind to children: they become sick and die; the adults in their lives who are supposed to care for them sometimes cause chaos in their lives instead; and the societies they live in are at times dysfunctional. Why, for example, do children find the impetus to play during times of war and natural disasters? Why does play still emerge when children are hospitalized for surgery or chronic illness and why do children play despite experiencing some of the random tragedies that can scar a person's life? What is the function and power of *as if* when children find themselves living under and within these "startling circumstances"? How does the *as if* power to transform and consider alternative realities, and to distance oneself from the here and now help children (and, yes, adults), make it through the 'dark and stormy nights' of life?

Making it through the dark days of natural disasters

SOMETIMES IT'S NOT people but forces of nature that disrupt and wreck havoc on children's lives. The suddenness of a hurricane or earthquake is frightening for all involved but for children the terror that is associated with the unforeseen destruction can be overwhelming, and brings with it ongoing fears, anxiety, changes in behaviors, and symptoms of post-traumatic stress disorder (PTSD). It's been suggested that "During natural disasters, children are one of the most vulnerable populations because their neurological systems are subject to permanent changes and their coping skills are not developed enough to manage catastrophic events." As the examples below illustrate, however, through *as if* play, children may find ways of coping and making sense of the experience in order "to create a concrete narrative of traumatic events so they can master frightening images."

Hurricane Katrina that devastated New Orleans and much of the Gulf area in 2005 was one of the deadliest and costliest natural disasters in the history of the United States. Over 1200 people died as a result of the hurricane and the extent of property damage has been estimated to exceed 100 billion dollars. Homes were destroyed, basic human services were disrupted, and families, when possible, were relocated to areas of safety. Children experienced it all.

There is evidence that after the terrible events of Hurricane Katrina children worked at making sense of the frightening experience through play. In one preschool, for example, children worked at building levees while engaged in mud play.

About that same time, Shonda dumped the 'gumbo' out of the pot, and it made a small lake in the mud and dirt near their feet. Hesiki examined the moving water and said, "The storm is coming!" The teacher asked what we needed to do about the storm. Hesiki replied, "We need to make levees."

During their free play time, some children took on the roles of people trying to help hurricane victims in their time of need. The teachers in this classroom had planned a curriculum unit on transportation which the children 'hijacked'; they kept steering the discussion to the various rescue vehicles they had seen on television. As one teacher said, "We kept trying to continue with the topic of transportation, but as far as the children were concerned, all roads led to Katrina."

Other examples of hurricane inspired play were observed by parents of young children after Hurricane Hugo hit the southeastern United States in 1989. A mother of a four-year-old reported that her child continually represented the destruction of trees during his play, using all sorts of objects to stand in for - to represent - the trees, including the spears of broccoli served at dinner. One parent of a three-year-old girl described her daughter's clever way of dealing with the bad behavior of Hurricane Hugo: the little girl repeatedly put Hugo in 'time out' as punishment for destroying her house.

Hurricanes aren't the only type of natural disaster that can impact a child's life and then become the focus of their imaginary, *as if*, play. After experiencing an earthquake, for example, children's play may take on the theme of objects in the physical environment being broken and therefore requiring repair. Some of these themes were still surfacing in the children's play months after the actual earthquake occurred.

Here, Cayden's pretend play is done by reference to broken buildings, a common occurrence in his current post-earthquake environment, where there is much rebuilding and cordoning off of buildings with the use of traffic cones.

Another child played out his earthquake experiences during therapy sessions by calling a toy dinosaur "the sea monster" and using the toy to ram into a 'doll family' and miniature doll furniture. During a subsequent therapy session, the boy used toy army men to kill the "sea monster."

This re-playing and reenacting of their experiences with natural disasters may have a positive benefit for children. One research study demonstrated the importance of this type of play by showing that children who were provided with the opportunity to work out their prior experience with an earthquake through play exhibited less post-experience anxiety than children who were not given that opportunity.

Making it through the days (and nights) of doctors, hospitals, and medical procedures

ONE OF THE ways in which life isn't always kind to children is the fact that children do get sick, become injured, and suffer from chronic illnesses that require varying degrees of medical attention. For some children, their experience with the world of medicine can include hospitalization, painful medical procedures, and the trauma of death and dying. Despite all of this, children living through difficult medical experiences still continue to play perhaps because "Play can help the hospitalized child better understand and interpret the imagery, sights, sounds, and the language of the hospital." Here is one example from the experience of a hospitalized child.

> Veronica set up a bed, croupette and a bedside stand. She brought in a medicine dropper and cup on a tray, placing them on the table. As she opened the croupette, she said to the two dolls, "I'm putting you two in bed together. You'll be happier that way. Now I have to put this flap back so I can get to you two with triple measles. Now, now, don't cry, this medicine is good for you. It tastes just like cookies, and you know you only get good cookies in the hospital, not like home.

Here is another story about children engaging in imaginary play in a hospital. It is about a number of children who were all patients on the same floor of the hospital. One of the children on the floor had died and the hospital staff had decided not to mention his death to the other children. Their rationale was that since no one had witnessed his death and no one had asked about him, there was no need to bring up the subject. The staff was then somewhat surprised to see what the children played out on their own.

> *Several of the boys between the ages of five and*
> *ten had constructed a coffin out of large building*
> *blocks and were playing mortician. Each boy carefully*
> *took turns lying in the box, arranging his head in a*
> *comfortable elevated position, crossing his arms and*
> *having a sheet gently placed over him.*

There is a group of professionals, called Child Life Specialists, who work in hospital and other medical settings to help children and families cope with the medical experience. Play is one of the main tools that Child Life Specialists use to support children in their efforts to make sense of, and cope with, all that is happening to them. Often the play occurs in specially designated activity rooms, play therapy rooms, or at bedside. Children may be provided with miniature replicas of the medical equipment they might encounter during their time in the hospital; for example, IV stands, hypodermic syringes, doctor's bags, and casts. By using these toys, children can reenact their sometime (or oftentimes) negative experiences and their "medical play involved a sense of mastery, as most characters [in their play] became healthy again." As one study found, "children with chronic illnesses and their siblings gravitated toward and benefitted from expressing and releasing their feelings while engaging in unstructured medical play."

Making it through random acts of violence

ONE OF THE most frightening experiences for children, or for anyone, is the random violence and tragedy that can enter a person's life.

Like the hurricane or earthquake, it seems to come out of nowhere, wreck its havoc, and then depart. But the horrors of the experience can have lasting effects. Here, too, play and the imagination can help children cope with the aftermath of the experience, as the following two examples of 'funeral play' illustrate. The first is a description of children's play in a Chicago housing project in the 1980s.

> The children played funeral every day for weeks. They
> would build a casket with blocks and take turns lying in
> the casket. The children took on the roles of the preacher,
> family members, and mourners. They would weep and cry
> for the person who died, saying, 'Don't take him!'

Children often bring the 'scripts' of their lives into their play; they take what they have observed or perhaps experienced firsthand and incorporate the details in their play. This is powerfully illustrated in the second example of children playing funeral, this time at school.

> Six-year-old James organizes his classmates to pick
> dandelions from the school lawn at recess. They create
> bouquets and stash them in their cubbies when they
> return to their first grade classroom. At their play and
> project time later in the day, the children construct a
> pretend casket from blocks complete with handles for
> pallbearers and enact a pretend funeral with James
> coaching them on prayers and songs. Other children join
> and the bouquets of dandelions are shared and thrown at
> the 'casket' as it is lowered into the grave site marked by
> tape on the classroom rug. James' 19-year-old aunt was
> killed in a drive-by shooting the previous Sunday.

Then there was the four-year-old boy who lived through the experience of a small plane crash landing on his street. As one might imagine, such an experience led to the development of fear and anxiety. Through a series of play therapy sessions, the boy was able to move past the fear and anxiety and was able to play with toy airplanes in ways that didn't involve crashes and destruction. It is possible that this "Postdisaster play appears to be similar to the mourning process, and is an effort to deal with the loss of parental protection, omnipotence, neighborhood and friends, as well as the threat of loss of home."

IN JULY OF 1976, twenty-six children living in Chowchilla, California, were kidnapped as they were riding the school bus home from school. The children, ages five through fourteen, along with the bus driver, were first forced into two different vans and then driven around the countryside for about eleven hours. After that initial ordeal, they were herded into another van of some sort, which was then buried underground, where they spent another sixteen hours. Led by the bus driver and a few of the older children, they all managed to escape with relatively little harm done to them physically. As one might imagine, however, the more than twenty-four hours spent in dark, cramped quarters, not knowing what was to become of them, took some toll on their young psyches. Once again, however, the impulse to play and reenact their experiences still survived.

Through the writings of the psychiatrist, Lenore Terr, who worked with twenty-five of the children for a number of years after the kidnapping, we learn that many of the children engaged in some interesting and recurring play and games related to what they had experienced that July. One of the girls, for example, was part of a recurring game of "kidnap tag" on her middle school playground. She was the "it" of the game and her friends were the kidnappers.

Another child would play "Bus Driver" by placing two chairs on the kitchen table and then coaxing her toddler sister up into the chair as a passenger. When asked if her bus was ever kidnapped, the girl replied, "No, this is a safe bus. There are no kidnappings here."

A number of the girls used their Barbie dolls as participants in their play. One girl would put her Barbie into the toy mobile home, load in clothes and accessories, and repeatedly drive the mobile home and her Barbie from one place to another. When asked if the Barbie ever did anything upon arriving at her destination, the child responded that, no, she never did anything; the whole point was to drive there and back safely. Another young girl, who was particularly affected and stressed by the dirt and grime that she had experienced during the kidnapping ordeal, would repeatedly play a game she called, "Barbie Goes to the Spa." Her Barbie dolls would be washed (in actual water) over and over again. She played "Barbie Goes to the Spa" so often that a couple of her Barbie dolls had to be discarded because they were damaged from their extended time in the water.

Making it through the stormy days and nights of war

WHERE THERE IS war, there is usually dislocation, destruction and death. Children can experience all that war has to offer, and "must cope with both the dangerous events of the war and the terror those events bring." Sometimes children experience the effects of war directly and sometimes the tragedies of war may touch them indirectly. People close to them may leave to be participants in the war and may or may not return. The institutions of their community - the actual physical structures of homes and shops, the societal structures of school, commerce, basic services, worship - may be disrupted or destroyed. Sometimes the terror and reality of war may force families to uproot themselves and move to locations of greater safety. As the 1996 report of the United Nations International Emergency Children's Fund (UNICEF) noted, "Children have, of course, always been caught up in warfare. They usually have little choice but to experience, at minimum, the same horrors as their parents."

And yet, children continue to play and use their imaginations despite the war related death and destruction that swirls around them.

During the American Civil War, for example, a Southern mother described how her son and friends would play *as if* they were Confederate soldiers. Note how their play included some of the more gory consequences of being a soldier fighting in the war.

> Almost their entire set of play have references to a state
> of war...He gets a stick and hobbles about...saying that he
> lost a leg at the Second Battle of Manassas; tells wonderful
> stories of how he cut off Yankee heads, bayoneted them, etc.

War does bring with it injury and death but it can also create heroes and stories of bravery and courage. Children's imaginary play can also reflect these aspects of the conflict, as illustrated by another description of Civil War inspired play.

> We felt thrilled through and through by accounts of the brave fighting our dear people were doing...We children were always drilling, marching, fighting...the whites as officers in the front rank, the blacks coming behind. The cows were the Yankees and I am afraid we didn't always drive them as slowly as Father wanted.

Make-believe war play during the Civil War even made it into the White House, the home of President Lincoln and his family. The Lincoln children were seen playing the following war inspired mini-drama: a doll was assigned the role of a treasonous soldier and the children then carried out an *as if* court martial. Once the 'soldier' was found guilty, he was to be executed and buried. One can only imagine how Lincoln's sons had learned about treason, courts-martial and executions.

All of the examples of war play just described are of children who had experienced and learned about the war indirectly. There were children, however, who had direct experiences with the terrors of war and brought those experiences into their imaginary play. For example, here are the words uttered by a young girl, the daughter of a Confederate family, while she was playing.

> Upon my word and 'honour, Sir, there are no letters and paper in this trunk at all.

Where did these words and the content they expressed come from? Were they simply the imaginary creation of a child at play? It turns out that this young girl was repeating the words she had heard her mother say to a Union soldier who was questioning her in their house.

The memories and stories of people who lived through the horrors of World War II also provide evidence of the ways in which imaginary play continues to exist during 'startling circumstances' and how perhaps this ability to engage in *as if* helped the children to cope and survive. Here are two examples of how children used the power of the imagination to lift themselves up from their present circumstances, to *distance themselves,* from the war-torn here and now, and for at least a moment, transport themselves to a happier place.

> *Every night before falling asleep, I give myself a little present. I make up a little story. Not just an ordinary story, but something really special. Something that doesn't have anything to do with ordinary life. Usually it is about a young prince who is handsome and rich. His life is perfect, only he is a bit lonely. That's why he always has himself driven around in his golden carriage. One day, when he happens to pass by, he sees me lying there and orders his coachman to stop. He steps out, comes nearer, and slides his strong arms around my back. In a moment he lifts me carefully as I am very fragile. And while I am asleep he carries me to the carriage.*

And here is another memory of using the imagination to transport oneself from the reality of the war.

> *But what I like most is to lie here with eyes shut. Then the only things I see are big white clouds. And then a white horse and carriage come driving up over the clouds. A handsome young prince and princess with long blond hair are sitting on the driver's box. When they come closer, I see that they are not a prince and princess at all, but my own Apu and Anyu [Hungarian for father and mother]. They drive on and on...I don't think they can see me, lying here in the cellar on my mattress. But then I feel myself lifted up very gently. And before I know it, I am sitting between them and together we fly about the white clouds in the blue sky.*

These are the memories of adults looking back at their childhoods during the war. There are also direct observations of children engaging in pretend play that reflected their experiences of the terrors of the war.

Anna Freud, Sigmund Freud's daughter, operated a nursery

school in London during World War II and the children who attended the school lived through England's involvement in the war and more specifically, the German blitz of London from September of 1940 to May of 1941. At one point, German airplanes dropped bombs on London for 57 consecutive days and ultimately more than 20,000 people lost their lives. Clearly many children would have experienced the fear, chaos, and destruction that was brought about by the Blitz. Anna Freud described how some of these children played out the aerial bombardment in her nursery school classroom.

> *War games play a part in our nursery as they do in others. Houses that are built are not simply thrown over as in former times, they are bombed from above, bricks being used as bombs. Playing train has given way to playing aeroplane; the noises of trains to that of flying planes. Games like these will come more into the forefront after air attacks, and give way to peace time games when things are normal again.*

It is interesting to note that an article in a 1942 issue of *Parents Magazine* endorsed this kind of war play and suggested that it might even be therapeutic for children. The authors of the article suggested that parents should consider a particular toy as a Christmas present: the 'Super Ack Ack Gun', a toy anti-aircraft weapon. The authors supported this suggestion by stating that, "child guidance workers agreed that it is best for children to be able to express freely through dramatic play what they hear and feel about war."

The Civil War and World War II are the wars of history books. The wars that are part of today's news also provide evidence that play continues despite all that war brings and that imagination and *as if* are still important in the lives of children making their way through the war zones of today.

Countries in the Middle East, for example, have seen more than their fair share of war over the past decades, with civil war striking Lebanon, Israelis and Palestinians inflicting violence on each other, and more recently, the conflicts in Afghanistan and Iraq. Despite the seemingly never-ending atmosphere of violence, instances of children playing and using their imaginations can still be found.

One example of *as if* play is drawn from the Persian Gulf War, when Israel was the target of Scud missile attacks launched from Iraq. Due to the threat of poison gas being delivered by these missiles, Israeli citizens were issued gas masks and some families also created 'sealed' rooms in their homes that hopefully would protect them from the poison gas attacks. A six-year-old Israeli girl described how she and a friend played together during this unsettling time.

> *Once my friend came to me for a short while. Her*
> *parents allowed her, if she took the box with gas mask*
> *on her shoulder. So we played a little in my room. We*
> *started puzzles but it did not work out. We dressed*
> *the dolls and put gas masks on them. And we rushed*
> *them into the Sealed Room.*

There were other examples of children engaging in re-enactment play during Israeli-Palestinian conflicts. Children in a Palestine refugee camp, for example, would play Intifada. Some of the Palestinian children would take on the roles of the refugees and these refugees would pretend to be protesting their living circumstances by throwing rocks at the 'Israeli soldiers,' who were played by other children in the camp. In another example, a five-year-old Palestinian girl had seen Israeli soldiers hold a knife to her grandmother's throat in order to force her to reveal some information; the girl later reenacted the scene with her own dolls.

The fact that imaginary play reflected the fighting and conflict surrounding the children can also be heard in the words of a nine-year-old boy living in Lebanon.

> *Whenever there was a lull [in the fighting] we would*
> *call our friends to come to our house and play*
> *together...Our favorite game was hide and attack. We*
> *made up machine guns and we had teams as armies*
> *so we throw bombs at them. We build barricades with*
> *chairs and pillow...*

This same boy also offered a 'simple' explanation for why this type of play might continue to exist.

> No, I don't like to be in a war and I don't like the killing of people. But it's okay to play; it's just a game.

Making it through some of the darkest days and nights of history

TWO OF THE darkest periods of human history were the days of slavery in the United States and years of the Holocaust in Europe before and during World War II. Yet despite the horrors of both of these times, evidence that children continued to play and imagine exists.

Play of slave children

WE KNOW FROM various accounts, particularly the slave narratives gathered through the Works Progress Administration (WPA) of the 1930s, that children living on the slave plantations of pre-Civil War America, both Black and White children, continued to play despite the tragic realities of slavery. The children of slaves played with each other and at times the children of slaves and the children of the slave owners played together. The children engaged in most of the types of play associated with childhood, including ball games, hide and seek, rough and tumble play, and play with toys, albeit homemade toys. The play that is most relevant to the present discussion, the play of the imagination and *as if*, also continued to be an important part of these children's lives.

One form of make-believe play on the plantations involved imitating the adults children saw around them. Sometimes this imitation consisted of dress-up play, as described by one former slave in her own words.

> Sum times we wud dress up in mammies dresses, an' play lak we wis find ladies. Sum times we wud break down er bush and hol' over our heads and lak dat wis er parasol.

191

Another example of the *as if* imitation of the adult world can be seen in this account of a make-believe funeral put on by the children, both the slave children and the plantation-owner's children.

> *[The boys] made a wagon of fig branches, and [used] four of them as horses. We tied a bow of black ribbon around the chicken's neck, and covered him with a white rag, and them marched in a procession singing...negro hymns, all the white children next to the hearses marching two by two, and the colored children following in the same order.*

As this accounting of the make-believe play of slave children suggests, when the adult world was imitated, when the children re-enacted their own experiences, the *as if* play included some of the stark realities of the world in which these children lived, e.g., the 'colored children' walking behind the white children. And when the Black and White children played a game of 'wagon,' it was the Black children who took on the roles of the mules. As Steven Mintz writes in his book, *Huck's Raft: A History of American Childhood*, "In fact many interracial games reenacted the relationship between masters and slaves, reinforcing the plantation hierarchy and accentuating the divide between the white and black children."

The urge, or perhaps the need, to reenact their reality did lead the slave children to engage in make-believe play that represented some of the more horrifying aspects of their experience. For example, there was a game called, "Hide the Switch," which on the surface might seem benign enough, with an object being hidden and searched for. The consequence for loser of the game, however, was a flogging. The Black children of the plantations also staged make-believe slave auctions and whippings.

Play of children during the Holocaust

THE EUROPEAN THEATER of World War II also brought with it the horrors of the Holocaust. The facts of this blight on human history are well known; the forced incarceration of Jews into ghettoes and concentration camps; the stripping of their possessions and wealth by the German authorities; the restrictions of freedoms; the deliberate and premeditated killing of 6,000,000 Jews and thousands of others, including gypsies, Catholics, and Russians. Many of us have seen the horrifying images of the Holocaust captured in photographs and on film. We have moving firsthand accounts described in the writings of Elie Wiesel, Viktor Frankl, and Anne Frank, among others. Yet despite the almost unimaginable horrors of the ghettoes and concentration camps, the play of the imagination did continue to exist.

George Eisen's book, *Children and Play in the Holocaust: Games Among the Shadows,* is an invaluable resource for understanding how play still managed to find expression in the ghettoes and concentration camps of Eastern Europe. It was Eisen who wrote that, "Finding play under these circumstances and conditions seems somewhat startling." But Eisen did find play still occurring under those startling circumstances and as Eisen notes, "Although their voices are haunting, it is important to listen to the children of the Holocaust, for they saw everything that grown-ups saw." Eisen also writes that, "In spite of their elders' desperate efforts to shelter them from the atrocities, their games in the ghettoes reflected, inevitably, the surrounding horror."

What, then, did the children see that was reflected in their make-believe and dramatic play? One example was the process of the camp inmates lining up each morning for the daily roll call. That became a script that could be incorporated into their play, as the memory of one camp survivor recalls.

> They play..."Roll Call," shouting "Caps Off!" They took on the roles of the sick who fainted during roll call and were beaten for it.

The same survivor also remembered how the children's play would imitate the abusive behavior of the German authorities.

> They played "Doctor"...who would take away food rations from the sick and refuse them help if they had nothing to bribe him with.

The daily drama of inmates returning from their assigned work details also found its way into children's play.

> Among the most popular ones [games] in Vilna was "Going Through the Gate," a game that enacted the experience of thousands of Jewish laborers who, returning from forced labor, were searched by the Jewish and German police, an experience similar to running the gauntlet.

After finding evidence of the continued presence of play and games under these 'startling circumstances', Eisen concluded that "Play activities thus came to provide everywhere a naturally reflective mirror of all the sorrow, dramas, and absurdities of the children's brief existence."

George Eisen wasn't the only researcher to find evidence of make-believe play existing in the ghettoes and concentration camps of the Holocaust. Yolanda Gampel, an Israeli psychoanalyst, conducted a study in which she interviewed twenty-five Jewish adults who lived through World War II in Europe as children. The memory of make-believe, *as if,* play told by one of her interview subjects fits right in with the examples of play discovered by Eisen in his research. It is also an example of how the horrors of reality can become the content of children's imaginary play.

> We used to play prisoners, the people of the camps against the SS, we would play shooting and "Hands up"...The boys... played the SS and we girls were prisoners...We pretended to cry. We played "make-believe." We pretended to plead, "No, don't rape us, we have small children."

Perhaps the 'horror among horrors' of the concentration camps were the ever-present possibility of being chosen for extermination. And children, because they were too young to be used for labor, were often among the first to be sent to the gas chambers. Yet children brought this aspect of their experience into their play as well, which led Eisen to write,

> Of all the play experiences it is the concept and even the notion of children's play in the extermination camps

that most tax the rationality of the human mind and imagination. The human mind is not always able to comprehend or assimilate the coexistence of atrocity and death and child's play.

But Eisen did find "numerous diaries and testimonies describing the heart-rendering scenes of children who played in the 'portal of death,'" as the following example illustrates.

Once they even play "Gas Chamber." They made a hole in the ground and threw stones in one after the other. Those were supposed to be people put in the crematoria, and they imitated their screams.

FORTUNATELY (OR UNFORTUNATELY, depending on one's perspective), there are a number of first-person accounts of living through the Holocaust that help us understand - and not forget - this unique period of human history. In perhaps the most well-known of these accounts, the author writes,

To enhance the image of this long-awaited friend in my imagination, I don't want to jot down the facts in this diary the way most people would do, but I want the diary to be my friend, and I'm going to call this friend Kitty.

Those are the written words of Anne Frank, whose book, *The Diary of Anne Frank*, has sold over 30 million copies and been translated into 70 languages. Anne was given a diary for her thirteenth birthday in June of 1942. One short month later, Anne and her family went into hiding in the now famous attic of a house in Amsterdam, Netherlands, and for the next two years she recorded her experiences in that diary. Anne took an *as if* approach to the diary, writing each day *as if* she were telling her innermost secrets to a good friend, albeit an imaginary one. Almost every entry in the diary begins with the words, "Dearest Kitty," and at different points Anne explains why this diary, or surrogate friend, was so important to her.

That's why I always wind up coming back to my diary - I start there and end there because Kitty's always patient.

Anne then goes on to write:

> Today I have two things to confess. It's going to take a long
> time, but I have to tell them to someone, and you're the
> most likely candidate, since I know you'll keep a secret, no
> matter what happens.

Like the children described in Chapter 5, Anne Frank conjured up an imaginary friend (in the form of her diary), a friend who would listen, be patient, and keep a secret. As children often do, Anne needed a certain kind of friend, one that didn't exist in the reality of that attic, so she used her imagination and lived her life *as if* that friend existed.

Three other well-known chroniclers of the Holocaust experience, Viktor Frankl, Elie Wiesel, and Primo Levi, also provide examples of how the *as if* quality of the imagination helped them cope with and survive the realities of their day-to-day existence.

Viktor Frankl was an Austrian psychiatrist who, along with his wife and parents, was deported to the Theresiendstadt concentration camp in September of 1942. He would spend most of the next three years in three different camps before being liberated in April of 1945. Tragically, the rest of his family - his wife and parents - perished in the camps.

Frankl detailed his experience in the concentration camps in his book, *Man's Search for Meaning*. Frankl's basic conclusion is that even in the worst of circumstances, it is possible to find meaning in life and finding that meaning is what can sustain you. And part of that meaning can be found, or nurtured, through the power of the imagination. You can, for example, conjure up the image of your wife, even though you do not know where, or how, she is.

> I did not know whether my wife was alive, and I had no
> means of finding out...but at that moment it ceased to
> matter. There was no need for me to know; nothing could
> touch the strength of my love, my thoughts, and the image
> of my beloved. Had I known then that my wife was dead,
> I think that I would still have given myself, undisturbed by

*that knowledge, to the contemplation of her image, and
that my mental conversation with her would have been
just as vivid and just as satisfying.*

Frankl believed that the workings of the inner life, the imagination, had the power to help the concentration camp inmate survive his or her circumstances. Of particular interest to Frankl was the power to remember and re-imagine past experiences.

*The intensification of inner life helped the prisoner find
refuge from the emptiness, desolation and spiritual poverty
of his existence, by letting him escape into the past. When
given free rein, his imagination played with past events,
often not important ones, but minor happenings and
trifling things.*

Frankl also describes how he used his imagination in essence to remove himself, to *distance* himself, if only for a moment, from the realities of his daily existence in the camps. In this case, he seems to use the imagination to actually put the present into the past, He even uses the words 'as if' in his description.

*I became disgusted with the state of affairs which
compelled me, daily and hourly, to think of only such trivial
things. I forced my thoughts to turn to another subject.
Suddenly, I saw myself standing on the platform of a well-
lit, warm and pleasant lecture room. In front of me sat an
attentive audience on comfortable upholstered seats. I was
giving a lecture on the psychology of concentration camps!
All that oppressed me at that moment became objective,
seen and described from the remote viewpoint of science.
By this method I succeeded somehow in rising above
the situation, above the sufferings of the moment, and I
observed them as if they were already in the past.*

The power to lie, the ability to engage in *as if* thinking and utter statements that aren't in fact true, also helped individuals survive the horrors of the concentration camps. Elie Wiesel was a teenager when he and his family - mother, father, and three sisters - were first forced to live in a ghetto in their home country of Romania and then were deported to a concentration camp. Wiesel and his two older sisters survived; his younger sister and parents perished in the camps. Wiesel wrote a number of books about his Holocaust experience with the slim volume, *Night*, perhaps being his most well-known.

In *Night*, Wiesel tells of a circumstance where he told a lie to another camp inmate who was a distant relative of Wiesel's. The relative asked Wiesel if he or any members of his family had any news of the man's wife, Reizel, and his two little sons. In answering, Wiesel chose to lie.

> *I knew nothing about them. Since 1940, my mother had not a single letter from them but I lied.*

Wiesel then goes on to describe the lie.

> *Yes, my mother's had news from your family. Reizel is very well. The children too.*

The man, according to Wiesel, "wept with joy" and later on says to Wiesel and Wiesel's father,

> *The only thing that keeps me alive...is that Reizel and the children are alive. If it wasn't for them, I couldn't keep going.*

Wiesel later describes an instance when perhaps lying to oneself in the form of pretending, an act of self-deception, may also be necessary for survival. Wiesel's father gave him this survival strategy when Wiesel found himself wondering about the fate of his mother and younger sister, Tzipora.

> *Your mother is still a young woman...She must be in a labor camp. And Tzipora's a big girl now, isn't she? She must be in a camp, too.*

Wiesel goes on to write about the necessity of this pretending.

> *How we should have liked to believe it. We pretended for what if the other one should still be believing it.*

Wiesel also tells the story of how he used the ability to lie as an act of self-preservation, in this case the preservation of a gold crown in his mouth. Wiesel was told to see the dentist in the camp and when there he asked the dentist what he was going to do. When the dentist replied that he was going to "simply take out your gold crown," Wiesel decided to pretend that he was sick and said, "You couldn't wait a few days, Doctor?...I don't feel very well. I've got a temperature." The dentist told him to come back when he was feeling better. Wiesel returned a week later, used the same excuse - told the same lie - and once again was spared the removal of his gold crown. Wiesel learned a few days later that the dentist had been put into prison, accused of selling the gold teeth he was extracting for his own profit.

Primo Levi was a twenty-five year old chemist when he was sent to Auschwitz in 1944. In his Holocaust memoir, *Surviving Auschwitz*, Levi also recalls instances when he found reasons to lie to another inmate and to himself.

Periodically, the concentration camp inmates were subject to the *selection process*. This was the process by which some inmates were put on a list for extermination in the gas chambers while other inmates were spared. Usually the determining criteria focused on age, health, and whether or not the inmate would be able to carry out assigned work responsibilities. The young, the old, and the infirm were often the ones most likely to be selected for the extermination list. On the eve of one selection process day, Levi was asked by an elderly inmate if Levi thought the man was at risk for being selected. Levi writes that, "I brazenly lied to old Wertheimer." Levi spoke *as if* he believed that the old man might survive the selection process because he wanted to give the man hope.

You could also lie to yourself as a means for maintaining hope and as a way to cope with the daily struggles of concentration camp life. You could act *as if* you believed you would survive whatever the camp conditions put you through. As to his own reaction to the selection process, Levi wrote:

> On this slender basis I also lived through the great
> selection of October 1944 with inconceivable tranquility.
> I was tranquil because I managed to lie to myself
> sufficiently.

As was discussed in Chapter 4, there are many reasons why we lie or tell deliberate untruths. We may want to deceive someone for our own gain, protect someone's feelings, or convince ourselves that a reality is a certain way when in fact it isn't. All of these reasons for lying were present in the concentration camps of the Holocaust. Regardless of the reason for lying, the power to lie emerges from our ability to act *as if* something is true when in fact it isn't.

These testaments from those who experienced the Holocaust firsthand provide strong evidence that, as Eisen writes " Play is far from a frivolous activity. It may take place in even the most hostile environments." The power of play in these hostile environments is captured by these words from a girl who lived in the Warsaw ghetto.

> When I am at play, I forget my hunger. I forget that outside such evil Germans are even existing. Early in the morning I rush to the child care center and I wish that the day would never end, because when it is getting dark, we all have to return home. In my room it is so full with dark shadows and black fear.

Play and its components of pretend and make-believe could lift that little girl out of the "dark shadows" and "black fear." Despite the conditions, the power of *as if* could provide children - and as we have seen, adults - with the ability to transform their reality. As Eisen wrote,

> Although the ghetto had the power to incarcerate the body, it could not clip the wings of imagination.

Why does 'as if' play continue under such startling circumstances?

BEFORE DISCUSSING SOME of the reasons why make-believe and imaginary play are powerful tools for coping with difficult circumstances, it is important to note that sometimes those circumstances are so difficult that children aren't able to play. Sometimes children are too scared, too hungry, too sick, or too injured to play.

Sometimes children have been separated from their parents or other important people in their lives and lack the basic sense of security that is needed to serve as a grounding for their play. At times the circumstances in which children live are such that the life force that provides the impulse to play may be dampened or even extinguished.

But as all of the examples discussed in this chapter suggest, we can find play existing under some very difficult circumstances so the question of 'why' is a legitimate one. What might *as if* play do for children? What purpose might it serve? What do children gain from make-believe and imaginary play and how might it help them cope with the dark and sometimes stormy nights? Many of the answers to these questions are directly related to the discussions of *as if* play found in the earlier chapters of this book.

Reality isn't the only option

MANY OF THE examples described in this chapter show children using play and the imagination to suspend and transform the reality in which they find themselves, be it the reality of the slave plantation, concentration camp, or hospital. Children can use the powers of *as if* to distance themselves from the difficulties of those realities, even if it might be for just a moment. Children engage in make-believe to "call upon the power of their imagination to create metaphors for their circumstances and simultaneously distance themselves from their circumstances by identifying with their imaginative creation." And as we saw in the life stories of Elie Wiesel and Primo Levi, this distancing from reality can also take the form of lies, those told to others and those told to oneself.

Controlling a little corner of your life

A CHILD LIVING under the oppressive conditions of the slave plantation, the horrifying daily existence of the concentration camp, or the oftentimes bewildering and scary circumstances of the hospital, gets to control very little in that experience. Daily life is dictated and

regimented by adults and sometimes painful experiences are inflict-
ed upon them by those very same adults. For some children living
under those circumstances, the play of the imagination may be the
only time when they can be in control of their lives.

The psychologist, Erik Erikson, talked about play occurring in the
microcosms of one's experience. In this little corner children can try
out ideas, try on roles, express their feelings and fears, and have life
come out the way in which they would like it to happen; all taking
place in a 'safe context,' because reality has been suspended. James
Marten, who wrote about children's experiences during the Civil
War, highlighted this function of children's play.

> In their play worlds, children can feel freedom as well
> as control, reliving pleasant experiences and reducing
> painful incidents to meaningful and bearable lessons
> and memories. In some cases, particularly in 'dramatic
> play,' happy endings can be invented, emotional release is
> achieved, and frustrations and disappointments tempered.

Writing about slave children on the plantations, Steven Mintz
concluded that for these children play could be much more than just
'wiling away the time.'

> Children were not simply slavery's victims; they were
> also active agents, who managed to resist slavery's
> dehumanizing pressures...enslaved African-American
> children did not simply play games to escape their misery;
> instead their games mirrored their surroundings. Games
> like "Hide the Switch," which concluded with the loser
> being flogged, and "auction," in which children staged
> slave auctions allowed black children to reenact what they
> saw around them in order to understand and cope with
> slavery's stresses.

This same sense of taking control and mastering experience can be
seen in medical settings as well, since "Medical play can be a vehicle
for a 'working through process' whereby children cope with stressful medical experiences and report mastery through the creation of
positive outcomes where characters can overcome illness and pain."

Sometimes using the imagination to find a little corner of control involves creating an alternate reality to the one in which you find yourself trapped. Brian Grazer and Charles Fishman tell the story of a woman, Veronica De Negri, who was taken prisoner and tortured during the time of Pinochet's dictatorial and brutal rule in Chile. This is what they learned from an interview with this survivor.

> What Veronica told me is that to survive being tortured,
> hour after hour, every day for eight months, she had to get
> into a state of flow as well, but a flow state of an alternate
> reality, that has its own narrative. That's how she survived.
> She couldn't control the physical world, but she could
> control her psychological reaction to it.

Lawrence Thornton, in his novel, *Imagining Argentina,* also provides a description of how *as if* and the imagination can give a person a feeling of control over what otherwise may seem to be uncontrollable circumstances.

Thornton's novel is set in the 1970s when the military government of Argentina was abducting those citizens who were opposing and speaking out against its rule; those who were abducted were referred to as the *disappeareds.* The protagonist of Thornton's story, Carlos, a theater director, has experienced this firsthand: his wife has disappeared. He goes about looking for his wife, and others who have disappeared, by imagining where they might be.

At one point in the story, Carlos is talking with an Auschwitz concentration camp survivor who had made his way to Argentina after the war. When asked how he and his wife had survived the horrors of Auschwitz, the survivor offers these thoughts.

> So a paradox. If you are forced to live in a nightmare, you
> survive by realizing that you can reimagine it, that some
> day you can return to reality.

Later in the story, Carlos expands on how the imagination can help one survive and even defeat ones enemies, the 'they' of the following statement.

*They can see everything they want to, but never forget
that they cannot see beyond the distortion of their
imagination where there is no color and everything
exists in black and white. And that is why we will survive,
because they do not have what is necessary to defeat us.
The real war is between our imagination and theirs, what
we can see and what they are blinded to. Do not despair.
None of them can see far enough, and so long as we do
not let them violate our imagination we will survive.*

This stands for that

AS DISCUSSED IN Chapter 2, play is an early - and powerful - form of representation or the understanding that one thing, be it an object, gesture, or word, can stand in for an idea or feeling. Much of children's imaginary play is characterized by the use of symbols to represent their ideas and feelings. The power of symbolism and representation is particularly important for children experiencing the difficult circumstances described in the present chapter.

A young child may have mastered the rudiments of her language but the ability to translate or transform ideas and feelings, especially difficult ones, into sentences to be communicated to another person is still developing. And the challenging circumstances may make that expression even more difficult. Focusing on the medical world, Nabors and her colleagues wrote that

*Telling a story through play also can provide a child with a
sense of emotional release, which can be a relief for a child
who does not have the ability to directly express all of the
emotions that he or she may be feeling related to having
an illness or experiencing medical interventions.*

At times, the symbolism and representations that emerge in imaginative play may serve as a window into a child's mind and feelings because "Following a trauma, young children may appear mute and withdrawn, and some elements of the traumatic event may show up in the child's play activities."

Vivian Paley, who has written extensively about the importance of play for young children, relates an anecdote about children's play after the 2001 World Trade Center tragedy. The children were explaining how they had to swim to safety in order to escape the exploding bullfrog. Paley comments that, "Grownups may speak often of that terrible time and there will be repeated reports and replays on television, but children must be able to imagine themselves swimming safely and using their jackets as pillows." The words of Anna Freud, who along with colleagues operated a nursery school program in London during World War II, echoes this notion: "When adults go over their experiences in conscious thought and speech, children do the same in play."

Just being human

THE DRIVE TO continue imagining other possibilities may be part of what it means to be human. It may be, as James Garbarino and his colleagues wrote in their study of children living in war zones, that children continue to play because "children with any shred of childhood left to them play." Betty Lifton, in her biography of Janusz Korczak, the Polish pediatrician who could have saved his own life but went to the gas chambers at the Treblinka concentration camp with the orphan children he wouldn't abandon, wrote that, "Despite the carnage, despite the power of man's destructiveness, the mighty life force goes on." It seems that this "mighty life force" may be the power to imagine, the power to engage in *as if* thinking. Again, as George Eisen wrote about the play he discovered existing in the ghettoes and concentration camps of the Holocaust: "Although the ghetto had the power to incarcerate the body, it could not clip the wings of the imagination."

I will let the last words of why play continues to emerge under startling circumstances come from a child herself, a 10-year-old girl living in what was then war-torn Lebanon.

> *We got a small blackboard and we were drawing and*
> *we had so much fun running and chasing each other. I*

was trying to play so much. I told my mother later I was playing as much as I could because I had a feeling that if something happened and the fighting and shelling came back, I may die and I will never get another chance to play.

Chapter 9

Being A Head Taller

We academics sometimes latch onto an idea or statement and return to it time and time again in our professional work; these are ideas that show up often in our teaching and writing. For me, one of those ideas was captured in a frequently cited statement by the Russian psychologist, Lev Vygotsky. Vygotsky believed that make-believe play was a fundamental process in the forward momentum of children's developmental growth. In discussing the importance of pretense, of *as if*, Vygotsky wrote, "In play a child always behaves beyond his average age, above his daily behavior; in play it is *as though he were a head taller than himself.*" (Italics added) There are more than three decades of university students out there who listened to me discuss the importance of Vygotsky's statement and now I am going to conclude this book by returning to it again.

How might a child behave *as if* she were a head taller? Vygotsky offered the example of a child engaged in a role-playing activity in which she is acting out the part of a sister. In this play the child needs to behave as a sister might; at least according to the child's understanding of what it means to be a sister. And that's where "being a head taller" comes in. If you were to ask this child in a non-play situation to define and explain what it means to be a sister, she might not have the verbal and conceptual skills to do so very logically. But within the play frame, she is able to act out her nascent understandings about sibling relationships. As Paul Harris wrote in his book about the importance of the imagination, "The child who pretends to bathe a doll needs to know something about water and baths." This child who pretends to bathe a doll may not be able to verbally articulate what she knows about water and baths (and babies taking baths) but the knowledge she does have is able to be expressed in the 'language' of play. The child who pretends to be a sister needs to know something about sisters. The child, however, may not have the language and conceptual ability needed to express that knowledge; she can, however, express it in the language of play.

Children, then, are often *acting out* their conceptual understandings in play; understandings that they wouldn't be able to explain outside of the play frame. The child who ties a towel around his neck and claims to be Superman, for example, might not be able to articulate in words what a superhero is or does but "in play, [is] able to express the various characteristics that [he] didn't necessarily know [he] knew." And a three-year-old who may find sharing a toy with another child on parental demand a difficult behavior to produce, manages to demonstrate the ability within a make-believe play interaction.

Vygotsky also believed that children are able to control their impulses within the play frame in ways that may elude them in everyday, non-playing life. Vygotsky wrote that "A child's greatest self-control occurs in play. He achieves the maximum display of willpower when he renounces an immediate attraction in the game." Play, according to Vygotsky, "continually creates demands on the child to act against immediate impulse." As was discussed earlier in the book, during play children must *distance* themselves from the immediate and conventional understandings of objects, people, events, and themselves. In play, "thought is separated from objects and actions and arises from ideas rather than things; a piece of wood begins to be a doll and a stick becomes a horse. Action according to rules begins to be determined by ideas and not by objects themselves." Controlling those impulses and distancing oneself from the immediate reality are all examples of behaving a head taller than yourself.

Parents helping their children be a head taller

CHILDREN ARE HELPED to be a head taller by their parents who engage in a bit of *as if* pretend play of their own. In this pretend play parents act *as if* their children are in fact a head taller. Here are a couple of examples.

The human baby is born rather helpless and dependent on adults to provide for her survival. Without us, the stark truth is that a human baby, unlike snake, alligator, or guppy babies, will die. But the human baby isn't really born totally helpless; she is born with certain reflexes that will help her enter the community of persons. Some of these reflexes lay the foundation for the development of important skills and abilities and some seem to have no real purpose and disappear as the young infant matures.

One of the important innate reflexes is the grasping reflex. Put an object in the tiny palm of a baby and those little fingers will close around the object. It isn't intentional or thoughtful on the part of the baby; it is an inborn, reflexive response. The object and the pressure the object puts on the smooth skin of that tiny palm triggers the reflex. The baby - the hand - can't help but close. Muscles automatically move, pulling bones, cartilage, and skin with them, and grasp whatever it is that triggered the response. Muscles, cartilage, bones, skin, neurons firing, synapses connecting - it's all reflexive, instinctual, and beyond the baby's control.

But the mother looking down at her baby lying in the crib doesn't see neurons firing and synapses connecting; she sees a person. She leans over and smiles, and she just wants to touch this new person she has recently brought into the world. She takes her finger and lightly places it in the palm of her baby's hand. The tiny fingers curl tenderly around the mother's finger, muscles automatically moving, pulling bones, cartilage, and skin with them. The grasping of the mother's finger is not intentional or deliberate, except of course to the mother. She doesn't see muscles, cartilage, and skin; she sees a person, a social being. As a result, the mother says, "Oh, you want to hold my hand, do you?"

The baby is not holding the mother's hand in the social, mommy and baby sense. It is only a reflex doing what a reflex does. But the mother is doing what a mother does; she is attaching meaning to the movements of that tiny hand and in some sense saying to her child that you don't know it yet but one day you will be holding my hand as a social being, and for now, I will help you act a head taller than you really are.

The second example comes from the domain of language development and illustrates how parents help their children become users of their native language.

Imagine this common scene from the local supermarket. A father is pushing a shopping cart around the market with his infant son safely strapped in the cart. The child is old enough to be sitting up by himself but has not yet developed much language. As they move about the store, the father is carrying out a conversation with his son.

"Should we have beans or carrots for dinner?" asks the father as he holds up two different jars of baby food. "Which would you like tonight?"

No words come from his child but the child's eyes do dart between the father's face and the jars being held up in the father's hands. A little smile shows on the baby's face. That's enough of an answer for the father.

"Oh, you want carrots tonight. Good choice."

This is an example of what has been called, "alter ego talk." Before children are old enough to fully comprehend language, let alone intelligibly produce it, parents often maintain both ends of the conversation. The parent takes any little gesture, glance, or babble on the part of the child as an effort to communicate and then makes an interpretation of what the child is intending and trying to say. You may not be able to communicate and express your meaning quite yet, the father is thinking, but I am going to pretend, to act *as if,* you can. I am going to assume that you are a head taller than you really are.

Kenneth Kaye, in his study of the social development of infants, wrote that, "In a way, parents are entertaining a fiction, but it is a fiction with a function." What is this fiction entertained by parents? It is the fiction that the newborn infant is holding the mother's hand and it is the fiction that infant in the shopping cart understood that the father was asking about dinner choices and then made a choice about the menu. In both cases, the parent acted *as if* the baby were more capable than he or she actually was. In the first case, the mother acted *as if* the baby had social intentions when in fact it was just the innate reflex at work. In the second case, the father acted *as if* the baby understood the language being used and was answering the question with her smile and gaze. The function of this parental make-believe, according to Kaye, is that ultimately the parent is creating the child, the person, she is pretending exists in the first place. In other words, parents pull children to new abilities by acting *as if* they are already capable of the abilities and that they are a head taller than they really are. As Kaye writes, "Evolution has produced infants who can fool their parents into treating them as more intelligent than they really are...it is precisely because parents play out this fiction that it eventually comes true."

These are examples from the world of developing children. Since this book is about the importance of make-believe, of *as if*, for all human beings and not just children, I thought it would be interesting to present some examples of adult members of the species also acting *as if* they were a head taller.

Lying to ourselves, about ourselves

IN CHAPTER 4, the discussion focused on the lies that we tell other people. Lying to other people isn't the only type of lie we can and do tell, however; we are equally adept at lying to ourselves. Self-deception may be as prevalent - and powerful - as deception that is directed at others. Why do we lie to ourselves? The reason may be as simple as the fact that "lying to ourselves...helps us accept our fraudulent behavior" and that "self-deception evolves in the service of deception - the better to fool others." In other words, we often deceive ourselves about the lie we foisted on someone else. As Robert Trivers writes in his book, *The Folly of Fools: The Logic of Deceit and Self-deception in Human Life,* we may "deceive ourselves the better to deceive others."

Trivers goes on to suggest that there are number of categories of self-deception including: the creation of false personal narratives, self-inflation, having an illusion of control, assuming a stance of moral superiority, and the derogation of others. One theme in the human penchant for self-deception is the idea that somehow we are better than other people.

> *There exists a pervasive tendency to see the self as better than others. Individuals judge positive personality attributes to be more descriptive of themselves than of the average person but see negative personality attributes as less descriptive of themselves than of the average person.*

It seems that "Most people consider themselves to be smarter than the average person, and more attractive, and a better driver, and so forth." This does sound a bit like seeing yourself as being a head taller than you really are.

At first blush, lies in the service of self-deception may seem to be, like most types of lies, a form of moral transgression and therefore should be viewed in a negative light. There are some levels of self-deception, however, that may in fact be positively related to healthy emotional development and feelings of happiness. There may be some forms of self-deception that are really our attempts at pretending to be a head taller for self-beneficial reasons. It has been suggested, for example, that "The mentally healthy person appears to have the enviable capacity to distort reality in a direction that enhances self-esteem, maintains beliefs in personal efficacy, and promotes an optimistic view of the future." In this "capacity to distort reality" we see another example of how we humans do not simply accept reality as the only option; in the case of lying to ourselves, we apparently believe that "regular doses of self-deception are good for you." Self-deception serves the purpose of being a head taller in that "By exaggerating your assessment of your chances of success, you can actually improve those chances." In other words, if I deceive myself into thinking I am more talented than I am, I may in fact achieve success with the talent that I do have.

Wearing the 'as if' coat

ONE OF MY most treasured colleagues from my years at the University of North Dakota shared a small office suite with me. There were only two offices in the suite so we saw a good deal of each other over the years and had some wonderful conversations about teaching and learning. He was one of the science educators in our college of education and taught classes on the teaching of science in elementary and high school to our undergraduates.

I noticed early on in my tenure at the college that right before he left his office for the classroom in which he taught, he would take off his sport coat and put on a white lab coat. This was his regular routine and ritual. I asked him about this routine and he told me that it was his way of making the transition from simply being a faculty member sitting in his office to being the scientist/science educator in the classroom. He said it was his way of changing his mindset and focus. In the writing of this book, I learned that he was perhaps onto something important about the act of *as if*.

In a 2012 article in the *Journal of Experimental Social Psychology* titled, "Unclothed Cognition," the authors examined the hypothesis that "wearing a piece of clothing and embodying its symbolic meaning will trigger associated psychological processes." They were interested in how the wearing of certain clothes might affect people's ability to sustain focus on a task with a minimum of errors in accomplishing the task. The specific article of clothing they were interested in was the doctor's white lab coat. They posited that "Wearing a lab coat...signifies a scientific focus and an emphasis on being careful and attentive - attributes that involve the importance of paying attention to the task at hand and not making errors." In other words, the doctor's lab coat *represented* certain qualities of mind; the lab coat *stood for* those qualities. Using the terms discussed in Chapter 2, the lab coat is the *signifier* and the attributes of scientific focus and careful attentiveness are the *signifieds*.

In this study, the investigators divided the research subjects into three treatment conditions: one group wore a doctor's white lab coat; a second group saw but did not wear a doctor's coat; and the third group wore a painter's coat. After administering the task that tested attention and focus, the results indicated that the group who actually put on and wore the doctor's lab coat performed the best; just seeing the doctor's coat did not have the same effect. The study's authors concluded that "wearing clothes causes people to 'embody' the clothing and its symbolic meaning."

Unlike young children playing doctor, the subjects in this research study were not role-playing doctors; they simply donned an article of clothing frequently associated with being a doctor. Apparently at some subconscious level of awareness the lab coat carried meaning with it, meaning that suggested a cognitive approach to an immediate experience, i.e., the experimental task. Because the research subjects put on these doctors' lab coats, they perhaps entered the research setting *as if* they carried with them the scientific focus of doctors. As a result, they behaved a head taller when completing the task. Vygotsky's concept of being a head taller never came up in my conversations with my colleague but I have a hunch he might have seen himself in his white lab coat in the same way.

Fake it until you make it

VYGOTSKY'S BELIEF THAT the playing child is acting a *head taller* than herself echoes the common maxim of *fake it until you make it*. And *fake it until you make it* brings to mind a statement by William James who is often called the father of American psychology. James is quoted as saying: "If you want a quality, act as if you already had it." In other words, pretend you can do something and someday you may just succeed. Here are some examples of people who claim to have put that principle into practice.

Theodore Roosevelt, 26th president of the United States, was well-known for having the self-discipline and determination to transform himself both physically and intellectually. Part of his process at self-transformation seems to reflect the idea of acting a head taller and faking it, as evidenced by his approach to facing his own fears: "There were all kinds of things of which I was afraid at first but by acting as if I was not afraid I gradually ceased to be afraid."

Judd Apatow, a very successful movie director and producer wrote the following about his first foray into heading up a writing staff for a television show: "Slowly I figured out how to run a writing staff and edit, but I was faking it. I was faking it for a long time."

Amy Cuddy, social psychologist and author of the book, *Presence: Bringing Your Boldest Self to Your Biggest Challenges*, tells the story of her first year in graduate school when she experienced great fear at the prospect of giving a speech. She described this anxiety in a meeting with her advisor and admitted that she was considering withdrawing from the graduate program. Her advisor replied by saying: "No, you're not. You're going to do the talk. And keep doing it - even if you have to fake it - until you have a moment when you realize that you can do it."

The singer-songwriter, James Taylor, has been part of the cultural music scene for more than fifty years. He is recognized for his distinctive guitar style and for writing and singing such classic songs as "Fire and Rain" and "Carolina in My Mind," and he was inducted into the Rock & Roll Hall of Fame in 2000. Like any other accomplished person, however, Taylor was once a novice at his chosen art form and profession. He, too, invokes the idea of pretending and playing *as if* when describing his own development as both a guitar player and song writer. In a documentary film about his life and career, Taylor said this about his learning process: "You just pretend you could play the guitar and then maybe you could...and then you pretend you could write a song and maybe you could."

Steve Jobs, the co-founder of Apple Computers, was legendary for his management style during his tenure at Apple. His extreme focus on the details of product design and manufacturing resulted in a leadership personality that could be curt, dismissive, and what some former Apple employees might characterize as abrasive, if not cruel. But like James Taylor, Jobs was also once a beginner and novice in his chosen field. Before founding Apple, Jobs worked at Atari under another legendary figure in the world of computer technology, Nolan Bushnell. Bushnell was a mentor of sorts to Jobs and at one point gave Jobs the following advice about how to behave when you have the responsibility of leading others. Bushnell is quoted as saying: "I taught him [Jobs] that if you act like you can do something, then it will work. I told him, 'Pretend to be completely in control and people will assume that you are.' "

Notice how both James Taylor and Nolan Bushnell used the word *pretend* and Teddy Roosevelt spoke of *acting as if*. Their words express the sense of *self deception* that was discussed earlier in this chapter. Even though you might not have the skills, confidence or experience needed to perform a task at an accomplished level, sometimes if you make believe you do, if you deceive yourself into thinking and acting *as if* you do have those skills, your performance will begin to develop and improve. If you act based on a "set of interrelated positive illusions - namely, unrealistically positive self-evaluations, exaggerated perceptions of control or mastery, and unrealistic optimism," then what you are pretending to be able to be and do may become what you can actually be and do. Or, in the words of Amy Cuddy, "Don't fake it 'till you make it, fake it 'till you become it."

"Smile, (or walk) tho' your heart is aching"

THERE ARE TWO songs in the American musical canon that tell us to look and act happy even if we are not feeling that way. The first is from the Broadway musical, "Bye Bye Birdie," that opened in 1960 and gave us the instructions to "Put on a happy face," even when you're feeling low.

> Pick out a pleasant outlook
> Stick out that noble chin.
> Wipe off the full of doubt look
> Slap on a happy grin.

The second song had music composed by the great comedian, Charlie Chaplin. Simply put, the song suggests the despite whatever is troubling and bringing you down, if you find a way to smile you will feel better about your circumstances.

> *Smile, 'tho your heart is aching*
> *Smile, even tho' it's breaking*
> *When there are clouds in the sky*
> *You'll get by*
> *If you*
> *Smile, through your fear and sorrow...*
> *Smile, what's the use of crying*
> *You'll find that life is still worthwhile*
> *If you'll just smile.*

The message in both of these songs is that if we act a head taller than how we may be feeling at the moment - by smiling - we actually may be able to change the way we are feeling. Although it may be true that we smile because we are experiencing positive emotions (the smile is the signifier and the emotions are the signified), it may also be possible that if we consciously and deliberately put a smile on our faces we can potentially change our emotions from negative to positive. As the psychologist William James wrote, "I don't sing because I'm happy. I'm happy because I sing."

It actually turns out that the sentiments put forth by Charlie Chaplin and "Bye Bye Birdie" may be supported by some scientific research. Consider, for example, the effect of holding chopsticks in your mouth.

Intuitively we might think that we smile for one of two reasons: one, something positive has happened in our external experience; for example, we just received a loving hug from a granddaughter. The second reason we smile comes from an internal source, for example, a pleasant memory of the hug we received during the last visit by the granddaughter. In both cases, our smile is a consequence and representation of the experience. We feel positive so we smile. There has been a line of research, however, that suggests it may be possible for the relationship between smiling and feelings to work in the opposite direction; we will experience positive emotions *if* we smile. That's where the chopsticks come in.

Imagine a chopstick held horizontally between your lips, as far back in your mouth as possible. The physical presence of the chopstick in your mouth causes your facial muscles to move *as if* they are forming a smile; a smile that was not produced by the experience of a positive emotion but by the chopsticks. A number of research studies have looked at the effect of this artificially produced smile on emotions.

One line of smile research looked at the effect of smiling on the response to stress. A commonly occurring indicator for the experience of stress is an elevated heart rate. Two of the stress inducing methods used in the research studies included: subjects submerging their hands in frigid water for a period of time, and subjects completing a very challenging task, for example, copying a design using their non-dominant hand while only being able to see the mirror image of what they were drawing. Clinical measures, i.e., elevated heart rate, suggested that both of these conditions were indeed stressful. Holding chopsticks in the mouth in order to induce the physical characteristic of a smile had the effect of alleviating stress in the individuals, i.e., reducing their elevated heart rates.

There have also been studies that look at the effects of induced smiling on participants' perceptions of humor. Subjects were shown a series of cartoons and asked to rate them in terms of perceived humor or 'funniness.' Some of the subjects saw the cartoons *after* having their smiles provoked by chopsticks; subjects in a control group were presented the cartoons without first experiencing the provoked smile. The results here showed the positive effect of smiling; the subjects who experienced the chopstick smiling generally rated the cartoons as funnier than the subjects in the control group. In other words, smiling - even smiling artificially produced - caused the subjects to be more receptive to humor.

Smiling even when you don't feel like it may not be the only way to fool yourself into feeling better. Walking *as if* you are happy may do the trick as well.

Research has found that people who are depressed often have a different walking pattern than individuals who are not depressed. Some of the characteristics of 'depressed walking' include: a slower walking speed, more movement side to side, a slumped posture, and less vigorous arm swings. A provocative research study examined whether inducing this 'depressed walking' pattern in people could actually affect people's recall of either emotionally negative or positive words.

The participants in this study were asked to walk on a treadmill while watching a gauge mounted in front of them. They were given the task of walking on the treadmill so that the gauge would move either to the right or to the left. (The direction depended on which group they were in.) Unbeknownst to the participants, the gauge would move right or left depending on whether their walking gait mimicked the gait of depressed or non-depressed individuals.

While the subjects were walking, they were given a list of words to recall, words that were either negative or positive in their emotional tone. The research aim was to assess what is called *affective memory bias*, which would be determined by the difference between the number of negative and positive words recalled. The participants were asked to recall these words while still walking on the treadmill.

The main result of the study was that, "memory for negative words did in fact change substantially with walking pattern." In other words, those participants who were manipulated into adopting a 'depressed walking' pattern did recall significantly more negative words than the 'non-depressed' walkers. The 'non-depressed' walking group remembered more positive terms than the 'depressed' group but the difference between the groups was not statistically significant.

Like so many other experimental, laboratory-based research studies, the results of the walking study and the smiling studies can only be viewed as 'interestingly suggestive.' But like the Langer study on aging discussed in Chapter 7, pretending to be a head taller really doesn't cost or risk very much, just like the young child isn't risking very much in her pretend play. If acting *as if* you are younger may result in feeling younger; and if smiling and walking *as if* you are happy may cause you to feel happier, it certainly seems to be worth the pretending.

Being a head taller in school

IN A 2011 report, titled, "Let's pretend: Solving the education crisis in America," two psychologists, Fred Newman and Lenora Fulani, suggest that the key to improving the educational outcomes for children who typically don't succeed in school is to pretend that they can. They believe that "projects like the Harlem Children's Zone, the KIPP schools and many other charter schools succeed where much else fails because the teams running those projects are collectively pretending that the kids can become learners." Much like parents treating their young children *as if* they are social and *as if* they can participate in a conversation, the children in these types of schools are "actively related to as learners - even though they have not yet become that."

Newman and Fulani are invoking Vygotsky's notion of being a head taller for their analysis of how some schools are successfully getting children to see themselves as capable learners and then performing as capable learners. This idea of performance is central to their position on teaching and learning. They write that, "in our view, a fundamental tool for education reformers is the tool of performance. The act of pretending to be something other than you are, used self-consciously and collectively is a tool for growth."

Newman and Fulani are not reticent about the power of performing, pretending, and acting *as if* you are a head taller in the context of education and schooling. In their minds, the problems of underachieving children and underachieving schools would be solved by a focus on children being treated *as if* they were capable learners.

We believe that if such a national 'performance' were created, the education crisis in America would be over. Children, having developed the capacity to pretend to be who they are not, i.e., good learners, also develop the capacity to become the thing they are pretending to be. And, thus, if we could all together assist poor and minority kids in pretending that they are classroom achievers, they could choose to become that.

Writing as if you are a head taller

AS I APPROACHED the final words of this book and reflected on the process of putting my thoughts down on paper all these years, I came to realize that in many ways this book itself was an act of *as if*, an act of being a head taller. First, I worked on this book *as if* I had something important to say. When I encountered moments of self-doubt, of which there were many, I was able to re-motivate myself by believing (or at least pretending) that my overall idea for the book was somewhat unique and could offer an interesting perspective on how we think about the human ability to engage in make-believe. The fact that the book was finally completed is a testament to the fact that I was able to convince myself of that premise. I was able to continue entering the 'writing frame' and act *as if* my beliefs about the value of the project were true.

I also continued to work on this book *as if* there would be an audience out there who might find the book someday and choose to read it. I made believe that you, the reader, might actually exist. You, this pretend and hoped for reader, was my imaginary friend - and sometime muse - throughout the writing process. I have to say that there were many moments when you didn't hold up your end of the bargain and you refused to show up; those moments led to times when I couldn't find the motivation to enter the 'writing frame.' But eventually I was able to conjure you back up again and you agreed to sit there on my desk, or just above the laptop screen, and I continued with my make-believe. I also remembered the words of Richard Rodriguez who reflected on his own writing process in his book, *Hunger of Memory*: "I write very slowly because I write under the obligation to make myself clear to someone who knows nothing about me." I certainly wrote slowly; you, the reader, can decide if I wrote clearly.

So, if someone (a real someone) out there is now holding this book, I guess all of my make-believe play paid off. Whatever self-deception in which I engaged - being overly confident, exaggerating a sense of my abilities - allowed me to stay with the project despite numerous periods of self-doubt. And keeping you, my imaginary friend and reader, in mind helped me act a head taller than I actually was and let me become the person who actually wrote this book. I guess you really can fake it until you make it.

Notes

Introduction

PAGE

2 *I saw her that Saturday morning...*This anecdote was a personal observation.

3 *Browse through the research oriented journal, Child Development...*

Tamis-LeMonda, C., Shannon, J. D., Cabrera, N. J., & Lamb, M. E. (2004). Fathers and mothers at play with their 2- and 3-year-olds: Contributions to language and cognitive development. *Child Development, 75*(6), 1806-1820.

Howe, N., Petrakos, H., Rinaldi, C. M., & LeFebvre, R. (2005). "This is a bad dog, you know...": Constructing shared meanings during sibling pretend play. *Child Development, 76*(4), 783-794.

3 *Browse the shelves of the local bookstore...*

Brown, S. (2009). *Play: How it shapes the brain, opens the imagination, and invigorates the soul.* NY: Avery.

Paley, V. (2004). *A child's work: The importance of fantasy play.* Chicago: The University of Chicago Press.

3 *Consult the policy and position statements of the National Association for the Education of Young Children...*

Copple, C., & Bredekamp, S. (Eds.) (2009). *Developmentally appropriate practice.* Washington, DC: NAEYC. (p. 328)

4 *As Brian Sutton-Smith...*

Sutton-Smith, B. (1997). *The ambiguity of play.* Cambridge, MA: Harvard University Press. (p. 1)

6 *One dictionary defines the word, empathy...*
Pocket Oxford American Dictionary, Second Edition, 2008, NY.

8 *...under what one author called some very startling circumstances.*

Eisen, G. (1988). *Children and play in the Holocaust: Games among the shadows.* Amherst, MA: The University of Massachusetts Press. (p. 22)

8 *President Theodore Roosevelt suggested that the way to conquer a fear...*

Goodwin, D. K. (2013). *The bully pulpit: Theodore Roosevelt, William Howard Taft, and the golden age of journalism.* NY: Simon & Schuster. (p. 40)

9 *As the psychologist Alison Gopnik has written...*

Gopnik, A. (2005, December 20). The real reason children love fantasy: Kids aren't escapists, they're little scientists. slate.com.

(https://slate.com/culture/2005/12/children-s-love-of-fantasy.html)

Chapter 1: As If, or Reality Isn't the Only Option

PAGE

12 *As the psychologist Alison Gopnik has written...*

Gopnik, A. (2009). *The philosophical baby: What children's minds tell us about truth, love, and the meaning of life.* NY: Farrar, Straus, and Giroux. (p. 19)

12 *And as Jonathan Gottschall has written...*

Gottschall, J. (2012). *The storytelling animal: How stories make us human.* Boston: Houghton Mifflin Harcourt. (p. xiv)

15 *The English anthropologist and linguist Gregory Bateson...*

Bateson, G. (1971). The message "This is Play." In R. E. Herron & B. Sutton-Smith (Eds.). *Child's play* (pp. 261-266). NY: John Wiley & Sons.

15 *...what Peter Gray refers to...*

Gray, P. (2013). *Free to learn: Why unleashing the instinct to play will make our children happier, more self-reliant, and better students for life.* NY: Basic Books. (p. 150)

15 *...children can "draw on forms of thinking and logic..."*

Engel, S. (2005). *Real kids: Creating meaning in everyday life.* Cambridge, MA: Harvard University Press. (p. 103)

16 *As Stuart Brown wrote in his book...*

Brown, S. (2009). *Play: How it shapes the brain, opens the imagination, and invigorates the soul.* NY: Avery. (p. 97)

16 *..."the child who pretends to bathe a doll..."*

Harris, P. (2000). *The work of the imagination.* Malden, MA: Blackwell Publishing. (p. 2)

16 *As Paul Harris writes in his book...*

Harris, P. (2000). (p. 25)

16 *..."we use the predetermining elements of the life space..."*

Newman, F., & Holzman, L. (1993). *Lev Vygotsky: Revolutionary scientist.* NY: Routledge. (p. 101)

18 *As Bateman writes...*

Bateman, C. (2014). What are we playing with? Role-taking, role play, and story play with Tolkein's legendarium. *International Journal of Play, 3*(2), 107-118. (p. 111)

20 *"much of their play..."*

Engel, S. (2005). *Real kids: Creating meaning in everyday life.* Cambridge, MA: Harvard University Press. (p. 83)

20 *Lenore Terr, a psychiatrist who has worked with...*

Terr, L. C. (1991). Childhood traumas: An outline and overview. *American Journal of Psychiatry,* 148, 10-20.

Terr, L. C. (1981). "Forbidden Games": Post-traumatic child's play. *Journal of the American Academy of Child Psychiatry,* 20, 741-760.

21 *..."reinvent [this] experience in order to learn...*

Erikson, E. H. (1972). Play and actuality. In M. W. Piers (ed.), *Play and development* (pp. 127-167). NY: W. W. Norton & Company. (p. 132)

21 *The essayist Roger Rosenblatt...*

Rosenblatt, R. (2013). *The boy detective: A New York childhood.* NY: HarperCollins. (p. 217)

21 *As the Russian psychologist Lev Vygotsky wrote...*

Vygotsky, L. S. (1978). The role of play in development. In L. S. Vygotsky, *Mind in society: The development of higher psychological processes* (pp. 92-104). Cambridge, MA: Harvard University Press. (pp. 96-97)

21 ..."the imagination liberates us..."

Singer, D. G., & Singer, J. L. (1990). *The house of make-believe: Children's play and the developing imagination*. Cambridge, MA: Harvard University Press. (p. 20)

21 *Children even distance themselves...*

Harris, P. (2000). *The work of the imagination*. Malden, MA: Blackwell Publishing. (p. 18)

22 *When children enter the play frame...*

Berk, L. E. (1994). Vygotsky's theory: The importance of make believe. *Young Children, 50*(1), pp. 30-39. (p. 32)

22 *As bad as that would be for we adults...*

Bloom, P. (2013). *Just babies: The origins of good and evil*. NY: Crown Publishers. (p. 21)

22 *The human being's ability...*

Singer, D. G., & Singer, J. L. (1990). *The house of make-believe: Children's play and the developing imagination*. Cambridge, MA: Harvard University Press. (p. 19)

22 *It is the "special mystery..."*

Singer, D. G., & Singer, J. L. (1990). (p. vii)

23 *If the play is to be maintained...*

Harris, P. (2000). *The work of the imagination*. Malden, MA: Blackwell Publishing. (p. 111)

23 *As Vygotsky wrote...*

Vygotsky, L. S. (1978). The role of play in development. In L. S. Vygotsky, *Mind in society: The development of higher psychological processes* (pp. 92-104). Cambridge, MA: Harvard University Press. (p. 94)

24 *Vygotsky went as far as stating that...*

Vygotsky, L. S. (1978). (p. 99)

25 *The child's play, in other words...*

Saler, M. (2012). *As if: Modern enchantment and the literary prehistory of virtual reality*. NY: Oxford University Press. (p. 20)

Chapter 2: This Stands for That

PAGE

29 *What is significant about deferred imitation...*

Fein, G. G. (1975). A transformational analysis of pretending. *Developmental Psychology, 11*(3), 291-296. (p. 291)

32 *They didn't have real weapons...*

Berger, M. (1941, November 23). American soldier - One year after. *New York Times,* pg. SM3 (3-4; 29-30).

41 *"The telegraph had given [him] a power..."*

Wheeler, T. (2008). *Mr. Lincoln's T-Mails: The untold story of how Abraham Lincoln used the telegraph to win the Civil War*. NY: HarperCollins. (p. 65)

43 *"the history of mankind had been controlled..."*

Wheeler, T. (2008). (p. xvi)

43 *"The spirits of the leaders past..."*
Wheeler, T. (2008). (p. 1)

44 *"precise vocabulary of stitches and colors"*
Abbott, K. (2014). *Liar, temptress, solider, spy: Four women undercover in the Civil War*. NY: Harper. (p. 113)

44 *If news about President Lincoln...*
Abbott, K. (2014). (p. 25)

45 *"a significant factor hastening the Allied victory..."*
Nez, C. (2011). *Code talker*. NY: Penguin Books. (p. iv)

46 *"a completely undiscovered and unsuspected dimension..."*
Adkins, L. (2003). *Empires of the plain: Henry Rawlinson and the lost languages of Babylon*. NY: St. Martin's Press. (p. xxiii)

47 *As the author Wallace Stevens wrote..."*
Geary, J. (2011). *I is an other: The secret life of metaphor and how it shapes the way we see the world*. NY: HarperCollins. (Epigraph)

49 *Justice Rehnquist wrote...*
https://www.law.cornell.edu/supremecourt/text/491/397#writing-USSC_CR_0491_0397_ZD

50 *Similarly, Justice Stevens argued...*
https://www.law.cornell.edu/supremecourt/text/491/397#writing-USSC_CR_0491_0397_ZD

52 *what the psychologist D. W. Winnicott called...*
Winnicott, D. W. (1971). *Playing and reality*. NY: Penguin.

52 *As Susan Linn wrote in her book...*
Linn, S. (2008). *The case for make believe: Saving play in a commercialized world*. NY: New Press. (p. 74)

52 *"Not so much the object used as the use of the object."*
Winnicott, D. W. (1971). *Playing and reality*. NY: Penguin. (p. xii)

Chapter 3: Standing in the Other Person's Shoes

PAGE

55 *In his book, Copernicus "defied common sense..."*
Sobel, D. (2011). *A more perfect heaven: How Copernicus revolutionized the cosmos*. NY: Walker & Company. (p. 3)

56 *Jean Piaget, wrote that children themselves experience...*
Piaget, J. (1968). *Six psychological studies*. NY: Vintage Book. (p. 9)

58 *..."an individual has a theory of mind..."*
Astington, J. W. (1993). *The child's discovery of the mind*. Cambridge, MA: Harvard University Press. (p. 4)

59 *One morning he wanted to read...*
dePaolo, T. (1978). *Pancakes for breakfast*. Orlando, FL: Harcourt.

60 *As the author Richard Rodriguez stated...*
Rodriguez, R. (1982). *Hunger of memory*. Boston: David R. Godine. (p. 186)

64 ...*as Goleman writes...*

Goleman, D. (2013). *Focus: The hidden driver of intelligence.* NY: Harper. (p. 119)

65 *The psychologist Martin Hoffman offers this definition of empathy.*

Hoffmann, M. (2000). *Empathy and moral development: Implications of caring and justice.* NY: Cambridge University Press. (p. 29)

66 *that our species could be called Homo empathic...*

Kryznaric, R. (2014). *Empathy: Why it matters and how we get it.* NY: Perigee. (p. xiii)

66 *For example, Goleman discusses a research study...*

Goleman, D. (2013). *Focus: The hidden driver of intelligence.* NY: Harper.

67 *"Pretense is important to theory of mind because in pretend play..."*

Lillard, A. (2001). Pretend play as Twin Earth: A social-cognitive analysis. *Developmental Review, 21,* 495-531. (p. 514)

67 *Role play is striking because children...*

Harris, P. L. (2000). *The work of the imagination.* Malden, MA: Blackwell. (p. 30)

69 *The psychologist Alan Leslie...*

Astington, J. W. (1993). *The child's discovery of the mind.* Cambridge, MA: Harvard University Press. (p. 55-6)

69 *And two other researchers, Judy Dunn and Claire Hughes...*

Dunn, J., & Hughes, C. (2001). "I got some swords and you're dead!" Violent fantasy, antisocial behavior, friendship, and moral sensibility in young children. *Child Development, 72*(2), 491-505. (p. 492)

70 *As Tracy Gleason, a professor psychology...*

Gleason, T. (2016, April 6). Why make-believe play is an important part of childhood development.

http://theconversation.com/why-make-believe-play-is-an-important-part-of-childhood-development-49693.

70 *There is some suggestion from research studies...*

Youngblood, L. M., & Dunn, J. (1995). Individual differences in young children's pretend play with mother and sibling: Links to relationships and understanding of other people's feelings and beliefs. *Child Development, 66,* 1472-1492.

71 *"are due to the fact that children..."*

Lillard, A. (2001). Pretend play as Twin Earth: A social-cognitive analysis. *Developmental Review, 21,* 495-531. (p. 499)

71 *As Lillard wrote, "When children pretend..."*

Lillard, A. (2001). (p. 512)

71 *The psychologist Steven Pinker...*

Pinker, S. (2012). *The better angels of our nature.* NY: Penguin Books. (p. 175-176)

71 *The novelist Julian Barnes...*

Kryznaric, R. (2014). *Empathy: Why it matters and how we get it.* NY: Perigee. (p. 131)

71 *And another novelist, Meg Rosoff...*

Rosoff, M. (2017, September 15). What Richard Dawkins could learn from Goldilocks and the Three Bears. *Guardian.* https://www.theguardian.com/books/2017/sep/15/meg-rosoff-point-of-view-fairytales.

72 *And as the main character in Lloyd Jones' novel...*

Jones, L. (2008). *Mister Pip*. NY: Dial Press. (p. 231)

73 *Mind-mindness has been defined as...*

Meins, E., Fernyhough, C., Arnold, B., Leekam, S. R., & de Roseau, M. (2013). Mind-mindness and theory of mind: Mediating roles of language and perspectival symbolic play. *Child Development, 84*(5), 1777-1790. (p. 1778)

76 *"our enemies - to acknowledge..."*

Kryznaric, R. (2014). *Empathy: Why it matters and how we get it*. NY: Perigee. (p. xv)

78 *As Robert Kennedy wrote...*

Kennedy, R. (1971). *Thirteen days: A memoir of the Cuban missile crisis*. NY: W. W. Norton & Co. (p. 95)

Chapter 4: The Truth Isn't the Only Option

PAGE

82 *A study conducted by the Science Museum of London...*

Poulson, K. (2010, September 8). Lying may be distasteful but it's also a right. *USA Today,* pg. 11A.

82 *In a research study carried out in the United States...*

Feldman, R. (2009). *The liar in your life: The way to truthful relationships*. NY: Twelve. (p. 14)

82 *Lying is so pervasive...*

Poulson, K. (2010, September 8). Lying may be distasteful but it's also a right. *USA Today,* pg. 11A.

82 *We might think that our doctor's office...*

Iezzoni, L. I., Sowmya, R., Rao, C. M., DesRoches, C. V., & Campbell, E. G. (2012). Survey shows that at least some physicians are not always open or honest with patients. *Health Affairs, 31*: pp. 383-391.

83 *A 2006 study...*

Sprinks, J. (2013). Nurses warned of ethical perils of lying to patients with dementia. *Nursing Standard, 28*(1), p. 5.

83 *In his memoir about his life as a neurosurgeon...*

Marsh, H. (2015). *Do no harm: Stories of life, death, and brain surgery*. NY: Thomas Dunne Books. (p. 173)

85 *According to a survey of 2000 people...*

Open thread: The most lied-about books. *Guardian* (2003). https://www.theguardian.com/books/booksblog/2013/sep/09/have-you-ever-lied-about-a-book?CMP=twt_gu

85 *...the novelist Russell Banks...*

By the Book, NYTimes.com, January 2, 2014. https://www.nytimes.com/2014/01/05/books/review/russell-banks-by-the-book.html

86 *Broadly speaking, we lie for one of three reasons...*

Vasek, M. E. (1986). Lying as a skill: The development of deception in children. In R. W. Mitchell & N. S. Thompson (Eds.), *Deception: Perspectives on human and nonhuman deceit* (pp. 271-293). NY: State University of New York Press.

86 *Harry Truman, before he became president...*

McCullough, D. (1992). *Truman*. NY: Simon & Schuster. (p. 68)

88 *For example, Sissela Bok...*

Bok, S. (1978). *Lying: Moral choice in public and private life*. NY: Vintage. (p. 13)

89 *As one article looking at the difference between lying and pretending pointed out...*

Taylor, M., Lussier, G. L., & Maring, B. L. (2003). The distinction between lying and pretending. *Journal of Cognition and Development, 4*(3), 299-323. (p. 300)

90 *"Human beings are the grandmasters of mendacity...*

Smith, D. L. (2004). *Why we lie: The evolutionary roots of deception and the unconscious mind*. NY: St. Martin's Press. (p. 10)

90 *Paul Ekman suggests that...*

Ekman, P. (1989). *Telling lies: Clues to deceit in the marketplace, politics, and marriage*. NY: W. W. Norton & Company. (p. 66)

90 *And according to Robert Feldman...*

Feldman, R. (2009). *The liar in your life: The way to truthful relationships*. NY: Twelve. (p. 64)

91 *The use of lies in raising children...*

Heyman, G. D., Luu, D. H., & Lee, K. (2009). Parenting by lying. *Journal of Moral Education, 38*(3), 353-369.

92 *Parents in Tzeltal-speaking...*

Heyman, G. D., Luu, D. H., & Lee, K. (2009). (p. 363)

92 *"Taken together, our findings suggest..."*

Heyman, G. D., Hsu, A. S., Fu, G., & Lee, K. (2012). Instrumental lying by parents in the US and China. *International Journal of Psychology*, pp. 1-9. (p. 8)

93 *I looked at Mum and realized...*

Buckley, C. (2009). *Losing Mum and Pup: A memoir*. NY: Twelve. (p. 55)

93 *The first lies of children are generally produced in response...*

Vasek, M. E. (1986). Lying as a skill: The development of deception in children. In R. W. Mitchell & N. S. Thompson (Eds.), *Deception: Perspectives on human and nonhuman deceit* (pp. 271-293). NY: State University of New York Press.

93 *The earliest lies of children...*

Feldman, R. (2009). *The liar in your life: The way to truthful relationships*. NY: Twelve. (p. 64)

93 *It doesn't take long...*

Talwar, V., Murphy, S. M., & Lee, K. (2007). White lie-telling in children for politeness purposes. *International Journal of Behavioral Development, 31*(1), 1-11.

93 *As Feldman writes in his book...*

Feldman, R. (2009). *The liar in your life: The way to truthful relationships*. NY: Twelve. (p. 64)

99 *Young children are prone to what has been called semantic leakage...*

Talwar, V., Gordon, H. M., & Lee, K. (2007). Lying in the elementary years: Verbal deception and its relation to second-order belief understanding. *Developmental Psychology, 43*(3), 804-810. (p. 804)

99 *It is quite common for children to peek under the cloth...*

Feldman, R. (2009). *The liar in your life: The way to truthful relationships*. NY: Twelve.

99 *It has been suggested that the development of semantic leakage control...*

Talwar, V., Gordon, H. M., & Lee, K. (2007). Lying in the elementary years: Verbal deception and its relation to second-order belief understanding. *Developmental Psychology, 43*(3), 804-810.

100 *The liar must be "aware of his listener's knowledge..."*

de Villiers, J. G., & de Villiers, P. A. (1978). *Language acquisition*. Cambridge, MA: Harvard University Press. (p. 164)

100 *"Must be able to have an appropriate assessment..."*

Talwar, V., Gordon, H. M., & Lee, K. (2007). Lying in the elementary years: Verbal deception and its relation to second-order belief understanding. *Developmental Psychology, 43*(3), 804-810. (p. 804)

100 *Paul Harris in his book...*

Harris, P. L. (2000). *The work of the imagination*. Malden, MA: Blackwell. (p. 47)

101 *For Harris, "the study of early pathology..."*

Harris, P. L. (2000). (p. 6)

101 *Baron-Cohen's concept of mind blindness...*

Baron-Cohen, S. (1995). *Mindblindness: An essay on autism and theory of mind*. Cambridge, MA: The MIT Press.

101 *...and Wolfberg's suggestion that...*

Wolfberg, P. J. (1999). *Play & Imagination in children with autism*. NY: Teachers College Press. (p. 18)

101 *Feldman goes as far as saying...*

Feldman, R. (2009). *The liar in your life: The way to truthful relationships*. NY: Twelve. (p. 73)

101 *"Autistic children don't know about cheating"*

Park, C. C. (1982). *The siege: The first eight years of an autistic child*. Boston: Little, Brown and Company. (p. 310)

101 *"The inability to lie convincingly..."*

Park, C. C. (2001). *Exiting Nirvana: A daughter's life with autism*. Boston: Little, Brown and Company. (p. 57)

101 *Feldman notes the irony of this situation when he writes..."*

Feldman, R. (2009). *The liar in your life: The way to truthful relationships*. NY: Twelve. (p. 73)

Chapter 5: Real Friends Aren't the Only Option

PAGE

107 *His name was William Martin.*

Macintyre, B. (2010). *Operation Mincemeat: How a dead man and a bizarre plan fooled the Nazis and assured an Allied victory.* NY: Crown.

108 *memorialized as the "man who never was"*

Montagu, E. (1953). *The man who never was.* Philadelphia: Lippincott.

108 *The intelligence agents...*

Macintyre, B. (2010). *Operation Mincemeat: How a dead man and a bizarre plan fooled the Nazis and assured an Allied victory.* NY: Crown. (p. 296)

110 *The artist Frida Kahlo wrote the following...*

Herrera, H. (1983). *Frida: A biography of Frida.* NY: Perennial. (p. 15)

110 *"We were quite cruel about her leg..."*

Herrera, H. (1983). (p. 15)

111 *She would encounter this friend by entering another world.*

Herrera, H. (1983). (p. 15-16)

111 *while she danced...*

Herrera, H. (1983). (p. 15-16)

111 *When I returned to the window...*

Herrera, H. (1983). (p. 16)

112 *In one research study, for example, not a single child...*

Gleason, T., Sebanc, A. M., & Hartup, W. W. (2000). Imaginary companions of preschool children. *Developmental Psychology, 36*(4), 419-428.

112 *There is also research finding that children without imaginary friends...*

Gopnik, A. (2009). *The philosophical baby: What children's minds tell us about truth, love, and the meaning of life.* NY: Farrar, Straus, and Giroux. (p. 52)

112 *These differences may develop because "children with imaginary companions..."*

Trifoni, G., & Reese, E. (2009). A good story: Children with imaginary companions create richer narratives. *Child Development, 80*(4), 1301-1313. (p. 1310)

112 *"children has sole knowledge of their imaginary companions..."*

Trifoni, G., & Reese, E. (2009). (p. 1310)

113 *"He doesn't have a bike, I go much faster than him."*

Coetzee, H., & Shute, R. (2003). "I run faster than him because I have faster shoes.": Perceptions of competence and gender role stereotyping in children's imaginary friends. *Child Study Journal, 33*(4), 257-271. (p. 263)

113 *This type of relationship produces such comments as...*

Coetzee, H., & Shute, R. (2003). (p. 264)

113 *a view that the psychologist Alison Gopnik...*

Gopnik, A. (2009). *The philosophical baby: What children's minds tell us about truth, love, and the meaning of life.* NY: Farrar, Straus, and Giroux. (p. 51)

114 *Marjorie Taylor, who has conducted extensive research...*

Taylor, M. (1999). *Imaginary companions and the children who create them.* NY: Oxford University Press. (p. 60)

114 *One child, whose imaginary friend was named Whisper...*

Meltz, B. (2000, October 12). Johnny's imaginary friends should be welcome anytime. *Boston Globe.*

http://archive.boston.com/lifestyle/family/articles/2000/10/12/johnnys_imaginary_friends_should_be_welcome_anytime/

114 *"distance themselves from 'Bad me' percepts as well as hold onto..."*

Friedberg, R. D. (1995). Allegorical lives: Children and their imaginary companions. *Child Study Journal, 25*(1), 1-21. (p. 3)

114 *The novelist Anthony Marra...*

Marra, A. (2013). *A constellation of vital phenomena: A novel.* NY: Hogarth. (p. 119)

115 *"Whisper is so angry with you, Daddy."*

Meltz, B. (2000, October 12). Johnny's imaginary friends should be welcome anytime. *Boston Globe.*

http://archive.boston.com/lifestyle/family/articles/2000/10/12/johnnys_imaginary_friends_should_be_welcome_anytime/

115 *"Interactions with imaginary companions often include..."*

Taylor, M. (1999). *Imaginary companions and the children who create them.* NY: Oxford University Press. (p. 84)

115 *This function of control...*

Erikson, E. (1972). Play and actuality. In M. W. Piers (Ed.), *Play and development* (pp. 127-167). NY: W. W. Norton & Company.

115 *"allow children to explore issues of control..."*

Gurian, A. (2010). When your child's new friend is imaginary. http://www.education.com/reference/article/Ref_When_Your_Childs_New/

115 *The child doesn't have to worry about...*

Taylor, M. (1999). *Imaginary companions and the children who create them.* NY: Oxford University Press. (p. 64)

115 *Consider this reflection...*

Weaver, L. H. (1983). Forbidden fancies: A child's vision of Mennonite plainness. *Journal of Ethnic Studies, 1*(3), 51-59. (p. 55)

116 *"To insiders, plainness constitutes normality...*

Weaver, L. H. (1983). (p. 51)

116 *But as Laura also recognized...*

Weaver, L. H. (1983). (p. 53)

116 *"As a Mennonite child..."*

Weaver, L. H. (1983). (p. 54)

116 *"Some of us children began..."*

Weaver, L. H. (1983). (p. 52)

116 *As an adult, Laura..."*

Weaver, L. H. (1983). (p. 58)

116 *"My adult distress as the lack of versatility..."*

Weaver, L. H. (1983). (p. 55)

117 *Well, yes, I say definitely that Elwood drinks...*

Chase, M. (1971). *Harvey*. NY: Dramatists Play Service. (p. 14)

117 *Marjorie Taylor, for example, tells the story of a 3-year-old...*

Harris, P. (2000). *The work of the imagination*. Malden, MA: Blackwell Publishing. (p. 58)

118 *The writer, Adam Gopnik tells the story of Charlie Ravioli...*

Gopnik, A. (2002, September 30). Bumping into Mr. Ravioli. *The New Yorker, 78*(29). (p. 80)

119 *Other parents come to understand that the friend they keep hearing about...*

Meltz, B. (2000, October 12). Johnny's imaginary friends should be welcome anytime. *Boston Globe.*

http://archive.boston.com/lifestyle/family/articles/2000/10/12/johnnys_imaginary_friends_should_be_welcome_anytime/

119 *In her book...*

Taylor, M. (1999). *Imaginary companions and the children who create them*. NY: Oxford University Press. (p. 21)

120 *"throw some parents for a loop"*

Meltz, B. (2000, October 12). Johnny's imaginary friends should be welcome anytime. *Boston Globe.*

http://archive.boston.com/lifestyle/family/articles/2000/10/12/johnnys_imaginary_friends_should_be_welcome_anytime/

120 *Taylor and her colleague Anne Mannering...*

Taylor, M., & Mannering, A. M. (2007). Of Hobbes and Harvey: The imaginary companions of children and adults. In A. Goncu & S. Gaskins (Eds.), *Play and development: Evolutionary, sociocultural and functional perspectives* (pp. 227-245). Mahwah, NJ: Lawrence Erlbaum. (p. 236)

120 *When parents do attempt to discourage...*

Taylor, M. (1999). *Imaginary companions and the children who create them*. NY: Oxford University Press.

120 *If you want to know how your child...*

Taylor, M. (1999). (p. 78)

121 *Play with an imaginary companion...*

Taylor, M., & Mannering, A. M. (2007). Of Hobbes and Harvey: The imaginary companions of children and adults. In A. Goncu & S. Gaskins (Eds.), *Play and development: Evolutionary, sociocultural and functional perspectives* (pp. 227-245). Mahwah, NJ: Lawrence Erlbaum. (p. 234)

122 *"invented universes with distinctive languages..."*

Gopnik, A. (2009). *The philosophical baby: What children's minds tell us about truth, love, and the meaning of life*. NY: Farrar, Strauss, and Giroux. (p. 53)

122 *"The shift...to paracosms may..."*

Gopnik, A. (2009). (p. 61)

122 *fewer children create paracosms...*

Root-Bernstein, M., & Root-Bernstein, R. (2006). Imaginary worldplay in childhood and its impact on adult creativity. *Creativity Resesarch Journal, 18*(4), 405-425.

122 *As a teenager, Wilson was fascinated...*

Berg, A. S. (2013). *Wilson*. NY: G. P. Putnam's Sons. (p. 44)

122 *"began imagining that he was an admiral..."*

Berg, A. S. (2013). (p. 44)

123 *He fantasized once again about what he dubbed...*

Berg, A. S. (2013). (p. 48-49)

123 *"virtual universes...consisting of histories...*

McGreevy, A. (1993). The parsonage children: An analysis of the creative early years of the Brontes of Haworth. *Gifted Child Quarterly, 39*(3), 146-153. (p. 150)

123 *According to one study...*

Root-Bernstein, M., & Root-Bernstein, R. (2006). Imaginary worldplay in childhood and its impact on adult creativity. *Creativity Resesarch Journal, 18*(4), 405-425.

124 *Juan Pujol Garcia was a Spaniard...*

Macintyre, B. (2012). *Double cross: The true story of the D-Day spies.* NY: Crown Publishers.

124 *His imaginary agents "began recruiting their own sub-agents..."*

Macintyre, B. (2012). (pp. 116-117)

125 *"simply too well placed for [his] own good..."*

Macintyre, B. (2012). (p. 126)

126 *"for deception...imaginary agents..."*

Macintyre, B. (2010). *Operation Mincemeat: How a dead man and a bizarre plan fooled the Nazis and assured an Allied victory.* NY: Crown. (p. 61)

126 *"Real agents tended to become truculent..."*

Macintyre, B. (2010). (p. 61-62)

126 *"Sometimes those friends were real..."*

Collins, J. (2014, November 19). I'm out. *Players Tribune.*

https://www.theplayerstribune.com/en-us/articles/jason-collins-retires

126 *"West had the furniture covered with drop cloths..."*

Clarke, T. (2013). *JFK's last hundred days: The transformation of a man and the emergence of a great president.* NY: The Penguin Press. (p. 245)

127 *The Greeks had called her daemon...*

Moore, C. (2012). *Sacre Bleu: A comedy d'Art.* NY: William Morrow. (p. 321)

128 *Which is why I like waiting for what we call The Muse...*

Kenower, W. (2015, December 14). Waiting for the muse. *Huffington Post.*

https://www.huffingtonpost.com/william-kenower/waiting-for-the-muse_b_8801274.html

128 *Dicks in his lovely novel...*

Dicks, M. (2012). *Memoirs of an imaginary friend.* NY: St. Martin's Press. (p. 139)

129 *Not much is known about how these fantasies...*

Taylor, M. (1999). *Imaginary companions and the children who create them.* NY: Oxford University Press. (p. 7)

130 *"contemporary wisdom is that imaginary..."*
> Trifoni, G., & Reese, E. (2009). A good story: Children with imaginary companions create richer narratives. *Child Development, 80*(4), 1301-1313. (p. 1301)

130 *As parents it may be easy to be resistant...*
> Gopnik, A. (2009). *The philosophical baby: What children's minds tell us about truth, love, and the meaning of life.* NY: Farrar, Strauss, and Giroux. (p. 61)

130 *"Human beings have a unique capacity to love..."*
> Taylor, M., & Mottweiler, C. M. (2008). Imaginary companions: Pretending they are real but knowing they are not. *American Journal of Play, 1*(1), 47-54. (p. 47)

Chapter 6: Superheroes, Tales Of Fairies, And Monsters

PAGE

131 *"Children's play is clearly about many things..."*
> Gottschall, J. (2012). *The storytelling animal: How stories make us human.* Boston: Houghton Mifflin Harcourt. (p. 33)

131 *"There is a universal grammar..."*
> Gottschall, J. (2012). (p. 55)

132 *But don't underestimate me..."*
> "Fly," music and lyrics by Robbie Schaeffer; on the album, *In the Flesh.* Little Star Records, 2004.

133 *"as much a part of our communal DNA..."*
> Tye, L. (2012). *Superman: The high-flying history of America's most enduring hero.* NY: Random House. (p. xiii)

133 *"You'd have to live in a cave..."*
> Rosenberg, R. S. (Ed.), *Our superheroes, ourselves.* NY: Oxford University Press. (p. xiii)

133 *The results of one research study...*
> Galbraith, J. S. (2007). *Multiple perspectives on superhero play in an early childhood classroom.* Doctoral dissertation, The Ohio State University. (p. 21)

134 *"the findings from the school culture..."*
> Galbraith, J. S. (2007). (p. i-ii)

134 *"Children usually know more than their teachers..."*
> Jones, E., & Cooper, R. M. (2000). *Playing to get smart.* NY: Teachers College Press. (p. 66)

134 *Nobody urges children to read about Superman...*
> Mackenzie, C. (1943, July 11). Children and the comics. *The New York Times,* p. SM23.

135 *We had begun the journey that day...*
> Chabon, M. (2008, March 10). Secret skin. *The New Yorker,* p. 64.

137 *Think about the universal pleasure of chasing games...*
> Gray, P. (2013). *Free to learn: Why unleashing the instinct to play will make our children happier, more self-reliant, and better students for life.* NY: Basic Books. (p. 172)

137 *"children seemed to be obsessed..."*

Gronlund, G. (1992). Coping with Ninja Turtle play in my kindergarten class-room. *Young Children, 48*(1), 21-25. (p. 22)

137 *"no matter how creative and analytical they might be..."*

Langley, T. (2013, September 13). The psychology of superheroes (and villains): What we learn about personality when we analyze good guys, bad guys - and ourselves. *The Boston Globe.*

https://www.bostonglobe.com/ideas/2013/09/13/the-psychology-super-heroes-and-villains/43ukfWyuIHdeOKC5wv8P9M/story.html

138 *Gerard Jones, in his book...*

Jones, G. (2002). *Killing monsters: Why children need fantasy, super heroes, and make-believe violence.* NY: Basic Books. (p. 181)

138 *"But the evidence suggests that repeated play..."*

Jones, G. (2002). (p. 181)

139 *The story was told by the therapist who was working with the young girl.*

Rubin, L. C. (2013). Are superhero stories good for us?: Reflections from clinical practice. In Rosenberg, R. S. (Ed.), *Our superheroes, ourselves* (pp. 37-52). NY: Oxford University Press. (pp. 46-7)

140 *In Philadelphia, for example...*

Campbell, B. (2017, April 22). Power rangers bring mighty morphin delight to kids in hospital. *NPR Now.*

https://www.npr.org/sections/thetwo-way/2017/04/22/525149796/power-rangers-bring-mighty-morphin-delight-to-kids-in-hospital

140 *At a children's medical center in Austin, Texas...*

Straeter, K. (2015, October 13). Superheroes flew into this Children's Medical Center - and you've gotta see the villain they catch for these kids!! *FaithIt.com.* https://faithit.com/superheroes-flew-into-this-childrens-medical-center-youve-gotta-see-villain-catch-these-kids/

141 *In 2013, nursing students at Baylor University in Texas...*

Baylor University Media (2016, July 18). Baylor nursing alumni help turn hospitalized children into superheroes. *Baylor Media and Public Relations*

https://www.baylor.edu/mediacommunications/news.php?action=story&story=171153

141 *A cancer center in Brazil...*

Fradkin, C., Vanderlei Weschenfelder, G., & Yunes, M. A. M. (2016). Shared adversities of children and comic superheroes as resources for promoting resilience. *Child Abuse & Neglect, 51,* 407-415. (p. 409)

141 *The kids that my team and I chose have been through hell and back...*

Zhang, M. (2017, August 26). Photographer turns sick and disabled kids into Justice League superheroes. *PetPixel.* https://petapixel.com/2017/08/26/photographer-turns-sick-disabled-kids-justice-league-superheroes/

142 *"Generations of children [have been] soothed..."*

Jones, G. (2002). *Killing monsters: Why children need fantasy, super heroes, and make-believe violence.* NY: Basic Books. (p. 129)

142 *Marina Warner writes in her book...*

Warner, M. (2014). *Once upon a time: A short history of fairy tale.* NY: Oxford University Press.

142 *One tally found that the gruesomeness...*

Gottschall, J. (2012). *The storytelling animal: How stories make us human.* Boston: Houghton Mifflin Harcourt. (p. 44)

143 *As Bruno Bettelheim wrote...*

Bettelheim, B. (1976). *The uses of enchantment: The meaning and importance of fairy tales.* NY: Vintage Books. (p. 40)

143 *"In the traditional fairy tale..."*

Bettelheim, B. (1976). (p. 144)

144 *"The child is unaware of his inner processes..."*

Bettelheim, B. (1976). (p. 149-150)

144 *"finds his own solutions, through contemplating..."*

Bettelheim, B. (1976). (p. 25)

144 *"As he listens to the fairy tale, the child..."*

Bettelheim, B. (1976). (p. 75)

144 *Superhero stories were Sammy's fruitcakes, so to speak...*

Dyson, A. H. (1997). *Writing superheroes: Contemporary childhood, popular culture, and classroom literacy.* NY: Teachers College Press. (p. 47-48)

145 *what one author called, "cultural capital"*

Giugni, M. (2006). Conceptualizing Goodies and Baddies through narratives of Jesus and Superman. *Contemporary Issues in Early Childhood, 7*(2), 97-108. (p. 101)

145 *Rebecca Kantor and her colleagues...*

Kantor, R., Elgas, P. M., & Fernie, D. E. (1993). Cultural knowledge and social competence with a preschool peer culture group. *Early Childhood Research Quarterly, 8,* 125-147.

146 *"Fear is a wonderful thing, in small does."*

Popova, M. (2014, March 20). Neil Gaiman on why scary stories appeal to us, the art of fear in children's books, and the most terrifying ghosts haunting society. *Brain Pickings.*
https://www.brainpickings.org/2014/03/20/neil-gaiman-ghost-stories/

146 *As Susan Linn wrote...*

Linn, S. (2008). *The case for make believe: Saving play in a commercialized world.* NY: New Press. (p. 142)

147 *Stephen Asma, in his book...*

Asma, S. (2009). *On monsters: An unnatural history of our worst fears.* NY: Oxford University Press. (p. 284)

147 *It is one of the places where horror and scary fiction work...*

Lee, F. R. (2014, June 13). A literary expert on driving in the dark: Neil Gaiman follows the guiding light of instinct. *The New York Times.* https://www.nytimes.com/2014/06/14/books/neil-gaiman-follows-the-guiding-light-of-instinct.html

148 *In a significant sense, monsters are part of our attempt...*

Asma, S. (2009, October 30). Monsters and the moral imagination. *The Chronicle of Higher Education*, Section B, B11-B12.

148 *Christopher Golden reflected on how he learned...*

Golden, C. (2016). The weight of four-color justice. In L. Mignogna (Ed.), *Last night, a superhero saved my life* (pp. 43-51). NY: Thomas Dunne Books. (p. 47-48)

148 *The author of Killing Monsters...*

Jones, G. (2002). *Killing monsters: Why children need fantasy, super heroes, and make-believe violence.* NY: Basic Books. (p. 60)

148 *Finally, the biologist E. O. Wilson...*

Capuzzo, M. (2001). Epigraph. *Close to shore: The terrifying shark attacks of 1916.* NY: Broadway Books.

149 *Jane Katch in her book...*

Katch, J. (2001). *Under deadman's skin: Discovering the meaning of children's violent play.* Boston: Beacon Press. (pp. 86-87)

149 *"Jason's use of movies to master his fears..."*

Katch, J. (2001). (pp. 87-88)

150 *Many adults tend to take literally...*

Bettelheim, B. (1976). *The uses of enchantment: The meaning and importance of fairy tales.* NY: Vintage Books. (p. 179)

150 *This is exactly the message that fairy tales get across...*

Bettelheim, B. (1976). (p. 8)

152 *Here is my 10-year-old son, Owen...*

Doerr, A. (2014, December 1). A year in reading: Anthony Doerr. themillions.com. https://themillions.com/2014/12/year-in-reading-anthony-doerr.html

152 *And listen to this mother describe her son's use of pretend power...*

Jones, G. (2002). *Killing monsters: Why children need fantasy, super heroes, and make-believe violence.* NY: Basic Books. (p. 190)

153 *When I was at boarding school...*

Sacks, O. (2015). *On the move: A life.* NY: Alfred A. Knopf. (p. 3)

153 *I feel like I'm a real kinda superhero...*

Stone, A. L. (2008). Superhero play among preschool children. Thesis. The Humboldt State University. (p. 63)

Chapter 7: The Simulation of Reality, (and the Reality of Simulation)

PAGE

157 *Children can "enact what people might do..."*

Harris, P. (2000). *The work of the imagination.* Malden, MA: Blackwell Publishing. (p. 41)

157 *"a theoretical construct defined as behavior..."*

Fein, G. G. ((1981). Pretend play in childhood: An integrative review. *Child Development, 52,* 1095-1118. (p. 1096)

157 *"pretense involving an imaginary companion is a simulation of reality..."*

Gleason, T. R. (2017). The psychological significance of play with imaginary companions in early childhood. *Learning Behavior, 45*, 432-440. (p. 437)

158 *"this extra practice, albeit imagined..."*

Gleason, T. R. (2017). (p. 439)

158 *"practices at being other people"*

Lillard, A. (2001). Pretend play as Twin Earth: A social-cognitive analysis. *Developmental Review, 21*, 495-531. (p. 514)

158 *We end the year with a simulation game of the Oregon Trail.*

Post, L. Oregon Trail Simulation, *National Educational Association* (NEA.org). http://www.nea.org/tools/tips/oregon-trail-simulation.html

159 *The Wikipedia entry for Sim City offers this description of the game.*

https://en.wikipedia.org/wiki/SimCity

159 *Second Life users (also called residents) create virtual representations...*

https://en.wikipedia.org/wiki/Second_Life

159 *Just the other day I watched a television commercial for a drug company...*

https://www.enbrel.com/joint-damage-simulator

160 *"There is one major thing that separates simulators from real life...*

Lucero II, L., & Gomez, M. (2018, August 12). Richard Russell stole a plane in Seattle and crashed it: How'd he learn to fly? NYTimes.com. https://www.nytimes.com/2018/08/12/us/richard-russell-q400-flight-simulator.html

160 *A lot of soldiers enter the training sessions...*

Mead, C. (2013). *War play: Video games and the future of armed conflict*. Boston: Houghton Mifflin Harcourt. (p. 114)

161 *"It's a video game created by the U.S. Army to win over the hearts..."*

CBS News (2004, March 30). https://www.cbsnews.com/news/army-recruits-video-gamers/

161 *The Army's own website describes the player's experience this way.*

https://www.goarmy.com/downloads/americas-army-game.html

161 *"Everything from the direction and velocity of shell ejection..."*

Kennedy, B. (2002, July 1). Uncle Sam wants you (to play this game). NYTimes.com. https://www.nytimes.com/2002/07/11/technology/uncle-sam-wants-you-to-play-this-game.html

161 *The designers, primarily the Modeling, Virtual Environments and Simulation Institute...*

Kennedy, B. (2002, July 1). Uncle Sam wants you (to play this game). NYTimes.com https://www.nytimes.com/2002/07/11/technology/uncle-sam-wants-you-to-play-this-game.html

161 *The VAE was a "mobile mission simulator"...*

Allen, R. (2009). The Army rolls through Indianapolis: Fieldwork at the Virtual Army Experience. *Transformative Works and Cultures, 2*.

162 *"the camera goes into the Humvee..."*

Allen, R. (2009).

162 *It has kinetic hammers that, when an explosion goes off...*

Allen, R. (2009).

162 *Some of the tasks that the recruit can practice...*

Conners, M. (2014, May 16). Army releases Virtual Battle Space 3 Computer Game. *The Amplifier Magazine*. https://div46amplifier.com/2014/05/16/army-releases-virtual-battle-space-3-computer-game/

162 *"She said it's easier to get lost..."*

McBride, W. (2012, October 16). Fort Jackson training new Soldiers with Virtual Battle Space 2 Simulator. U. S. Army Releases. https://www.army.mil/article/88897/fort_jackson_training_new_soldiers_with_virtual_battlespace_2_simulator

163 *And as one Army captain said...*

Lopez, T. C. (2014, April 3). Latest "Virtual Battle Space" release adds realism to scenarios, avatars. *Army News Service*. https://www.army.mil/article/123316/latest_virtual_battle_space_release_adds_realism_to_scenarios_avatars

163 *"rehearse what they would be doing out there..."*

Stark, S. (2014, July-September). Virtual Battlespace 3 bring greater realism to the not-quite-real-fight. *Army AL&T Magazine*, p. 52.

163 *Or as one Army captain said...*

Lopez, T. C. (2014, April 3). Latest "Virtual Battle Space" release adds realism to scenarios, avatars. *Army News Service*. https://www.army.mil/article/123316/latest_virtual_battle_space_release_adds_realism_to_scenarios_avatars

163 *The greatest power of virtual reality is the ability to try and fail..*

Rosen, R. (2008). The history of medical simulation. *Journal of Critical Care*, 23, 157-166. (p. 62)

164 *"see which tools can fit down which corridors"*

Weintraub, K. (2016, June 5). Simulation center aids surgeons, medical teams. usatoday.com. https://www.usatoday.com/story/life/2016/06/05/simulation-lab-boston-childrens-hospital/84982842/

164 *"Like flight simulators for pilots..."*

Weintraub, K. (2016, June 5). Simulation center aids surgeons, medical teams. usatoday.com. https://www.usatoday.com/story/life/2016/06/05/simulation-lab-boston-childrens-hospital/84982842/

165 *(Leslie Jamison has written a very interesting book...)*

Jamison, L. (2014). *The empathy exams*. Minneapolis, MN: Graywolf Press.

167 *"It's like it's plugged back in!"*

Ramachandran, V. S. (2011). *The tell-tale brain: A neuroscientist's quest for what makes us human*. NY: W. W. Norton & Company. (p. 34)

168 *"restoring the congruence between motor output and sensory input"*

Ramanchandran, V. S., & Altschuler, E. L. (2009). The use of visual feedback, in particular mirror visual feedback, in restoring brain function. *Brain*, 132, 1693-1710. (p. 1697)

168 *Ramachandran calls this process an "optical trick."*

Ramanchandran, V. S., & Altschuler, E. L. (2009). (p. 1697)

168 *The application "mixes animation and magical realism..."*

Suellentrop, C. (2016). This video game will break your heart. nytimes.com. https://www.nytimes.com/2016/02/06/arts/that-dragon-cancer-video-game-will-break-your-heart.html.

168 *places the player as Ryan, a distraught father...*

Campbell, C. (2013, May 9). Gaming's new frontier: Cancer, depression, suicide. *polygon.com.* https://www.polygon.com/2013/5/9/4313246/gamings-new-frontier-cancer-depression-suicide.

169 *Players found themselves in a hospital room...*

Tanz, J. (2016, January). Playing for time. *Wired.* https://www.wired.com/2016/01/that-dragon-cancer/

169 *"In a stark hospital scene..."*

Stanton, R. (2016, January 18). That Dragon, Cancer review - you've never played anything like it. *The Guardian.* https://www.theguardian.com/technology/2016/jan/18/that-dragon-cancer-review-youve-never-played-anything-like-it.

169 *Scenarios such as these can be overwhelming...*

Stanton, R. (2016, January 18). That Dragon, Cancer review - you've never played anything like it. *The Guardian.* https://www.theguardian.com/technology/2016/jan/18/that-dragon-cancer-review-youve-never-played-anything-like-it

169 *"We went from caring for Joel to making everybody care about Joel."*

CBS News (2017, March 12). That Dragon, Cancer: A game for Joel. https://www.cbsnews.com/news/that-dragon-cancer-a-game-for-joel/

170 *"Neglect of the future self can arise..."*

Hershfield, H. E., Goldstein, D. G., Sharpe, W. F., Fox, J., Yeykelis, L., Carstensen, L., & Bailenson, J. N. (2011). Increasing saving behavior through age-processed renderings of the future self. *Journal of Marketing Research, 48,* S23-S37. (p. S24)

170 *"visual analog of a 70-year-old..."*

Hershfield, H. E., Goldstein, D. G., Sharpe, W. F., Fox, J., Yeykelis, L., Carstensen, L., & Bailenson, J. N. (2011). (p. S26)

170 *The researchers hypothesized that "the participants..."*

Hershfield, H. E., Goldstein, D. G., Sharpe, W. F., Fox, J., Yeykelis, L., Carstensen, L., & Bailenson, J. N. (2011). (p. S26)

171 *which is defined by the "replacement of natural sensory information..."*

Fox, J., & Bailenson, J. N. (2009). Virtual self-modeling: The effects of vicarious reinforcement and identification on exercise behaviors. *Media Psychology, 12,* 1-25. (p. 6)

171 *Participants then observed these virtual selves...*

Fox, J., & Bailenson, J. N. (2009). (p. 2)

172 *"virtual humans [serve as] models..."*

Fox, J., & Bailenson, J. N. (2009). (p. 6)

172 *"Participants witnessed [their virtual self] gain or lose weight..."*

Fox, J., & Bailenson, J. N. (2009). (p. 6)

172 *It turns out that "exposure to virtual cause-and-effect..."*

Hershfield, H. E., Goldstein, D. G., Sharpe, W. F., Fox, J., Yeykelis, L., Carstensen, L., & Bailenson, J. N. (2011). Increasing saving behavior through age-processed renderings of the future self. *Journal of Marketing Research, 48*, S23-S37. (p. S29)

172 *My students and I devised a study...*

Langer, E. J. (2009). *Counter-clockwise: Mindful health and the power of possibility.* NY: Ballantine Books. (p. 5)

173 *"to 'act as if' it is 1959..."*

Langer, E. J. (2009). (p. 9)

175 *Using the rubber hand illusion, we induced...*

Maister, L., Sebanz, N., Knoblich, G., & Tsarkis, M. (2013). Experiencing ownership over a dark-skinned body reduces implicit racial bias. *Cognition, 128*, 170-178. (p. 176)

177 *As the Wikipedia entry states...*

https://en.wikipedia.org/wiki/Simulation_hypothesis.

177 *"he wouldn't be surprised if we were to find out..."*

Loria, K. (2016, April 22). Neil deGrasse Tyson thinks there is a 'very high' chance the universe is just a simulation. BusinessInsider.com. https://www.businessinsider.com/neil-degrasse-tyson-thinks-the-universe-might-be-a-simulation-2016-12.

Chapter 8: Making It Through the Dark and Stormy Night
PAGE

179 *"startling circumstances"*

Eisen, G. (1988). *Children and play in the Holocaust: Games among the shadows.* Amherst, MA: The University of Massachusetts Press. (p. 22)

180 *"During natural disasters, children are one of the most..."*

Baggerly, J., & Exum, H. A. (2008). Counseling children after natural disasters: Guidance for family therapists. *The American Journal of Family Therapy, 36*, 79-93. (p. 80)

180 *"to create a concrete narrative of traumatic events..."*

Baggerly, J., & Exum, H. A. (2008). (p. 87)

181 *About the same time, Shonda dumped the 'gumbo' out of the pot...*

Aghayan, C., Schellhaas, A., Wayne, A., Burts, D. C., Buchanan, T. K., & Benedict, J. (2005). Project Katrina. *Early Childhood Research & Practice, 7*(2). http://ecrp.uiuc.edu/v7n2/aghayan.html

181 *"We kept trying to continue with the topic of transportation..."*

Aghayan, C., Schellhaas, A., Wayne, A., Burts, D. C., Buchanan, T. K., & Benedict, J. (2005). Project Katrina. *Early Childhood Research & Practice, 7*(2). http://ecrp.uiuc.edu/v7n2/aghayan.html

181 *A mother of a four-year-old reported...*

Saylor, C. F., Swenson, C. C., & Powell, P. (1992). Hurricane Hugo blows down the broccoli: Preschoolers' post-disaster play and adjustment. *Child Psychiatry and Human Development, 22*(3), 139-149.

181 *After experiencing an earthquake, for example...*

Bateman, A., Danby, S., & Howard, J. (2013). Living in a broken world: How young children's well-being is supported through playing out their earthquake experiences. *International Journal of Play 2*(3), 202-219.

181 *Here, Cayden's pretend play...*

Bateman, A., Danby, S., & Howard, J. (2013). (p. 212)

182 *During a subsequent therapy session...*

Bateman, A., Danby, S., & Howard, J. (2013).

182 *One research study demonstrated the importance of this type of play...*

Baggerly, J., & Exum, H. A. (2008). Counseling children after natural disasters: Guidance for family therapists. *The American Journal of Family Therapy, 36,* 79-93.

182 *"Play can help the hospitalized child better understand..."*

Haiat, H., Bar-Mor, G., & Schochat, M. (2003). The world of the child: A world of play even in the hospital. *Journal of Pediatric Nursing, 18*(3), 209-214. (p. 210)

182 *Veronica set up a bed...*

Petrillo, M., & Sanger, S. (1980). *Emotional care of hospitalized children: An environmental approach, 2nd. ed.* Philadelphia: J. B. Lippincott Company. (p. 176)

183 *Several of the boys between the ages of five and ten...*

Petrillo, M., & Sanger, S. (1980). (p. 164)

183 *"medical play involved a sense of mastery...*

Nabors, L., Bartz, J., Kichler, J., Sievers. R., Elkins, R., & Pangallo, J. (2013). Play as a mechanism of working through medical trauma for children with medical illnesses and their siblings. *Issues in Comprehensive Pediatric Nursing, 36*(3), 212-224. (p. 221)

183 *As one study found, "children with chronic illnesses..."*

Nabors, L., Bartz, J., Kichler, J., Sievers. R., Elkins, R., & Pangallo, J. (2013). (p. 221)

184 *The children played funeral every day for weeks...*

Garbarino, J., Kostelny, K., & Dubrow, N. (1991). *No place to be a child: Growing up in the war zone.* Lexington, MA: D. C. Heath and Company. (p. 149)

184 *Six-year-old James organizes his classmates...*

Van Hoorn, J., Nourot, P. M., Scales, B., & Alward, K. R. (2007). *Play at the center of the curriculum, 4th ed.* Upper Saddle River, NJ: Pearson/Merrill Prentice Hall. (p. 72)

184 *"Postdisaster play appears to be similar to the mourning..."*

Sugar, M. (1988). A preschooler in a disaster. *American Journal of Psychotherapy, 42*(4), 619-629. (p. 624)

185 *Through the writings of Lenore Terr...*

Terr, L. C. (1991). Childhood traumas: An outline and overview. *American Journal of Psychiatry, 148,* 10-20.

Terr, L. C. (1981). "Forbidden games: Post-traumatic child's play. *Journal of the American Academy of Child Psychiatry, 20,* 741-760.

186 *"must cope with both the dangerous events of the war..."*

Assal, A., & Farrell, E. (1992). Attempts to make meaning of terror: Family, play, and school in time of civil war. *Anthropology and Education Quarterly, 23*(4), 275-290. (p. 275)

186 *As the 1996 report of the United Nations...*

UNICEF (1996). The state of the world's children 1996: Children in war. https://www.unicef.org/sowc/archive/ENGLISH/The%20State%20of%20the%20World's%20Children%201996.pdf

186 *Almost their entire set of play have references to a state of war...*

Marten, J. (1998). *The children's Civil War.* Chapel Hill, NC: The University of North Carolina Press. (p. 165)

187 *We felt thrilled through and through by accounts of brave fighting...*

Werner, E.E. (1998). *Reluctant witnesses: Children's voices from the Civil War.* Boulder, CO: Westview Press. (p. 55)

187 *Make-believe play during the Civil War even made it into the White House...*

Marten, J. (1998). *The children's Civil War.* Chapel Hill, NC: The University of North Carolina Press. (p. 162)

187 *Upon m word and 'honour,' Sir...*

Marten, J. (1998). (p. 165)

188 *Every night before falling asleep, I gave myself a little present...*

David, K. (1989). *A child's war: World War II through the eyes of children.* NY: Avon Books, 1989. (pp. 77-78)

188 *But what I like most is to lie here with my eyes shut...*

David, K. (1989). (p. 201)

189 *War games play a part in our nursery as they do in others...*

Freud, A., & Burlingham, D. T. (1943). *War and children.* NY: Medical War Books. (pp. 23-24)

189 *It is interesting to note that an article in a 1942 issue...*

Werner, E.E. (2000). *Through the eyes of innocents: Children witness World War II.* Boulder, CO: Westview Press. (p. 74)

190 *Once my friend came to me for a short while. Her parents allowed her to...*

Bat-Zion, N. (1995). Play in wartime: The case of Israeli children under missile attack. In E. Klugman (ed.), *Play, policy & practice* (pp. 119-144). St. Paul, MN: Redleaf Press. (p. 126)

190 *Children in a Palestine refugee camp, for example, would play Intifada...*

Garbarino, J., Kostelny, K., & Dubrow, N. (1991). *No place to be a child: Growing up in the war zone.* Lexington, MA: D. C. Heath and Company. (p. 12)

190 *In another example, a five-year-old Palestinian girl...*

Garbarino, J., Kostelny, K., & Dubrow, N. (1991). (p. 116)

190 *Whenever there was a lull in the fighting...*

Assal, A., & Farrell, E. (1992). Attempts to make meaning of terror: Family, play, and school in time of civil war. *Anthropology and Education Quarterly, 23*(4), 275-290. (pp. 280-281)

190 *No, I don't like to be in war and I don't like the killing of people...*

Assal, A., & Farrell, E. (1992). (p. 281)

191 *Sum times we wud dress up...*

Chudacoff, H. P. (2007). *Children at play: An American history*. NY: New York University Press. (p. 55)

192 *[The boys] made a wagon of fig branches...*

King, W. (1995). *Stolen childhood: Slave youth in Nineteenth-century America*. Bloomington, IN: Indiana University Press. (p. 30)

192 *And when the Black and White children played a game of 'wagon'...*

Mintz, S. (2004). *Huck's raft: A history of American childhood*. Cambridge, MA: Belknap Press. (pp. 104-105)

192 *As Steven Mintz writes in his book...*

Mintz, S. (2004). (pp. 104-105)

192 *The Black children of the plantations also staged make-believe...*

Marten, J. (1998). *The children's Civil War*. Chapel Hill, NC: The University of North Carolina Press.

Mintz, S. (2004). *Huck's raft: A history of American childhood*. Cambridge, MA: Belknap Press.

193 *George Eisen's book...*

Eisen, G. (1988). *Children and play in the Holocaust: Games among the shadows*. Amherst, MA: The University of Massachusetts Press.

193 *Finding play under these circumstances and conditions...*

Eisen, G. 1988. (p. 22)

193 *Although their voices are haunting...*

Eisen, 1988. (p. 58)

193 *In spite of their elders' desperate efforts to shelter them...*

Eisen, 1988. (p. 79)

193 *They play..."Roll call," shouting "Caps Off!...*

Eisen, G. (1988). (p. 80)

193 *They played "Doctor"...*

Eisen, 1988. (p. 81)

194 *Among the most popular ones...*

Eisen, 1988. (p. 77)

194 *Eisen concluded that "Play activities thus came to provide..."*

Eisen, 1988. (p. 77)

194 *We used to play prisoners, the people of the camps against the SS...*

Gampel, Y. (1988). Facing war, murder, torture, and death in latency. *The Psychoanalytical Review, 75*, 504-505. (pp. 504-505)

194 *Of all the play experiences it is the concept and even the notion...*

Eisen, G. (1988). *Children and play in the Holocaust: Games among the shadows*. Amherst, MA: The University of Massachusetts Press. (p. 66)

195 *Once they even played "Gas Chamber"...* (pp. 80-81)

195 *To enhance the image of my long-awaited friend...*

Frank, A. (1996). *The diary of a young girl: The definitive edition*. NY: Anchor Books. (p. 6)

195 *That's why I always wind up coming back to my diary...*
Frank, A. (1996). (p. 142)

196 *Today I have two things to confess...*
Frank, A. (1996). (p. 159)

196 *I did not know whether my wife was alive...*
Frankl, V. E. (1984). *Man's search for meaning.* NY: Washington Square Press. (pp. 56-58)

197 *The intensification of inner life...*
Frankl, V. E. (1984). (p. 58)

197 *I became disgusted with the state of affairs...*
Frankl, V. E. (1984). (pp. 73-74)

198 *I knew nothing about them...Yes, my mother's had news from your family...*
Wiesel, E. (1960). *Night.* NY: Bantam Books. (p. 41)

198 *The only thing that keeps me alive...*
Wiesel, E. (1960). (p. 42)

198 *Your mother is still a young woman...*
Wiesel, E. (1960). (p. 42-43)

198 *How we should have liked to believe it...*
Wiesel, E. (1960). (p. 43)

198 *Wiesel also tells the story of how he used the ability to lie...*
Wiesel, E. (1960). (pp. 49-50)

199 *Levi writes that, "I brazenly lied to old Wertheimer...*
Levi, P. (1996). *Survival in Auschwitz: The Nazi assault on humanity.* NY: Simon & Schuster. (p. 125)

199 *On this slender basis I also lived through the great selection...*
Levi, P. (1996). (p. 125)

200 *...as Eisen writes, "Play is far from a frivolous activity..."*
Eisen, G. (1988). *Children and play in the Holocaust: Games among the shadows.* Amherst, MA: The University of Massachusetts Press. (p. 6)

200 *When I am at play, I forget my hunger...*
Eisen, G. (1988). (p. 101)

200 *Although the ghetto had the power to incarcerate the body...*
Eisen, G. (1988). (p. 75)

201 *Children engage in make-believe to "call upon the power of their imagination..."*
Fearn, M., & Howard, J. (2012). Play as a resource for children facing adversity: An exploration of indicative case studies. *Children & Society, 26,* 456-468. (p. 463)

202 *The psychologist, Erik Erikson, talked about play occurring...*
Erikson, E. H. (1972). Play and actuality. In M. W. Piers (ed.), *Play and development* (pp. 127-167). NY: W. W. Norton & Company.

202 *In their play worlds, children can feel freedom as well as control...*
Marten, J. (1998). *The children's Civil War.* Chapel Hill, NC: The University of North Carolina Press. (p. 159)

202 *Children were not simply slavery's victims...*

Mintz, S. (2004). *Huck's raft: A history of American childhood.* Cambridge, MA: Belknap Press. (p. 104)

202 *"Medical play can be a vehicle..."*

Nabors, L., Bartz, J., Kichler, J., Sievers. R., Elkins, R., & Pangallo, J. (2013). Play as a mechanism of working through medical trauma for children with medical illnesses and their siblings. *Issues in Comprehensive Pediatric Nursing, 36*(3), 212-224. (p. 213)

203 *What Veronica told me is that to survive being tortured...*

Grazer, B., & Fishman, C. (2015). *A curious mind: The secret to a bigger life.* NY: Simon & Schuster. (p. 74)

203 *So a paradox. If you are forced to live a nightmare...*

Thorton, L. (1987). *Imagining Argentina.* NY: Bantam Books. (p. 79)

204 *They can see everything they want to...*

Thorton, L. (1987). (p. 99)

204 *Telling a story through play also can provide a child...*

Nabors, L., Bartz, J., Kichler, J., Sievers. R., Elkins, R., & Pangallo, J. (2013). Play as a mechanism of working through medical trauma for children with medical illnesses and their siblings. *Issues in Comprehensive Pediatric Nursing, 36*(3), 212-224. (p. 213)

204 *"Following a trauma, young children may appear mute..."*

Kalantari, M., Yule, W., Gardner, F. (1993). Protective factors and behavioral adjustment in preschool children of Iranian martyrs. *Journal of Child and Family Studies, 2*(2), 97-108. (p. 99)

205 *"Grownups may speak often..."*

Paley, V. (2004). *A child's work: The importance of fantasy play.* Chicago: University of Chicago Press. (p. 7)

205 *"When adults go over their experiences..."*

Freud, A., & Burlingham, D. T. (1943). *War and children.* NY: Medical War Books. (p. 67)

205 *It may be, as James Garbarino and his colleagues wrote...*

Garbarino, J., Kostelny, K., & Dubrow, N. (1991). *No place to be a child: Growing up in the war zone.* Lexington, MA: D. C. Heath and Company. (p. 12)

205 *Betty Lifton, in her biography of Janusz Korczak...*

Lifton, B. (1988). *The King of Children: A biography of Janusz Korczak.* NY: Schocken Books. (p. 251)

205 *"Although the ghetto had the power to incarcerate the body..."*

Eisen, G. (1988). *Children and play in the Holocaust: Games among the shadows.* Amherst, MA: The University of Massachusetts Press. (p. 75)

205 *We got a small blackboard and we were drawing...*

Assal, A., & Farrell, E. (1992). Attempts to make meaning of terror: Family, play, and school in time of civil war. *Anthropology and Education Quarterly, 23*(4), 275-290. (p. 281)

Chapter 9: Being A Head Taller

PAGE

207 *"In play a child always behaves beyond his average age..."*

Vygotsky, L. S. (1978). The role of play in development. In L. S. Vygotsky, *Mind in society: The development of higher psychological processes* (pp. 92-104). Cambridge, MA: Harvard University Press. (p. 102)

207 *As Paul Harris wrote in his book about the importance of imagination...*

Harris, P. L. (2000). *The work of the imagination.* Malden, MA: Blackwell Publishing. (p. 2)

208 *"in play [is] able to express the various..."*

Galbraith, J. S. (2007). *Multiple perspectives on superhero play in an early childhood classroom.* Doctoral dissertation. The Ohio State University. (p. 40)

208 *"And a three-year-old who may find sharing a toy..."*

Berk, L. E., Mann, T. D., & Ogan, A. (2006). Make-believe play: Wellspring for development of self-regulation. In D. G. Singer, R. M. Golinkoff, & K. Hirsh-Pasek (eds.), *Play=learning: How play motivates and enhances children's cognitive and social-emotional growth* (pp. 74-100). NY: Oxford University Press. (p. 78)

208 *Vygotsky wrote that "A child's greatest self-control..."*

Vygotsky, L. S. (1978). The role of play in development. In L. S. Vygotsky, *Mind in society: The development of higher psychological processes* (pp. 92-104). Cambridge, MA: Harvard University Press. (p. 99)

208 *Play, according to Vygotsky...*

Vygotsky, L. S. (1978). (p. 99)

208 *In play, "thought is separated from objects and actions..."*

Vygotsky, L. S. (1978). (p. 97)

210 *"In a way, parents are entertaining a fiction..."*

Kaye, K. (1982). *The mental life and social life of babies: How parents create persons.* Chicago: The University of Chicago Press. (p. 131)

211 *As Kaye writes, "Evolution has produced infants..."*

Kaye, K. (1982). (p. 53)

211 *"lying to ourselves...helps us accept our fraudulent behavior"*

Smith, D. L. (2005). Natural-born liars. *Scientific American Mind, 16*(2), 16-23. (p. 22)

211 *"self-deception evolves in the service of deception..."*

Trivers, R. (2011). *The folly of fools: The logic of deceit and self-deception in human life.* NY: Basic Books. (p. 4)

211 *As Robert Trivers writes...*

Trivers, R. (2011). (p. 3)

212 *Trivers goes on to suggesst...*

Trivers, R. (2011). (p. 15)

212 *There exists a pervasive tendency to see the self...*

Taylor, S. E., & Brown, J. D. (1988). Illusion and well-being: A social psychological perspective on mental health. *Psychological Bulletin, 103*(2), 193-210. (p. 195)

212 *It seems that "Most people consider themselves..."*

Baumeister, R. F. (1993). Lying to yourself: The enigma of self-deception. In M. Lewis and C. Saarni (eds.), *Lying and deception in everyday life* (pp. 166-183). NY: The Guilford Press. (p. 167)

212 *"The mentally healthy person appears to have the enviable capacity..."*

Taylor, S. E., & Brown, J. D. (1988). Illusion and well-being: A social psychological perspective on mental health. *Psychological Bulletin, 103*(2), 193-210. (p. 204)

212 *"regular doses of self-deception are good for you"*

Baumeister, R. F. (1993). Lying to yourself: The enigma of self-deception. In M. Lewis and C. Saarni (eds.), *Lying and deception in everyday life* (pp. 166-183). NY: The Guilford Press. (p. 177)

212 *"By exaggerating your assessment of your chances..."*

Baumeister, R. F. (1993). (p. 178)

213 *In a 2012 article in...*

Adam, H., & Galinsky, A. D. (2012). Unclothed cognition. *Journal of Experimental and Social Psychology, 48,* 918-925. (p. 919)

213 *They posited that "wearing a lab coat..."*

Adam, H., & Galinsky, A. D. (2012). (p. 919)

214 *The study's authors concluded that "wearing clothes causes people..."*

Adam, H., & Galinsky, A. D. (2012). (p. 919)

214 *Theodore Roosevelt, 26th president of the United States...*

Goodwin, D. K. (2013). *The bully pulpit: Theodore Roosevelt, William Howard Taft, and the golden age of journalism.* NY: Simon & Schuster. (p. 40)

215 *Judd Apatow, a very successful movie director...*

Apatow, J. (2015). *Sick in the head: Conversations about life and comedy.* NY: Random House. (p. 314)

215 *Amy Cuddy, social psychologist and author of the book...*

Cuddy, A. (2015). *Presence: Bringing your boldest self to your biggest challenges.* NY: Little, Brown and Company. (p. 104)

215 *The singer-songwriter, James Taylor...*

PBS American Masters Documentary: Troubadours: Carole King/James Taylor & the Rises of the Singer-Songwriter.

215 *Steve Jobs, the co-founder of Apple Computers...*

Isaacson, W. (2011). *Steve Jobs.* NY: Simon & Schuster. (p. 55)

216 *"set of interrelated positive illusions...*

Taylor, S. E., & Brown, J. D. (1988). Illusion and well-being: A social psychological perspective on mental health. *Psychological Bulletin, 103*(2), 193-210. (p. 193)

216 *Or in the words of Amy Cuddy...*

Cuddy, A. (2015). *Presence: Bringing your boldest self to your biggest challenges.* NY: Little, Brown and Company. (p. 295)

217 *As the psychologist William James wrote...*

Cuddy, A. (2015). (p. 174)

218 *One line of smile research looked at the effect of smiling on the response to stress.*

Kraft T. L., & Pressman, S. D. (2012). Grin and bear it: The influence of manipulated facial expression on the stress response. *Psychological Science, 23*(11), 1372-1378.

218 *There have also been studies that look at the effects of induced smiling...*

Strack, F., Martin, L. L., & Stepper, S. (1988). Inhibiting and facilitating conditions of the human smile: A non obtrusive test of the facial feedback hypothesis. *Journal of Personality and Social Psychology, 54*(5), 768-777.

219 *Research has found that people who are depressed often have a different walking...*

Michalak, J., Rohde, K., & Troje, N. (2015). How we walk affects what we remember: Gait modifications through biofeedback change negative affective memory bias. *Journal of Behavior Therapy and Experimental Psychiatry, 46*, 121-125. (p. 124)

220 *"projects like the Harlem Children's Zone..."*

Newman, F., & Fulani, L. (2011). Let's pretend: Solving the education crisis in America. A Special Report. All Stars Project, Inc. (p. 2)

220 *"actively related to as learners..."*

Newman, F., & Fulani, L. (2011). (p. 3)

220 *"in our view, a fundamental tool for education..."*

Newman, F., & Fulani, L. (2011). (p. 7)

221 *We believe that if such a 'performance' were created...*

Newman, F., & Fulani, L. (2011). (p. 2)

222 *"I write very slowly because I write under the obligation..."*

Rodriguez, R. (1982). *Hunger of memory: The education of Richard Rodriguez.* Boston: David R. Godine. (p. 186)

About the Author

LAUREN HAREL

AFTER BEGINNING HIS academic career at the University of North Dakota, David Kuschner retired as an associate professor emeritus of early childhood education at the University of Cincinnati. He is the author of the recently published book, *Being In Time With Children: Reflections On the Moments Between Us*, co-author of *The Child's Construction of Knowledge: Piaget for Teaching Children*, and an editor of three collections of readings on the topic of play. He was the co-creator and co-host of a weekly radio show entitled, *Considering Children*, for which he conducted interviews with the likes of Dr. Benjamin Spock, Bob Keeshan (Captain Kangaroo), and Alex Haley, author of *Roots*. In 2014 he was the recipient of the Brian Sutton-Smith Play Scholar Award from *The Association for the Study of Play*. He lives with his wife, Leslie, in Philadelphia, Pennsylvania and can be contacted at BeingInTime2019@gmail.com.

www.ingramcontent.com/pod-product-compliance
Lightning Source LLC
Chambersburg PA
CBHW022103280326
41933CB00007B/237